366 readings from
JUDAISM

Also in the Global Spirit Library

366 readings from Islam

366 readings from Buddhism

366 readings from Christianity

366 readings from Taoism and Confucianism

366 readings from Hinduism

THE GLOBAL SPIRIT LIBRARY

366 readings from
JUDAISM

edited by

ROBERT VAN DE WEYER

THE PILGRIM PRESS
CLEVELAND, OHIO

ARTHUR JAMES
NEW ALRESFORD, UK

First published in USA and Canada by
The Pilgrim Press,
700 Prospect Avenue East, Cleveland, Ohio 44115

First published in English outside North America by
Arthur James Ltd,
46a West Street, New Alresford, UK, SO24 9AU

Copyright © 2000 Arthur James Ltd

Translation, compilation and editing
© 2000 Robert Van de Weyer

05 04 03 02 01 00   5 4 3 2 1

A catalogue record for this book is available from
the Library of Congress and the British Library.

North America ISBN 0-8298-1391-8
English language outside North America ISBN 0 85305 455 X

Typeset in Monotype Joanna by
Strathmore Publishing Services, London N7

Printed by
Tien Wah Press, Singapore

CONTENTS

Series Introduction   page vii

Introduction   page ix

Sacred History   before 1/1

Prophetic Vision   before 4/24

Jewish Wisdom   before 6/11

Jewish Philosophy   before 11/18

Bibliography   page 371

Index of Writers   page 373

.

SERIES INTRODUCTION

The Global Spirit Library is the first comprehensive collection of the spiritual literature of the world, presented in accessible form. It is aimed at people who belong to a particular religious community, and wish to broaden their spiritual outlook; and at the much larger group, perhaps the majority of people in the world today, who have little or no attachment to a religious community, but seek spiritual wisdom. Each book contains the major writings of one of the world's spiritual traditions.

Much of the world's spiritual literature was designed to be read or heard in small portions, allowing ample time for personal reflection. Following this custom, the books in *The Global Spirit Library* each consist of an annual cycle of daily readings. Two or more books may be read in parallel at different times of the day; or an entire book may be read straight through. Again following a time-honoured practice, many of the original texts have been condensed.

Spiritual traditions differ from one another in their theological formulations; and the history of humankind is blighted by rivalry between different religious communities. Yet theology is no more than human speculation about truths that are beyond the grasp of the human mind. The writings in these books amply demonstrate that, as men and women actually experience these truths within themselves and others, divisions and rivalries fade, and unity is found. May the third millennium be an era of spiritual unity across the globe.

INTRODUCTION

A Jew is someone who, through having a Jewish mother, can claim descent from the great Hebrew patriarchs, Abraham, Isaac and Jacob. Judaism is the ancient religion of the Jewish people.

The origin of Judaism lies with the decision by Abraham, probably in the nineteenth century BCE, to leave his ancestral home in Mesopotamia (modern Iraq), and travel west. His descendants formed a nation that eventually conquered the land of Canaan on the coast of the Mediterranean. Abraham believed himself to be guided by God, and the Hebrews came to regard themselves as chosen by God as a light in the world. They established Jerusalem as their capital, and twice built a temple there. The second temple was destroyed in 70 CE, and the Jewish people dispersed across Europe and the near East. Wherever they went they maintained their ancient customs, remained culturally distinct – and never lost their sense of being a chosen people. In 1947 the Jewish homeland was re-established as the state of Israel.

Jesus and his early followers were Jews, and Christianity recognizes the Hebrew Bible as its Old Testament. Islam regards the Hebrew patriarchs and prophets as forerunners of Muhammad. Thus the two largest world religions are spiritually descended from Judaism.

SACRED HISTORY

The core of the Hebrew Bible is the history of the Hebrew people from the beginnings of the world to the first rebuilding of their temple. The authors are unknown, although the first five books are traditionally attributed to Moses; but their common purpose was to show the relationship between human behaviour and divine action. They also record the laws which governed ancient Hebrew society, and which Jews in different circumstances over the centuries have striven to observe.

The creation of heaven and earth

In the beginning God created heaven and earth. The earth was formless and desolate, and darkness covered the surface of the ocean; the Spirit of God was hovering over the waters.

God said: 'Let there be light.' And there was light. God saw that the light was good, and he separated the light from the darkness. He named the light 'day', and the darkness 'night'. Evening passed and morning came. That was the first day.

God said: 'Let there be a dome to divide the waters in two.' So God made a dome, separating the water below it from the water above it. He named the dome 'sky'. Evening passed and morning came. That was the second day.

God said: 'Let the water under the sky be gathered into one place, and let dry ground appear,' And it was so. God named the dry ground 'land' and the waters 'seas'. And he was pleased with what he saw. Then he said: 'Let the land produce all kinds of plants, those that bear grain and those that bear fruit.' And it was done. So the land produced all kinds of plants, and God was pleased with what he saw. Evening passed and morning came. That was the third day.

God said: 'Let lights appear in the sky to separate day from night, and to mark the seasons, days and years. They will shine in the sky to give light to the earth.' He made the two larger lights, the sun and moon, and he also made the stars. God was pleased with what he saw. Evening passed and morning came. That was the fourth day.

Genesis 1.1–16, 18b–19

The creation of living things

God said: 'Let the waters teem with living things, and let birds fly across the sky.' So God fashioned the great monsters and all the fish that live in the sea; and he made the birds that fly in the air. He was pleased with what he saw. Evening passed and morning came. That was the fifth day.

God said: 'Let the land produce all kinds of animal, domestic and wild, large and small.' And it was so. God was pleased with what he saw. Then he said: 'Now we shall make human beings in our own image, to resemble us. They shall rule over the fish of the sea, the birds of the air, and the animals that move on the land.' So God created human beings, fashioning them like himself. He made them male and female, blessed them, and said: 'Be fruitful and multiply; fill the earth and subdue it. Rule over the fish of the sea, the birds of the air, and the animals that move on the land. I have provided you with every kind of grain and fruit to eat; and for the animals and birds I have provided all sorts of green plants.' And it was so.

God saw all that he had made, and was very pleased. Evening passed and morning came. That was the sixth day.

By the seventh day God had completed his work, and he rested. He blessed the seventh day and made it holy.

Genesis 1.20−21, 23−24, 25b−31a; 2.2−3a

The tree of knowledge

God planted a garden in Eden, which is in the east, and he put there the first man and woman. In the middle of the garden stood the tree which gives life, and the tree that gives knowledge of good and evil. He said to the man and woman: 'You may eat the fruit of any tree in the garden, except the tree which gives knowledge of good and evil; if you eat the fruit of that tree, you will die the same day.'

The snake was the most cunning of all God's creatures. He asked the woman: 'Did God really say that you must not eat certain fruits?' The woman replied: 'We may eat the fruit from any tree in the garden except the one in the middle. God has told us not to eat the fruit of that tree; if we do, we shall die the same day.' The snake said: 'You will not die. God knows that when you eat this fruit, your eyes will be opened; you will become like God, knowing good and evil.'

The woman admired the beauty of the tree; she was convinced its fruit would be sweet, and would confer wisdom on her. She took some and ate it, and also gave some to her husband, who was with her. Their eyes were opened, and they realized they were naked; so they sewed fig leaves together, and covered themselves.

Genesis 2.8–9, 16–17; 3.1–7

God's judgement

That evening the man and the woman heard the Lord God walking in the garden, and they hid from him among the trees. The Lord God called to the man: 'Where are you?' The man replied: 'I heard you in the garden; I was afraid because I am naked, and I hid from you.' God asked: 'Who told you that you were naked? Have you eaten the fruit which I commanded you not to eat?' The man answered: 'The woman, whom you put here with me, gave me the fruit, and I ate it.' God said to the woman: 'Why did you do this?' The woman replied: 'The snake tricked me.'

The Lord God said to the woman: 'I shall increase the pains of pregnancy and childbirth. You will desire your husband, and yet you will be subject to him.'

Then he said to the man: 'Because of what you have done, the ground will be cursed. You will have to work hard all your life to gain enough food from it. It will produce thorns and thistles, and you will have to eat wild plants. By the sweat of your brow you will eat, until you return to the ground from which you came. You are made of dust, and to dust you will return.'

Adam, which means 'man', named his wife Eve, because she would be the mother of all human beings.

Then the Lord God said: 'Human beings are now like us, knowing good and evil. They must not be allowed to eat fruit from the tree of life, and live for ever.' So he banished them from the garden of Eden.

Genesis 3.8–13, 16–20, 22–23a

Cain and Abel

Adam had intercourse with his wife, and she became pregnant. She gave birth to a son, whom she named Cain. Later she gave birth to another son, Abel. When they grew up, Cain tilled the soil, while Abel became a shepherd.

One day Cain brought some of his crops as an offering to the Lord. Then Abel brought the first lamb of one of his sheep, killed it, and offered the best parts to the Lord. The Lord was pleased with Abel and his offering, but rejected Cain's offering.

Cain scowled with anger. The Lord said to him: 'Why are you angry? Why do you scowl? If you had acted rightly, you would be smiling. But because you have acted wrongly, sin is crouching at your door; it wants to overcome you, but you must master it.'

Then Cain said to his brother Abel: 'Let us go out to the fields.' When they were in the fields, Cain attacked his brother Abel, and killed him. The Lord asked Cain: 'Where is your brother Abel?' Cain answered: 'I do not know. Am I my brother's guardian?' The Lord said: 'Why have you done this? Your brother's blood cries out to me from the ground. Now you are cursed from the ground. You will become a restless wanderer on the earth.' Cain said: 'Your punishment is more than I can bear. Anyone who finds me, will kill me.' The Lord put a mark on Cain, to warn anyone who met him, not to kill him.

Genesis 4. 1a, 2–11a, 12b–13, 14b, 15b

The Flood

The Lord saw that human beings had become wicked, and their thoughts inclined constantly towards evil. He felt sorry that he had created them, and he was so filled with sadness that he declared: 'I shall wipe humankind from the face of the earth. I shall also wipe out the animals and the birds. I regret having made any of them.'

But the Lord was pleased with Noah, who had no faults, and was the only righteous man on earth. The Lord commanded Noah to build a boat. Then he said: 'I am going to send a flood on the earth to destroy all living beings; every creature will die. Go into the boat with your wife, your sons and their wives. Take with you a male and a female of every kind of animal and bird, in order to keep them alive. And take all kinds of food for you and for them.'

The rain continued for forty days; and as the waters rose, they lifted the ark high above the earth. The waters became so deep that they covered even the tallest mountains; and the boat drifted on the surface. The Lord destroyed every human being, animal and bird. Only Noah, and those who were with him, survived.

Genesis 6.5–8, 9b, 14a, 17–21; 7.17–19, 23

The rainbow

Then the rain stopped, and for a hundred and fifty days the waters gradually subsided. Finally the boat came to rest on the mountains of Ararat. Noah came out, with his wife, his sons and their wives. They were followed by all the animals and birds, one kind after another.

God said to Noah and his sons: 'I am now making a covenant with you and your descendants, and with all the animals and birds that came out of the boat with you – with every living creature on earth. With these words I make my covenant: I promise that never again will every living creature be destroyed by a flood; never again will a flood destroy the earth. This covenant between me and you and every living creature will last for all generations to come. As a sign I am setting my rainbow in the clouds. Whenever I cover the sky with clouds and the rainbow appears, I shall remember my promise to you and to all creatures.'

Genesis 8.3–4, 18–19; 9.8–15a

The Tower of Babel

At first the people of the world had one language, and spoke in the same way. As they moved eastwards, they came to a plain, and settled there. They said to one another: 'Let us make bricks, and bake them hard. And let us build ourselves a city, with a tower that reaches the sky. In this way we shall make a name for ourselves, and not be scattered across the earth.' So with bricks instead of stone, and tar as mortar, they began to build a city and a high tower.

The Lord came down to see their work, and said: 'As one people with one language there is no limit to what they can do. Let us go down and confuse their language, so they will not understand each other.'

So the Lord scattered them across the earth, and they stopped building the city. The city was called Babel, because there the Lord confused human language.

Genesis 11.1—9a

God's call to Abram

Abram was a descendant of Noah's son Shem. The Lord said to Abram: 'Leave your country, your relatives and your father's home, and go to the land I shall show you. I shall give you many descendants, and they will become a great nation. I shall bless those that bless you, and curse those that curse you; and through you I shall bless all the nations on earth.'

So Abram left, as the Lord had told him, and his nephew Lot went with him. He took his wife Sarai, and all the possessions and slaves they had acquired; and they set out for the land of Canaan. When Abram arrived in Canaan, the Canaanites themselves were still living there.

The Lord appeared to Abram, and said: 'I shall give this land to your descendants.' Abram built an altar to the Lord, and worshipped him. Then he continued towards the southern part of the country.

Genesis 12.1–2a, 3–4a, 5a, 6b–7a, 8b–9

God's covenant with Abram

Abram had a vision in which the Lord spoke to him: 'I shall be your shield, and I shall bestow upon you a great reward.' But Abram answered: 'Sovereign Lord, what good is your reward to me, since I have no children? One of my servants will inherit my property.' The Lord spoke again: 'A servant will not inherit your property; your own son will be your heir.' The Lord took him outside, and said: 'Look at the sky, and count the stars – if, indeed, you can count them. Your descendants will be as numerous as they are.'

Abram put his trust in the Lord; and the Lord was pleased with him, regarding him as righteous.

Genesis 15.1–6

Hagar and Ishmael

Sarai said to Abram: 'The Lord has kept me from having children. Go and lie with Hagar, my slave girl from Egypt. Perhaps she can bear a child on my behalf.' Abram agreed to Sarai's proposal. He had intercourse with Hagar, and she became pregnant.

When she found that she was pregnant, Hagar grew proud, and despised Sarai. So Sarai said to Abram: 'You are responsible for Hagar's contempt for me. I myself gave her to you. May the Lord judge between you and me.' Abram replied: 'She is your slave, and you can do what you wish with her.' Sarai treated Hagar so cruelly that she ran away.

The angel of the Lord met Hagar in the desert, and asked: 'Hagar, slave of Sarai, where have you come from, and where are you going?' Hagar replied: 'I am fleeing from my mistress.' The angel said: 'Go back to her, and submit to her.' Then he added: 'I shall give you descendants too numerous to count. You will bear a son, and you will name him Ishmael, because the Lord has heard your cry of distress. But your son will be like a wild donkey: he will be against everyone, and everyone will be against him. He will live apart from all his relatives.'

Hagar bore Abram a son, and he named him Ishmael.

Genesis 16.2, 4–6, 7a, 8–12, 15

The sign of the covenant

The Lord appeared to Abram, and Abram bowed down before him, his face touching the ground. Then God said: 'Your name will no longer be Abram, but Abraham, because I am making you the father of many nations. I shall be your God, and the God of your descendants. I shall give to you and your descendants this land of Canaan, in which you are now an alien; it will belong to you and your descendants for ever.

'You and your descendants must keep your covenant with me, for all generations. As a sign of the covenant between you and me, you must circumcise every boy, when he is eight days old.

'You should no longer call your wife Sarai; her name will be Sarah. I shall bless her, and I shall give you a son by her. She will become the mother of many nations; there will be kings among her descendants.'

Abram began to laugh, saying to himself: 'Can a man have a child when he is a hundred years old, as I am? Can Sarah have a child at the age of ninety?' He asked God: 'Why not allow Ishmael to be my heir?' God said: 'No. Your wife Sarah will bear you a son, and you will name him Isaac. I shall keep my covenant with him and his descendants forever. As for Ishmael, I have heard your request: I shall bless him, and give him many descendants; he will be the father of twelve rulers.'

That same day Abraham obeyed the Lord, circumcising his son Ishmael, and all the males in his household.

Genesis 17.1a, 3, 5, 7b–11, 15–20, 23a

Isaac's birth and Ishmael's banishment

The Lord blessed Sarah, as he had promised; she became pregnant, and bore a son. Abraham named him Isaac; and when Isaac was eight days old, Abraham circumcised him, as the Lord had commanded.

The child grew; and on the day he was weaned, Abraham held a great feast. Sarah saw Ishmael, the son whom Hagar had borne to Abraham, playing with Isaac. She said to Abraham: 'Send that slave girl and her son away. He must not inherit any of your wealth; my son Isaac must have it all.' Abraham was deeply distressed, but God said: 'Do not worry about the boy and the slave girl. Do whatever Sarah tells you, because it is through Isaac that your descendants will be named. I shall also give many descendants to Ishmael, and they will become a nation, because he too is your son.'

Early the next morning Abraham gave Hagar some food and a leather bag full of water. He put the boy on her back, and sent her away. She wandered through the desert of Beersheba. When the water was gone, she put the boy under a bush, and sat down some distance away. She began to sob, saying to herself: 'I cannot watch the child die.' God heard the boy cry, and an angel of the Lord spoke from heaven: 'Lift the boy up, and comfort him.' She opened her eyes, and saw a well. She filled her leather bag, and gave water to the boy.

The boy grew up in the desert, and became a skilful hunter.

Genesis 21.1–2a, 3–4, 8–17a, 18a, 19–20

God's test of Abraham

Some time later God tested Abraham. He said to Abraham: 'Take your son, your only son Isaac, whom you love, and go to the region of Moriah. There, on a mountain which I shall show you, offer him as a sacrifice to me.'

Early the next morning Abraham cut wood for the sacrifice and loaded it onto a donkey; then he and Isaac set out. On the third day Abraham saw their destination in the distance. They left the donkey, and Abraham ordered Isaac to carry the wood, while he himself carried a knife and live coals. As they walked along, Isaac asked: 'We have the coals and the wood to make the fire; but where is the lamb for the sacrifice?' Abraham answered: 'God himself will provide one.'

When they arrived at the mountain, Abraham built an altar, and arranged the wood on it. He tied up his son, and placed him on top of the wood. Then he lifted up his knife, in order to kill the boy. But at that moment the angel of the Lord called from heaven: 'Do not hurt the boy. Let him free. Now I know that you honour and obey God, because you have not kept back your son, your only son.'

Abraham looked round, and saw a ram caught in a bush by its horns. He took the ram, and offered it as a sacrifice in place of his son.

Genesis 22.1a, 2–3a, 4, 6, 7b–11a, 12–13

Esau and Jacob

Sarah and Abraham both died at a great age. When he was forty, Isaac married Rebecca. Isaac prayed for her, and she became pregnant with twins. They struggled against each other in her womb. Eventually she gave birth to two sons. The first was red, with hair all over his body; so he was named Esau. The second, who was born holding Esau's heel, was named Jacob.

As they grew up, Esau became a skilful hunter who loved the open country, while Jacob liked to remain quietly at home. Isaac preferred Esau, and enjoyed eating the animals that Esau killed, while Rebecca preferred Isaac.

One day, while Jacob was cooking some lentil soup, Esau came in from hunting, and exclaimed: 'I'm famished. Give me some of that red stuff you are cooking.' Jacob answered: 'I shall give it to you, if you will give me your rights as the first-born son.' Esau said: 'I am about to die of hunger. What good would my rights do me then?' Jacob insisted: 'Swear to me first.' So Esau swore an oath, giving his rights as first-born son to Jacob; and Jacob gave him bread and soup. Esau ate and drank, and then got up and left. Thus Esau showed that he despised his birthright.

Genesis 25.7, 20a, 21–22, 24–26a, 27–30a, 31–34

Isaac's blessing on Jacob

As Isaac grew old, he became blind. One day he called Esau, and said: 'Soon I shall die. Take your bow and arrows, and kill a wild animal for me; then cook it in the way that I like. After I have eaten it, I shall give you my blessing.'

Rebecca overheard Isaac's words, and said to Jacob: 'Go to the flock, and pick two fat young goats. I shall cook them in the way your father likes. Then you will take them to him, and he will give you his blessing.' Jacob replied: 'You know that Esau is hairy, while I am smooth. Perhaps my father will touch me, and discover I am deceiving him. Then I should bring a curse down on myself, rather than a blessing.' Rebecca said: 'Let any curse against you fall on me.'

When she had prepared the food, she put Esau's best clothes on Jacob; and she covered his arms and neck with goatskin. Jacob then took the food to his father. Isaac asked: 'How did you hunt an animal so quickly?' Jacob answered: 'The Lord your God gave me success.' Then Isaac asked Jacob to come closer; he touched Jacob, and said: 'Your voice is that of Jacob, but your hands are those of Esau. Are you really my son Esau?' 'Yes, I am,' Jacob replied. 'Draw near, and kiss me,' Isaac said. Jacob bent over, and kissed his father. When Isaac caught the smell of Esau's clothes, he blessed Jacob, and said: 'May those who curse you, be cursed; and may those who bless you, be blessed.'

Genesis 27. 1a, 2–5a, 6a, 9–13a, 14b–17,
20–22, 24, 26–27a, 29b

Jacob's dream

As Jacob left his father, Esau returned from hunting. He also cooked food for Isaac, and took it to him. 'Who are you?' Isaac asked. 'I am Esau, your elder son,' Esau replied. Isaac trembled violently, and said: 'Who was it, then, who killed an animal and brought it to me? I gave him my final blessing – and now he is blessed for ever.'

When Esau heard his father's words, he wept bitterly, and cried: 'Give me your blessing also, father.' Isaac answered: 'Your brother deceived me, and stole your blessing.' Esau said to himself: 'When my father has died, and the time of mourning is over, I shall kill Jacob.'

Esau told Rebecca of his intention; so she sent for Jacob, and said: 'Your brother Esau is consoling himself with the thought of killing you. My son, do what I say. Go at once to my brother Laban in Haran, and stay with him until your brother's anger cools.' So Jacob started out for Haran.

At sunset he lay down on the ground to sleep, with a stone for a pillow. In a dream he saw a stairway reaching from earth to heaven, with angels going up and coming down. Above the stairway stood the Lord, who said: 'I shall give to you and your descendants this land on which you are lying. I shall be with you, and protect you wherever you go, and bring you back to this land.'

Jacob awoke, and said: 'The Lord is here, and I did not know it.'

Genesis 27.30–31a, 32–35, 41–44; 28.10b–13, 15a, 16

Jacob's marriages

Jacob continued to travel eastwards, until he reached a well. He was talking to some shepherds there, when Rachel, the daughter of Laban, arrived with her father's flock of sheep. The shepherds told Jacob who she was; and he kissed her, crying for joy. 'I am your father's nephew,' he said. She ran and told her father, and he came to meet him. The two men embraced, and Jacob told Laban his plight.

When Jacob had stayed with Laban for a month, Laban said: 'Just because you are a relative, you should not work for me for nothing. What wages do you want?' Jacob was in love with Rachel, so he replied: 'I shall work for you for seven years, if you will give me Rachel in marriage.' Laban agreed. So Jacob worked for seven years to marry Rachel; but his love was so great, that they seemed like only a few days. Then Laban held a great wedding feast.

That night, instead of Rachel, he took his older daughter Leah to Jacob, and Jacob had intercourse with her. In the morning, when he saw Leah's face, he went to Laban, and demanded to know the reason for the deception. Laban replied: 'It is not our custom to give the younger daughter in marriage before the older. If you work for me for another seven years, I shall give you Rachel.'

Jacob agreed. Laban gave him Rachel as his wife, and he had intercourse with her also. Then he worked for Laban for another seven years.

> *Genesis* 29.1–2a, 6b, 9, 11–13a, 15, 18,
> 20, 22–23, 25–27, 28a, 30

Sons by Leah and Bilhah

When the Lord saw that Jacob loved Leah less than Rachel, he gave Leah the ability to have children, but left Rachel barren. Leah became pregnant, and gave birth to a son. She said: 'The Lord has responded to my misery, and now my husband will love me.' She named him Reuben. She became pregnant again, and gave birth to another son. She said: 'The Lord has heard that I am still not loved, so he has given me another son.' She named him Simeon. She became pregnant again, and gave birth to a third son. She said: 'Now my husband will become attached to me, because I have borne him three sons.' He was named Levi. She became pregnant again, and gave birth to a fourth son. She said: 'This time I shall praise the Lord.' She named him Judah. Then she stopped having children.

Rachel was jealous of her sister, and said to Jacob: 'Give me children, or I shall die.' Jacob became angry, and said: 'God has prevented you from having children. I cannot take his place.' Rachel said: 'Here is my slave girl Bilhah. Have intercourse with her, so she can have a child on my behalf. I shall become a mother through her.' Bilhah became pregnant, and gave birth to a son. Rachel said: 'God has vindicated me, and he has heard my prayer.' She named him Dan. Bilhah became pregnant again, and bore Jacob a second son. Rachel said: 'I have had a great struggle with my sister, and I have won.' She named him Naphtali.

Genesis 29.31–35; 30.1b–3, 5–8

Sons by Zilpah, Leah and Rachel

When Leah realized that she had stopped having children, she gave her slave girl Zilpah to Jacob; and Zilpah bore him a son. Leah said: 'I have been lucky.' She named him Gad. Zilpah bore Jacob another son; and Leah said: 'How happy I am. Now women will call me happy.' She named him Asher.

Reuben found in the fields some mandrake plants, which assist fertility. He took them to his mother Leah. Rachel said to her: 'Let me have some of your son's mandrakes.' Leah replied: 'Is it not enough that you have taken my husband's love? Now you are trying to take my son's mandrakes.' Rachel replied: 'If you give me your son's mandrakes, you can sleep with Jacob tonight.' In the evening, when Jacob came in from the fields, Leah went to meet him, and said: 'You will sleep with me tonight, because I have paid for you with my son's mandrakes.'

So Jacob had intercourse with Leah that night, and she bore him a fifth son. She said: 'God has rewarded me for giving my slave girl to my husband.' She named her son Issachar. Leah became pregnant again, and bore Jacob a sixth son. She said: 'God has presented me with a precious gift. My husband will now treat me with honour, because I have borne him six sons.' She named her son Zebulun.

Then God remembered Rachel. She gave birth to a son, and said: 'God has taken away my disgrace.' She named him Joseph.

Genesis 30.9–16, 17b–20, 22a, 23

Jacob's struggle with God

After the birth of Joseph, Jacob said to Laban: 'Allow me to return home.' Laban replied: 'The Lord has blessed me through you.' Jacob put his children and his wives on camels, and set off towards the land of Canaan.

When they reached the River Jabbok, he sent them across, but stayed behind alone. That night a man came and wrestled with him until dawn. When the man saw that he could not overpower Jacob, he struck Jacob on the hip, throwing it out of joint. Then the man exclaimed: 'Let me go, because the sun is rising.' Jacob replied: 'I shall not let you go, unless you bless me.' 'What is your name?' the man said. 'Jacob,' he answered. The man said: 'Your name will no longer be Jacob. You have wrestled with God and with men, and you have prevailed. Your name will be Israel.' Jacob said: 'Tell me your name.' The man answered: 'Why do you want to know my name?' Then he blessed Jacob.

Jacob said: 'I have seen God face to face, and I have survived.' As he left that place, he was limping.

Genesis 30.25, 27a; 31.17; 32.22b–29, 30b, 31b

Joseph and his brothers

Jacob settled in the land of Canaan, where his father had lived. Jacob loved Joseph more than his other sons, because he had been born to him in his old age. He made a robe for Joseph, with rich decorations. When his brothers saw that their father loved Joseph more than any of them, they hated Joseph, and became rude and hostile to him.

One night Joseph had a dream, and he told his brothers about it: 'We were in the field binding sheaves of corn. My sheaf rose and stood up straight. Your sheaves formed a circle round it, and bowed down.' This dream increased their hatred for him, and they said: 'Do you intend to be our king? Will you rule over us?' Then Joseph had another dream, which he related to his brothers: 'I saw the sun, the moon and eleven stars bowing down to me.'

He told his father about his dream, and his father rebuked him: 'What an absurd dream! Do you think that your mother, your brothers and I are going to bow to the ground before you?' But while his brothers were jealous of Joseph, his father pondered the matter.

Genesis 37.1, 3–8a, 9–11

Selling Joseph into slavery

One day, when Joseph's brothers were taking care of their father's flocks, they said to one another: 'When that dreamer comes, we shall kill him, and throw his body into one of the dry wells. We can say that a wild animal killed him.' Reuben pleaded: 'Spare his life. Just throw him into a well, but do not hurt him.'

When Joseph arrived, they ripped off his decorated robe, and threw him into a dry well. A little later, while they were eating, they saw a caravan on its way to Egypt, with camels loaded with spices and resins. Judah said to his brothers: 'What will we gain by killing Joseph, and then covering up our murder? Let us sell him to these people.' His brothers agreed; and they sold Joseph for twenty pieces of silver.

Then they slaughtered a goat, and dipped Joseph's cloak in its blood. They returned home, and handed the robe to their father, saying: 'We found this robe. Does it belong to Joseph?' Jacob exclaimed: 'Yes, it does! Some wild animal has killed him, and torn him to pieces.' He tore his clothes and put on sackcloth. In the following days and months many people, including his sons, tried to comfort him. But he declared: 'I shall continue mourning for my son until the day I die.'

Meanwhile the owners of the caravan arrived in Egypt, and sold Joseph to Potiphar, one of Pharaoh's officers, who was captain of the palace guard.

Genesis 37.12, 19–20a, 22a, 23–27a, 31–36

False accusation

The Lord blessed Joseph, giving success to his work for Potiphar. So Potiphar put Joseph in charge of all his affairs, concerning himself with nothing except the food he ate.

Joseph was well-built and handsome, and soon Potiphar's wife began to desire him. One day she called him, and said: 'Come to bed with me.' He refused, saying: 'Your husband has given me complete authority in this house, except over you. How could I do such a wicked thing, which is a sin against God?' She continued to ask Joseph day after day to come to bed with her, so he tried to avoid her presence.

One day, when he was working alone in the house, she caught him by his cloak, and said: 'Come to bed with me.' He ran out of the house, leaving the cloak in her hands. Then she called one of her servants, and cried: 'The Hebrew came into my room, and tried to rape me. I screamed as loudly as I could. So he ran out, leaving his cloak in my hands.'

When Potiphar returned home, she told him the same story. Potiphar was furious. He arrested Joseph, and threw him into Pharaoh's prison.

Genesis 39.2, 6–8a, 9–17a, 19b–20a

The prisoners' dreams

Some time later Pharaoh's wine steward and baker offended him, so he ordered them to be thrown into his prison. One night they each had a dream. In the morning Joseph noticed that they both looked upset, and he asked the cause. They answered: 'We each had a dream last night, but there is no one here to interpret them.' Joseph said: 'God gives the ability to interpret dreams. Relate them to me.'

The wine steward said: 'In my dream I saw a vine with three branches. As soon as the leaves came out, the blossoms appeared and the grapes ripened. I was holding Pharaoh's cup; so I squeezed the grapes into it, and gave it to him.' Joseph said: 'The three branches are three days. In three days Pharaoh will release you, and restore you to your position – so you will give him his cup, as you did before. Please speak well of me to Pharaoh, so I too may be released.'

Then the baker said: 'In my dream I was carrying three baskets on my head. In the top basket there were all kinds of pastries for Pharaoh, and the birds were eating them.' Joseph said: 'The three baskets are three days. In three days Pharaoh will impale you on a pole, and birds will eat your flesh.'

Three days later Pharaoh held a banquet to celebrate his birthday. He restored the wine steward to his position, and impaled the baker – just as Joseph had said. But the wine steward forgot all about Joseph.

Genesis 40.1–3, 5–14, 16b–23

Pharoah's dream

Two years later Pharaoh had a dream, which he related to his magicians and sages: 'I was standing by the River Nile, when seven sleek, fat cows came out of the water, and grazed among the reeds. Then seven thin, gaunt cows came out of the water – the poorest cows I have ever seen – and ate the fat ones. I woke up, but then fell back to sleep, and my dream continued. I saw seven ears of corn, full and ripe, growing on a single stalk. Then seven other ears sprouted; they were scorched and shrivelled by the desert wind. The shrivelled ears swallowed the full ears.'

None of Pharaoh's magicians and sages could interpret his dream. Then the wine steward remembered Joseph, and told Pharaoh how Joseph had correctly interpreted his own dream and that of the baker. So Pharaoh sent for Joseph, and said: 'I have had a dream, and no one can explain it. I have been told that you can interpret dreams.' Joseph replied: 'I cannot; but God will give Pharaoh the interpretation he desires.'

Pharaoh recounted his dream; and Joseph said: 'The two parts of the dream mean the same. There will be seven years of great plenty throughout Egypt, and then there will be seven years of famine. The repetition in your dream means that the matter has been firmly decided by God, and it will happen soon.'

Genesis 41.1–7a, 8, 9–12, 14a, 15–16, 25, 29–30a, 32

Governing Egypt

Then Joseph said to Pharaoh: 'You should choose a man of wisdom and insight, and put him in charge of the whole country. And you should appoint officials to take a fifth of the crops during the seven years of plenty, and store it in the cities under guard. This food can be used during the seven years of famine, to prevent the people from starving.'

Pharaoh approved the plan, and declared: 'We shall never find a better man than Joseph, who has God's Spirit within him. I now appoint him governor of all Egypt.' He took the signet ring from his finger, and put it on Joseph's finger; he dressed him in robes of fine linen, and put a chain around his neck; and he granted him the second royal chariot, with a guard of honour. He also gave Joseph a wife, Asenath, the daughter of a priest; and Joseph had two sons by her.

Joseph was aged thirty when he became governor of Egypt. During the seven years of plenty he visited each part of the country, collected corn, and stored it in barns in the nearest city. When the famine came, he opened the barns and sold the corn.

The famine also spread to Canaan. When Jacob heard that there was corn in Egypt, he ordered his sons to go there and buy some. But he did not send Joseph's full brother Benjamin, for fear that harm might come to him.

Genesis 41.33–38, 41–43a, 46–48, 50, 56; 42.1–4

Joseph's brothers in Egypt

When Joseph's brothers arrived in Egypt, they bowed to him, with their faces touching the ground. Although Joseph recognized them, they did not recognize him. He said: 'You are spies! You have come to see where our land is unprotected.' 'Sir,' they answered, 'we have come as your servants to buy food. We are twelve brothers – sons of the same man in the land of Canaan. One brother is dead, and the youngest has stayed with our father.' Joseph said: 'To test the truth of what you are saying, I shall keep one of you in prison here. The rest of you can purchase corn, and take it to your starving families. Then you must return, bringing your youngest brother with you.'

The brothers agreed to this, and they handed him silver to buy corn. Joseph picked out Simeon, and tied him up in front of them. Then he gave orders for their packs to be filled with corn, along with the silver.

When they arrived home, they told Jacob what had happened. Then they emptied their packs, and found the silver amongst the corn. They were afraid that Joseph would accuse them of stealing it. Jacob said: 'Do you want to deprive me of all my children? Joseph and Simeon have gone, and now you want to take away Benjamin. Everything is against me!' Then he added: 'I shall not allow my youngest son to go with you. He might come to some harm on the way. I am an old man, and the sorrow would kill me.'

Genesis 42.6b–7a, 9b–10, 13, 19–20,
24b–25, 29, 35–36, 38

Return to Egypt

The famine in Canaan grew worse. And when Jacob and his family had eaten all the corn which had been brought from Egypt, he said to his sons: 'Go back, and buy us a little more food. Take twice as much silver, so that you can return the silver that was in your packs. And take your brother Benjamin. Come back at once. May almighty God cause the governor to have pity on you, so that he will keep neither Benjamin nor Simeon.'

So the brothers, including Benjamin, took the gifts and twice as much silver, and hurried to Egypt. They presented themselves to Joseph. When Joseph saw Benjamin with them, he said to the steward of his house: 'Take these men to my house. They will eat with me at noon. Slaughter an animal, and prepare it.' The servant took the brothers to Joseph's house; and he brought Simeon to them.

When Joseph arrived, he inquired about their health. Then he said: 'You told me about your old father. How is he? Is he still alive and well?' They answered: 'Your humble servant, our father, is still alive and well.' They knelt down, and bowed before him. Joseph pointed to Benjamin, and said: 'So this is your youngest brother, whom you mentioned to me. May God bless you, my son.' At that moment Joseph was overwhelmed with love towards his brother; he rushed out of the room, and wept. Then he took control of himself, washed his face, and returned. He ordered the meal to be served. Benjamin was given five times as much food as the others.

Genesis 43.1–2, 12–17, 23b, 26–31, 34b

After the meal Joseph said to his steward: 'Fill the men's packs with as much food as they can carry, and put each man's money in the top of his pack. Also put my silver cup in the youngest brother's pack.' Early the next morning the brothers were sent on their way. A little later Joseph said to his steward: 'Hurry after those men. When you catch up with them, ask them why they have returned evil for good, by stealing my cup.'

When the steward caught up with them, he spoke as Joseph had instructed. The brothers replied: 'We swear that we have not stolen your master's cup. If any of us is found to have it, he will be put to death, and the rest of us will become your master's slaves.' The steward said: 'The one who has the cup will become my master's slave. The rest of you can go free.' The brothers lowered their packs to the ground, and opened them. The steward carefully searched each pack, starting with the eldest brother's pack, and finishing with the youngest. He found the cup in Benjamin's pack. The brothers tore their clothes, and returned to Joseph's house.

Judah said to Joseph: 'What can we say, my lord? How can we prove our innocence? God has uncovered our guilt. All of us are now your slaves – not just the one who was found to have the cup.' Joseph replied: 'I would not let all of you become my slaves. I want only the one who was found to have the cup. The rest of you may return safely to your father.'

Genesis 44.1–2a, 4, 6, 7b, 9–13, 16–17

Settling in Egypt

Judah pleaded with Joseph: 'If we return to Canaan without our youngest brother, our father will die. He is utterly devoted to the boy. He is so old that, as soon as he sees that he is missing, the sorrow will kill him. I cannot bear to see this happen. Let me stay here as your slave in place of our brother.'

Joseph could no longer control his emotions. He ordered his servants to leave the room; and then he told his brothers who he was. He wept so loudly that his servants heard him. He said to his brothers; 'This is only the second year of a famine that will last another five years. Hurry back to our father, and tell him that all his family can live here in Egypt, where I can provide food.' He threw his arms round Benjamin, and began to weep again; Benjamin also wept as they embraced. Then, still weeping, he kissed each of his brothers.

When Pharaoh heard that Joseph's brothers had come, he declared: 'Let them fetch their father and their families, and I shall give them the best land in the whole of Egypt.'

Thus Joseph's father and brothers settled in Egypt. The descendants of each of the twelve brothers formed a tribe; and all the twelve tribes of Israel prospered.

Genesis 44.30–31, 33–34; 45.1–2a, 6a, 9a,
11a, 14–16a, 18a; 47.27; 49.28

The oppression of the Israelites

As the years passed, the Israelites spread across Egypt. A new ruler, who knew nothing of Joseph, came to power, and declared: 'These Israelites have become too numerous and strong for us. In the event of war they might join our enemies and fight against us.' So he put them under slave-masters, in the hope of crushing their spirits with hard labour. The Israelites built the cities of Pithom and Rameses as supply centres for Pharaoh. Yet the more the Egyptians oppressed the Israelites, the more the Israelites increased in number, and the further they spread. So the Egyptians grew to fear the Israelites.

Then Pharaoh spoke to the midwives who helped the Hebrew women: 'When a Hebrew woman gives birth to a boy, kill him at once; only let the girls live.' But the midwives feared God, and refused to obey this command. When Pharaoh questioned them about their disobedience, the midwives said: 'The Hebrew are not like Egyptian women; they are vigorous, and give birth before we arrive.' So Pharaoh issued a command to all his people: 'Take every boy born to the Hebrews, and throw him into the river; but let every girl live.'

Exodus 1.8–10a, 11–12, 15–19, 22

The birth of Moses

A man from the tribe of Levi married a woman of the same tribe, and she bore him a son. She hid the boy for three months. But when she could hide him no longer, she took a basket made from bulrushes, and covered it with tar; then she placed the baby inside, and put it amongst the reeds on the edge of the river. The baby's sister stood at a distance to see what would happen.

Pharaoh's daughter came down to the river to bathe. She saw the basket among the reeds, and sent a slave girl to fetch it. She opened it, and saw the baby. He was crying, and she felt sorry for him. 'This is one of the Hebrew babies,' she said. The baby's sister asked: 'Shall I call a Hebrew woman to nurse the baby for you?' Pharaoh's daughter answered: 'Please do.' So the girl fetched the baby's own mother. Pharaoh's daughter said to her: 'Take this baby and nurse it; and I shall pay you.' The mother took the baby to her home, and cared for him.

When the boy grew older, she brought him to Pharaoh's daughter, who adopted him as her own son. Pharaoh's daughter said to herself: 'I pulled him out of the water; I shall name him Moses.'

Exodus 2.1–10

Escape and marriage

When Moses had grown up, he went to visit his own people, and observed how hard they were compelled to work. In Moses's presence an Egyptian killed a Hebrew. Moses glanced all around; and thinking that no one was watching, he killed the Egyptian, and hid his body in the sand.

The next day Moses returned, and saw two Hebrews fighting. He asked the one in the wrong: 'Why are you hitting a fellow Hebrew?' The man said: 'Who appointed you to rule and judge us? Are you going to kill me, just as you killed that Egyptian?' Moses was afraid, saying to himself: 'People have found out what I did.' When Pharaoh heard about Moses' action, he tried to kill him. But Moses escaped, and went to live in Midian.

The priest at Midian, called Jethro, had seven daughters. One day, when Moses was sitting by a well, the daughters came to draw water for their father's sheep and goats; but some shepherds drove them away. Moses came to their rescue, and drew water for them. When they returned home, they told their father that an Egyptian had protected them. Jethro said: 'Why did you leave this man? Go and invite him to eat with us.' Moses agreed to live with them; and Jethro gave him his daughter Zipporah in marriage.

The Israelites continued to suffer under slavery, and cried out for help. God heard their cry, and remembered his covenant.

Exodus 2.11–17, 19a, 20b–21, 23b–24a

God's call to Moses

One day, while he was tending Jethro's sheep and goats, Moses led them across the desert to the holy mountain of Sinai. There the angel of the Lord appeared to him as flames from within a bush. Moses saw that the bush was on fire, but did not burn up. He thought: 'This is strange. I must look more closely.'

When the Lord saw Moses move closer, he called to him from within the bush: 'Moses! Moses!' 'Here I am,' Moses replied. God said: 'Do not come any closer. Take off your sandals, for you are standing on holy ground. I am the God of your ancestors, of Abraham, Isaac and Jacob.' Moses covered his face, because he was afraid to look at God.

The Lord said: 'I have seen the misery of my people in Egypt. I have heard them cry out to be rescued from their slave-masters. I understand their sufferings, and I have come down to set them free. I shall take them from the hands of the Egyptians, to a rich and fertile land, flowing with milk and honey. I am sending you to Pharaoh, to lead my people out of his country.'

Moses said: 'Who am I, that I should go to Pharaoh, and bring my people out of Egypt?' God replied: 'I shall be with you. When you have brought the people out of Egypt, you will worship me on this mountain. That will be the sign that I have sent you.'

Exodus 3.1–8a, 10–12

God's name

Moses said to God: 'Suppose that I go to the Israelites, and say to them that the God of their ancestors has sent me to them. They will ask me your name. What should I tell them?' God replied: 'I am who I am. Say to the Israelites that "I am" has sent you to them. This is my name for ever; this is what all future generations will call me.'

Then Moses said: 'Lord, I have never been eloquent; and I have not become eloquent since you appeared to me. I am slow and hesitant in speaking.' The Lord said: 'Who gives people their mouths? Who can make them deaf and dumb? Who gives them sight, and can make them blind? It is I, the Lord. Now go! I shall help you speak, and I shall tell you what to say.'

Moses pleaded: 'Lord, please send someone else.' At this the Lord burned with anger, and said: 'What about your brother Aaron, the Levite. I know that he can speak well. He is already on his way to meet you, and will be glad to see you. You will put words in his mouth, and he will speak on your behalf.'

Moses went back to Jethro, and asked permission to return to his people. Then Moses put his wife and sons on a donkey, and set out for Egypt. Meanwhile the Lord had said to Aaron: 'Go into the desert and meet Moses.' So Aaron went to meet Moses at the holy mountain; and when they met, they embraced.

Exodus 3.13–14, 15b; 4.10–15a,
16a, 18a, 20a, 27

Bricks without straw

Then Moses and Aaron went to Pharaoh, and said: 'The Lord, the God of Israel says, "Let my people go, that they can hold a festival in my honour in the desert."' Pharaoh said: 'Who is the Lord, that I should listen to him, and let Israel go? I do not know the Lord, and I shall not let Israel go.' Moses and Aaron said: 'The Lord has revealed himself to us, and demands that we offer sacrifices to him.' Pharaoh exclaimed: 'How dare you suggest taking your people away from their labours! Your people have become more numerous than the Egyptians – and now you want to stop them from working.'

That same day Pharaoh issued this order to the slave-masters: 'Stop supplying the people with straw for making bricks. Let them gather straw for themselves. But require them to make the same number of bricks as before – not one brick less. They are lazy; that is why they are asking me to let them go and offer sacrifices to their God. Make them work harder, so they have no time to listen to lies.'

The Israelites spent so much time collecting straw, that they were unable to make the same number of bricks as before. So the slave-masters beat the Israelite foremen, and the foremen complained to Pharaoh. But Pharaoh refused to listen to their complaint. As the foremen were leaving Pharaoh, the foremen met Moses and Aaron, and said to them: 'The Lord will punish you for making Pharaoh and his officials hate us.'

Exodus 5. 1–2, 3a, 4–9, 14–15a, 17a, 20–21a

Snakes and blood

Moses turned to the Lord, and said: 'Why have you brought this trouble on your people? Why did you send me here? Ever since I went to Pharaoh to speak in your name, he has treated them with even greater cruelty. And you have done nothing to help them!' The Lord replied: 'You will see what I shall do to Pharaoh. My mighty hand will force him to release the people. I shall compel him to drive them out of his land.'

Then the Lord said to Moses: 'Go again to Pharaoh, and tell Aaron to throw his staff on the ground.' Moses and Aaron returned to Pharaoh, and Aaron threw his staff on the ground in front of him. The staff turned into a snake. Pharaoh summoned his sages and sorcerers. They each threw a stick on the ground, and by their magic powers their sticks also turned into snakes. Aaron's staff swallowed their sticks. But Pharaoh's heart grew hard, and still he would not listen to Moses and Aaron.

The Lord said to Moses: 'Return to Pharaoh when he goes to the river, and demand again that he lets my people go. If he refuses, tell Aaron to strike the surface of the river with his staff.' Moses and Aaron did as the Lord commanded. And when Aaron struck the surface of the river, the water turned to blood; the fish died, and it smelt so bad that the people could not drink from it. Pharaoh's sorcerers did the same thing by their magic powers; and Pharaoh's heart remained hard.

Exodus 5.22—6.1; 7.8–13, 15a, 16a,
20–21a, 22a

Locusts

The Lord said to Moses: 'Go to Pharaoh again. I have hardened his heart and the hearts of his officials, in order that I may perform miracles among them – and thus demonstrate to all people that I am the Lord.'

Moses and Aaron went to Pharaoh, and said: 'If you continue refusing to let our people go, locusts will appear tomorrow throughout your land. They will eat everything, even the remaining trees. They will fill your palaces and your homes.' Then Moses and Aaron turned and left.

Pharaoh's officials said to him: 'How long will this man torment us. Let the Israelite people go, so they may worship the Lord their God. Do you not realize that Egypt is ruined?' So Pharaoh summoned Moses and Aaron, and said: 'Your men may go and worship the Lord your God. But I shall never let you take your women and children. Clearly you are plotting to revolt.' Moses raised his staff, and the Lord caused a wind to blow across the land all day and night; and by morning the wind had brought the locusts. They covered the ground until it was black; and they devoured everything – the crops in the fields, and the fruit on the trees. Nothing green remained.

Pharaoh quickly called Moses and Aaron, and begged forgiveness. Moses prayed to God; and the wind changed direction, carrying away the locusts. But the Lord again hardened Pharaoh's heart, and he would not let the Israelites go.

Exodus 10.1, 2b, 3a, 4–6a, 7–8a, 10b,
13, 15, 16a, 17a, 19a, 20

Passing over the Israelites

The Lord said to Moses: 'I shall inflict only one more disaster on Pharaoh and his people. Then he will let you leave; indeed, he will drive you out of his country.' On the Lord's instructions Moses and Aaron said to the Israelites: 'Each household should kill a sheep or a goat, and smear some of its blood on the doorpost. During the night the Lord will move through the land of Egypt, killing every first-born male, both human and animal. The blood on the doorposts will mark the houses where Israelites live. When the Lord sees the blood, he will pass over that house.' The Israelites did what the Lord instructed.

At midnight the Lord killed all the first-born males in Egypt, from the son of Pharaoh, who was heir to the throne, to the sons of prisoners in Pharaoh's dungeons; and the first-born animals were also killed. There was loud wailing throughout the land, because not a single Egyptian family was spared.

That same night Pharaoh summoned Moses and Aaron, and said: 'Leave my country, you and the Israelites. Go and worship the Lord, as you have demanded. Take your sheep, goats and cattle with you. Also I beg you to bless me.'

So the Israelites set out from their homes in Egypt. There were about six hundred thousand men, plus their women and children.

Exodus 11.1; 12.6a, 7a, 12a, 13, 28–32, 37b

Israelite doubts

The Lord led the Israelites through the desert towards the Red Sea; they were armed for battle. During the day the Lord went ahead of them in a pillar of cloud, guiding them on their way; and at night he went ahead in a pillar of fire, giving them light. Thus they could travel night and day.

Once the Israelites had left, Pharaoh changed his mind, saying to his officials: 'What have we done? By letting the Israelites escape, we have lost their labour as slaves.' So he ordered his chariot to be made ready, and set out with his army. They pursued the Israelites across the desert, and caught up with them on the shore of the Red Sea.

When the Israelites saw Pharaoh and his army marching against them, they were terrified, and cried out to God for help. They said to Moses: 'Were there no graves for us in Egypt. Did you have to bring us to the desert to die? We told you to leave us alone, and let us serve the Egyptians. It would have been better to have remained as slaves than to perish here.' Moses replied: 'Do not be afraid. Stand firm, and you will see how the Lord will save you. The Lord will fight on your behalf; then you will never see these Egyptians again. Be still.'

Exodus 13.18, 21; 14.5–6, 9a, 10–14

Crossing the Red Sea

The Lord said to Moses: 'Why are you crying to me for help. Tell the people to move forward. Then stretch out your arm, and hold your hand over the sea.' So Moses held his hand over the sea; and all that night the Lord drove the sea back with a strong east wind, leaving dry land. Thus the water was divided. The Israelites walked across, with walls of water on both sides.

The Egyptians pursued them, going into the sea with their horses, chariots and drivers. The Lord caused the wheels of the chariots to stick, so they could only move with great difficulty. Then Moses again held his hand over the sea; and at dawn the water returned to its normal level. The Egyptians tried to escape, but the Lord caused the waters to cover them. Not a single member of the Egyptian army survived.

When the Israelites saw the great power that the Lord had displayed against the Egyptians, they stood in awe. They put their trust in the Lord, and in his servant Moses.

Exodus 14.15–16a, 21–23, 27, 28, 31

Manna and quails

The Israelites set out towards Sinai, and reached the desert of Sin. They complained again to Moses and Aaron: 'We wish that the Lord had killed us in Egypt. There we had ample food, and could eat as much as we wanted. But you have brought us into this desert, where we shall starve to death.' Moses replied: 'When you complain against us, you are really complaining against the Lord. He has heard you. In the evening he will give you meat to eat, and in the morning he will give you as much bread as you want.'

In the evening a flock of quails arrived, and covered the ground. In the morning there was a heavy dew; and when it had evaporated, there were thin flakes like frost. Moses said: 'This is the food which God has given you. The Lord commands that each of you should gather as much as you need. No one should keep any for tomorrow.' Some paid no attention to Moses, storing part of what they collected; but the following morning it was full of maggots, and smelt foul – and Moses was angry with them. So all the people gathered exactly what they needed; and when the sun grew hot, the rest melted on the ground.

The Israelites named the food 'manna'. It looked like a small white seed, and tasted like biscuits made with honey. They continued to eat manna for forty years, until they settled in the land of Canaan.

Exodus 16. 1b–2, 8, 13–14, 15b–16a, 19–21, 31, 35

Appointing judges

Jethro, Moses's father-in-law, heard what God had done through Moses for the Israelite people. So he came to Moses, bringing Zipporah, Moses's wife, and their two sons.

The day after Jethro's arrival, Moses was settling disputes among the people, and he was kept busy from dawn until dusk. Jethro asked Moses: 'Why are you doing this task alone?' Moses replied: 'I do it because people come to me, seeking God's will.' Then Jethro said: 'This is too much for one person; you will wear yourself out. Teach the people God's laws, explaining to them how they should live and what they should do. Then select some capable men, who fear God and cannot be bribed, and appoint them as leaders – leaders of thousands, hundreds, fifties and tens. Let them serve as permanent judges. They can bring the difficult cases to you, but they can resolve the simpler cases themselves. Thus they will share your burden, and make it lighter.'

Moses acted on Jethro's advice. Then Jethro returned to his home.

Exodus 18.1a, 2–3a, 13–14a, 15, 18, 20–22, 24, 27b

Climbing Mount Sinai

The Israelites left Rephidim, and camped near Mount Sinai. The Lord called to Moses from the mountain, and Moses went up to meet him. The Lord instructed him to say to the Israelites: 'If you will obey me and keep my covenant, I shall treat you as my most precious possession. All the nations belong to me; and I shall make you a nation of priests, dedicated to me alone.' Moses came down the mountain, summoned the leaders, and repeated the Lord's words. The leaders replied with one voice: 'We shall do everything the Lord commands.'

Moses went up the mountain again, and reported the leaders' response to the Lord. The Lord said: 'Tell the people to spend today and tomorrow purifying themselves.' Moses came down the mountain, and passed on this instruction.

Two days later, as the sun rose, thunder roared and lightning flashed. A thick cloud covered the mountain, and a loud trumpet blast was heard. The people trembled with fear. Moses led them to the foot of the mountain. The Lord descended to the top of the mountain, and called Moses. So Moses climbed the mountain, and the Lord said to him: 'Go down, and warn the people not to come and look at me. If they see me, many will perish. Then return with Aaron.' Moses did as the Lord commanded.

Exodus 19.2–3, 5–8, 10a, 16–17,
20–21, 24a, 25

The ten commandments

God spoke these words: 'I am the Lord your God, who released you from slavery, and brought you out of Egypt. Worship no god besides me. Do not make idols in the form of anything in heaven, on earth, or in the waters below. Do not bow down to any idol or worship it, because I am the Lord your God, and I tolerate no rivals. I punish those who hate me, but show love to those who love me and obey my commandments.

'Do not misuse my name. I, the Lord your God, punish those who misuse my name. Remember the Sabbath, and keep it holy. You should labour for six days, doing all your work; but the seventh day is dedicated to me. On that day no one should work.

'Respect your father and your mother, so that you may live long in the land that I am giving you.

'Do not murder. Do not commit adultery. Do not steal. Do not make false accusations against anyone. Do not desire for yourself another person's house or spouse, or anything else that another person owns.'

Exodus 20. 1–5a, 6a, 7–10a, 12–17

The covenant box and the calf

Some time later the Lord said to Moses: 'Come up to me on the mountain, and stay. I shall give you two stone tablets, on which are written my commandments.' So Moses prepared to go up the mountain. He said to the Israelite leaders: 'Wait here until we return. Aaron and Hur are with you; they can settle any disputes you may have.

As Moses climbed the mountain, a cloud covered it. Then the dazzling light of the Lord's presence descended onto it. After six days the Lord called to Moses from the cloud; and Moses remained on the mountain for forty days and nights. The Lord instructed Moses to make a box, in which the two stone tablets should be kept.

Moses spent so long on the mountain, that the people gathered round Aaron, and said: 'We do not know what has happened to this man Moses, who led us out of Egypt. So make us a god who can lead us.' Aaron replied: 'Take off the gold earrings that your wives, your sons and your daughters are wearing, and bring them to me.' So the people took off their gold earrings, and brought them to Aaron. He melted them down, and poured the molten gold into a mould, which was shaped like a calf.

When the people saw the golden calf, they exclaimed: 'Israel, this is our god, who led us out of Egypt!'

Exodus 24.12–13a, 14–18; 32.1–4

Moses's anger

Moses went back down the mountain, carrying the two tablets on which God's commandments were inscribed. As he approached the camp, he saw the people dancing around the golden calf; and he exploded with fury. He threw the tablets on the ground, shattering them. He took the golden calf, melted it, and ground it into fine powder; he mixed the powder with water, and forced the people to drink it.

Then he said to Aaron: 'What did these people do to you, that you led them into committing such a terrible sin?' Aaron replied: 'Do not be angry with me; you know how prone these people are to evil.' Moses saw that Aaron had lost control of the people, and allowed them to make fools of themselves.

The next day Moses said to the people: 'You have committed a terrible sin. But I shall again go up the mountain to the Lord, and seek forgiveness for you.' When Moses met the Lord, he begged the Lord to forgive the people, adding: 'If you cannot forgive them, remove my name from the book in which you record the names of your people.' The Lord replied: 'I shall only remove the names of sinners who do not repent.' The Lord punished the people by making them ill for a time.

Exodus 32.15a, 19–22, 25, 30, 32–33, 35a

The laws of God

The Lord then said to Moses: 'Cut two stone tablets, and I shall write on them the same words that were on the first tablets – which you broke. Be ready by dawn tomorrow, and come to meet me at the top of Mount Sinai. No one is to accompany you, or be seen on any part of the mountain; and no sheep and cattle are to graze at the foot of the mountain.' So Moses cut two more stone tablets, and early next morning he carried them up Mount Sinai, as the Lord had commanded.

The Lord came down in a cloud, and proclaimed his holy name. Then he passed in front of Moses, and declared: 'I, the Lord, am full of compassion and mercy. I am slow to anger, and overflow with love and faithfulness for every generation. I forgive sin and wickedness.' Moses bowed to the ground at once, and worshipped God. 'O, Lord,' he said, 'if I have found favour in your eyes, I beg you to go with us. These people are stubborn; but forgive their wickedness, and accept them as your own children.'

The Lord said to Moses: 'I now make a covenant with the people of Israel. In their presence I shall perform wonders, which have never been done in any nation of the world. All people will see how great is the work that I, the Lord, will do for you. Obey the laws which I give you today. And do not worship any other god, because I, the Lord, tolerate no rivals.'

Exodus 34. 1–7a, 8–11a, 14

Laws of love

The Lord gave these laws to the people of Israel: 'Be holy, because I, the Lord your God, am holy.

'Do not steal, or cheat, or lie. Do not make a promise in
my name, if you do not intend to keep it; that brings disgrace on my name. I am the Lord your God.

'Do not exploit others or defraud them. Do not hold back
the wages of someone you have hired, even for a single
night. Do not curse the deaf, or put rocks in front of the
blind, causing them to stumble. Fear me, for I am the Lord
your God.

'Do not pervert justice. Do not show partiality to the poor,
or favour to the rich, but be fair in your judgements.

'Do not slander others. And if someone is being accused
falsely, speak out in defence of that person. I am the Lord.

'Do not hate others. If someone has done wrong, speak
frankly – otherwise you will share that person's guilt.

'Do not bear grudges, or seek revenge against those who
have wronged you. Love your neighbour as you love yourself. I am the Lord.'

Leviticus 19. 1–2, 11–18

Laws of respect

'Keep the Sabbath, and honour the place where I am worshipped. I am the Lord.

'Do not seek the advice of those who consult the spirits of the dead; you will be defiled by such people. I am the Lord your God.

'Rise in the presence of old people, and show respect for them. Revere me, for I am the Lord your God.

'Do not mistreat foreigners who live in your land. Treat foreigners as you would treat compatriots; love them as you love yourselves. Remember that you were once foreigners in the land of Egypt. I am the Lord your God.

'Do not cheat others by using false measures of length, weight or quantity. Use honest scales, honest weights, and honest means of measuring length. I am the Lord your God, and I brought you out of Egypt.

'Obey all my laws and commands. I am the Lord.'

Leviticus 19.30—37

The Day of Atonement

'On the first day of the seventh month have a day of rest, to mark the new year. Blow the trumpet to summon the people for worship. Cook food, and offer it to the Lord. Do no work on that day.

   'The tenth day of the seventh month is the Day of Atonement. Fast on that day; eat nothing at all. Come together on that day, cook food, and offer it to the Lord. Do no work on that day, for it is the day when atonement is made for you before the Lord your God – the day when your sin is taken away. Anyone who eats anything on that day, or does any work on that day, will no longer be regarded as one of God's people. This instruction applies to all your descendants, wherever they may live. From sunset on the ninth day of the month, until sunset on the tenth day, you must rest and fast.'

Leviticus 23.24–32

The seventh and fiftieth years

'When you enter the land that I have promised to you, the land itself must observe a Sabbath in my honour. For six years sow your fields, prune your vines, and gather your crops. But in the seventh year let the soil rest; that year will be dedicated to me. Do not sow your fields or prune your vines. Although the soil will not have been cultivated during that year, it will provide enough food for you, for foreigners living among you, for your domestic animals, and for wild animals roaming on your land. Whatever the soil produces, may be eaten.

'Count seven Sabbath years, to reach forty-nine years. Then let a trumpet be blown throughout the land. Make the fiftieth year holy, proclaiming freedom for all who live in the land. During this year all property that has been sold must be restored to its original owner or his descendants; and all who have been sold as slaves should be released, so they can return to their families.

'Thus when you buy and sell property, fix the price according to the number of years before it will be restored to its original owner. If there are many years, the price should be higher; but if there are fewer years, the price should be lower. The price should reflect the number of years that the property can produce crops, before it is restored.'

Leviticus 25.1–4, 6a, 7–8, 9b–10, 14a, 15–16

Poverty and slavery

'If a neighbouring family becomes poor, and can no longer support itself, you must help that family, so that it can continue to live near you. When you lend money to the poor, do not charge any interest; simply take satisfaction in helping them to remain in their homes. And do not make any profit on food that you sell to the poor.

'If a neighbour falls into such dire poverty that he must sell himself to you as a slave, do not make him toil like a slave. Treat him as you would treat a hired worker, and let him serve you until the fiftieth year; then set him free, so that he can return to his family. The people of Israel are my slaves, because I brought them out of Egypt; they must not become slaves to any human master.

'Suppose a foreigner living near you grows rich, while a fellow Israelite becomes poor, and sells himself as a slave to that foreigner or to a member of his family. His relatives should strive to buy him back.

'Bless the people of Israel with these words: "May the Lord bless you and keep you. May the Lord make his face shine upon you, and be gracious to you. May the Lord turn his face towards you, and give you peace."'

Leviticus 25.25, 35, 36, 37*b*, 39–41*a*, 42, 47, 49*a*;
Numbers 6.22–26

The law of love

'People of Israel, remember this: the Lord, and only the Lord,
is your God; love the Lord your God with all your heart, with
all your soul, and with all your strength. Never forget the
laws that I give you. Teach them to your children. Repeat
them when you are at home and when you are travelling,
when you are resting and when you are working. Tie them
on your arms, and bind them on your foreheads, to remind
you of them. Write them on the doorposts of your houses
and on your gates.

'If you listen to my laws, and obey them faithfully, then
the Lord your God will keep his covenant of love with you,
as he promised your ancestors. He will love and bless you,
and give you many children. He will bless your fields, so that
you have ample corn, wine and olive oil; and he will bless
your calves and your lambs. No people in the world will be
as richly blessed as you.'

Deuteronomy 6.4–9; 7.12–13a, 14a

Passover and Harvest Festival

'Each year, on the night that the Lord your God rescued you from Egypt, celebrate the Passover. Slaughter one of your sheep or cattle for the Passover meal. Do not eat bread made with yeast; for seven days you should eat unleavened bread, as you did when you fled in haste from Egypt. This is the bread of affliction; by eating it, you will remember all the days of your life the time when you escaped from Egypt. For seven days no one throughout the land should possess any yeast. The meat of the animal slaughtered on the evening of the first day, must be consumed before dawn.

'Count seven weeks from the time when you begin to harvest the corn. Then celebrate the Harvest Festival. Honour the Lord your God by offering freely a proportion of the crop he has given you. Rejoice in God's presence – along with your children and your servants, and the foreigners, orphans and widows living near you.'

Deuteronomy 16.1b, 2b–4, 9–11a

Choice between good and evil

'My laws are not too difficult or beyond your reach. My laws are not written in the sky; so you do not have to fly in the sky in order to hear and obey them. Nor are they written on the other side of the ocean; so you do not have to cross the ocean in order to hear and obey them. No, my laws are close to you; they are in your mouth and in your heart. So you may easily obey them.

'Today I am giving you a choice between good and evil, between life and death. Today I invite you to love me, the Lord your God; I invite you to walk on my path, and keep my laws. If you accept my invitation, you will prosper and multiply; I shall bless you in the land that you are about to occupy. But if you refuse to obey my laws, and are drawn away to worship other gods, you will be destroyed. I warn you here and now: if you turn away from me, you will not live long in the land across the River Jordan that you will soon possess.

'Today I am giving you a choice between life and death, between my blessing and my curse; and may heaven and earth witness the choice which you make. Choose life. Love me, obey me, and be faithful to me. Then you and your descendants will live long in the land which I promised to your ancestors, Abraham, Isaac and Jacob.'

Deuteronomy 30.11–20

Joshua's appointment and Moses's death

When Moses had finished conveying God's laws to the people of Israel, he said: 'I am now too old to be your leader. The Lord has told me that I shall not cross the Jordan. The Lord your God will himself guide you into the land that you will possess. And he has said that Joshua will be your leader.'

Then Moses summoned Joshua, and said to him in the presence of all the people of Israel: 'Be determined and courageous. You will lead your people into the land that the Lord promised to our ancestors. The Lord himself will guide you. He will never fail you or abandon you; so do not be afraid or anxious.'

Moses wrote down God's laws. Then he gave what he had written to the descendants of Levi; they were the priests, who carried the Lord's covenant box. Moses said to the priests and to all the leaders: 'At the end of every seven years read aloud God's laws. Call together all the men, women and children, and all the foreigners who live among you; let them listen carefully, and thus learn to fear the Lord your God and to obey him.'

Moses went to the top of Mount Pisgah, east of Jericho. The Lord said to him: 'From here you can see the land which I promised to Abraham, Isaac and Jacob. Their descendants will occupy it; but you yourself will never enter it.' Then Moses died. At the time of his death he was still strong, and his eyesight was good. The people of Israel mourned for him for thirty days.

Deuteronomy 31.1–3a, 6–10a, 12–13a;
34.1a, 4–5a, 7b–8a

The fall of Jericho

Spies reported to Joshua that the people of Jericho were terrified of the Israelites. The next morning Joshua led the people to the River Jordan. When they had all crossed the river, Joshua pressed forward to Jericho.

The gates of Jericho were closed against the Israelites; no one could enter or leave the city. At the Lord's command, Joshua led his soldiers round the city once a day for six days. In front of them a group of priests carried the covenant box, with seven other priests carrying trumpets. On the seventh day the soldiers, led by Joshua, and the priests marched round the city seven times.

Then the priests blew their trumpets. As the soldiers heard the sound, they gave a loud shout – and the walls of the city collapsed. The soldiers charged into the city, and captured it.

Joshua summoned the two men who had served as spies. He told them to fetch Rahab and her family, and take them to safety near the Israelite camp. Then Joshua ordered his men to set fire to the city, and burn it to the ground.

Joshua 2.24b; 3.1a; 4.1a; 6.1–4a, 15a, 20, 22, 23b–24a

Joshua's final address

The Israelites gradually brought the whole of Canaan under their control. Then Joshua called together all the leaders, and spoke to them: 'I am now very old. You have seen what the Lord your God has done for you; he has been fighting on your behalf. You now possess all the land between the Red Sea in the east and the Mediterranean Sea in the west.

'Remain strong. Be careful to obey all the laws that Moses wrote down for you. Do not neglect a single law. Do not associate with those who do not obey those laws. Do not invoke the names of other gods, or swear by them; never bow down and worship any god but God. Hold fast to God, as you have done until now.

'As you have advanced through the land, the Lord has driven out great and powerful nations; no one has been able to stand against you. Any one of you can make a thousand men run away, because the Lord your God fights by your side – just as he promised. So be careful always to love the Lord your God.

'Now the time has come for me to die. You know in your hearts and souls that the Lord your God has kept all the promises he made to you; he has never failed you. But just as he has kept all his promises, so he will carry out all his threats. If you violate the covenant of the Lord your God, his anger will burn against you; and soon none of you will be left in this beautiful land that he has given you.'

Joshua 18.1a; 23.2–3, 4b, 6–11, 14–16

The birth of Samson

Joshua dismissed the people of Israel; and they each took possession of the land that he had assigned to them. As long as Joshua lived, the Israelites served the Lord. And after his death they continued to serve the Lord, so long as the old leaders remained alive – because they had seen for themselves the great things that the Lord had done for Israel. But when Joshua and those leaders had died, the next generation forgot the Lord, and sinned against him by serving other gods. So God let the Philistines defeat the Israelites, and rule over them for forty years.

At that time the Lord's angel appeared to an elderly woman, who belonged to the tribe of Dan. He said to her: 'Although you have been childless for many years, soon you will become pregnant. While you are pregnant, do not drink any wine or other fermented drink. You will give birth to a son. His hair must never be cut. From the day of his birth he will be dedicated to God, with the purpose of rescuing Israel from the Philistines.'

When the boy was born, the woman named him Samson. As he grew, the Lord blessed him, and the Spirit of the Lord gave him strength.

Judges 2.6–7, 10; 13.1, 3–4a, 5, 24–25a

Samson's riddle

One day Samson felt attracted to a young Philistine woman, and told his parents that he wanted to marry her. His parents said: 'Why must you go the heathen Philistines for a wife? Surely our own tribe contains a suitable woman.' But Samson was insistent, and he set off for the young woman's home.

On his way a young lion attacked him, roaring loudly. Suddenly the Spirit of the Lord came upon him, making him strong. He tore the lion apart with his bare hands, as if it were a young goat. When he reached the young woman's house, he talked with her, and liked her greatly. A few days later he married her, and took her back to his own home. On the way he left the road to look at the lion he had killed, and found a swarm of bees and some honey inside its carcass. He scraped the honey into his hands, and ate it as he walked along. Later he gave some to his parents.

Samson held a banquet in honour of his bride, to which thirty young Philistine men came. Samson said to them: 'Let me tell you a riddle. If you can give me the answer within seven days, I shall give you each a set of clothes made of fine linen.' The men accepted the challenge. So Samson told the riddle: 'Out of the eater came something to eat; out of the strong came something sweet.'

Judges 14. 1b–2a, 3a, 5b–6a, 7–9a, 10b–12, 14a

Solving Samson's riddle

For three days the thirty Philistine men could not find an answer to Samson's riddle. On the fourth day they said to Samson's wife: 'Trick your husband into revealing the answer – otherwise we shall set fire to your father's house, with you inside.'

So she went to Samson, burst into tears, and said: 'You do not love me; you hate me. You have challenged my people with a riddle, but you have not told me the answer.' Samson replied: 'Even my own parents do not know the answer. Why should I tell you?' She continued sobbing for seven days. Then Samson relented, telling her the answer; and she immediately told the Philistine men. The Philistine men went to Samson, and said: 'What could be sweeter than honey? What could be stronger than a lion?' Samson replied: 'If you had not ploughed with my cow, you would not have solved my riddle.'

Suddenly the Spirit of the Lord came upon him, making him strong. He went out and killed thirty Philistine men, and stripped them; and he gave their clothes to the thirty men who had answered the riddle. Then he returned home, burning with anger.

Judges 14.14b–15a, 16–17, 18b–19

Samson's revenge

Samson's wife left him, and returned to her father's house; he gave her to Samson's closest friend. Some time later, just before the harvest, Samson went to see his wife, taking a young goat. He said to her father: 'I want to visit my wife's room.' But her father would not let him enter, saying: 'I honestly believed that you hated her, so I gave her to your friend.'

Samson said: 'Now I shall take revenge on the Philistine people; I shall do them terrible harm.' He went out and caught three hundred foxes, and tied them tail to tail in pairs. Then he fastened a torch in each knot, lit the torches, and let the foxes loose in the Philistine fields. The foxes burnt the ripened corn, and then burnt the olive groves.

When the Philistines heard what had happened, they blamed Samson's father-in-law, because he had given Samson's wife to a friend. So they went and burnt down his house, with Samson's wife inside. Seeing what they had done, Samson roared at them: 'So this is the way you act! Now I shall take even greater revenge.' He attacked them viciously, and slaughtered a large number. Then he went to live in a remote cave.

Judges 14.20; 15.1–2a, 3–5, 6b, 8a

Defeating the Philistines

A group of Philistines marched to the tribe of Judah, and said: 'We want to take Samson prisoner, and treat him as he treated us. If you do not hand him over to us, we shall attack you.' So three thousand men of Judah went to the cave where Samson was living, and said to him: 'Do you not realize that the Philistines rule over us? What have you done to us?' Samson replied: 'I merely did to them what they did to me.' The men of Judah said: 'We have come to tie you up, and hand you over to the Philistines.' Samson said: 'Give me your word that you will not kill me yourselves.' They gave him their word. So they tied him up, and took him back.

When the Philistines saw him, they rushed towards him, shouting loudly. Suddenly the Spirit of the Lord came upon him, making him strong. He broke the ropes round his arms and hands as if they were burnt thread, and they dropped away. He saw on the ground the jawbone of a donkey that had recently died; he picked it up, and killed a thousand men with it.

He exclaimed: 'With the jawbone of a donkey I made donkeys of them!' Then he threw the bone away. The Israelite people now acknowledged Samson as their leader.

Judges 15.9b–16a, 17a, 20a

Delilah's trickery

Samson fell in love with a woman called Delilah. The Philistine rulers went to her, and said: 'Trick Samson into telling you the secret of his great strength – and how we could overpower him, tie him up, and render him helpless. Each one of us will give you eleven hundred pieces of silver.'

So Delilah asked Samson the secret of his strength, adding: 'If people wanted to tie you up and render you helpless, how could they do it?' Samson replied: 'If they were to tie me up with seven fresh bowstrings that have not yet been dried, I should be as weak as everyone else.' The Philistine rulers brought Delilah seven fresh bowstrings, and she tied Samson up. With the rulers hidden in an adjoining room, she shouted: 'Samson, the Philistines are coming!' But Samson snapped the bowstrings, as if they were thread snapping when fire touches it.

Delilah said to Samson: 'You have made a fool of me by lying to me. Tell me the truth.' Samson deceived her a second time, saying that if he were tied with new ropes, he would be helpless; and again he broke free.

Then she said: 'How can you say that you love me, when you refuse to confide in me?' She nagged him day after day to tell her the secret of his strength. Eventually he became so weary of her nagging, that he said: 'If my hair were cut, I should be as weak as everyone else.' She knew that he was telling the truth.

Judges 16.4a, 5–9a, 10a, 11, 12b,
15a, 16, 17b–18a

Samson's death

Delilah sent a message to the Philistine rulers, urging them to come back. They came, bringing the silver coins with them. She lulled Samson to sleep on her lap, and cut off his hair. Then she shouted: 'Samson, the Philistines are coming!' As he awoke, he thought: 'I shall shake myself free from them, as I have done before.' But when the Philistines attacked him, he found his strength had gone. They gouged out his eyes; then they took him to a prison, where they tied him in bronze chains, and forced him to grind corn. But his hair began to grow again.

Soon afterwards the Philistines assembled in their temple to celebrate their victory over Samson; and Samson was brought out of prison to entertain them. He was made to stand between the two central pillars of the temple, while the Philistine men and women jeered at him.

'Sovereign Lord,' Samson prayed, 'I beg you to remember me. Give me my strength just once more.' Then he put his hands on the two central pillars, and pushed against them with all his might, shouting: 'Let me die with the Philistines!' The building collapsed, killing three thousand people – including all the Philistine rulers.

Thus Samson killed more Philistines at his death than he had throughout his life.

Judges 16.18b–19a, 20–23a, 25b, 28a, 29–30

Ruth's loyalty

An Israelite widow called Naomi was living with her two sons in the country of Moab. Her sons married local women, Orpah and Ruth; but ten years later both sons died. So Naomi decided to return to her own land. She said to her daughters-in-law: 'Go back to your mothers. I cannot provide you with more sons to marry. The Lord has turned against me, and I do not want you to share my suffering.'

Orpah kissed Naomi, and departed. But Ruth clung to her cloak, saying: 'Do not urge me to leave you; let me go with you. Wherever you go, I shall go; wherever you live, I shall live. Your people will be my people, and your God will be my God. Wherever you die, I shall die – and that is where I shall be buried. May the Lord punish me if anything but death separates me from you!' When Naomi saw that Ruth was determined to go with her, she said nothing more.

They walked to Bethlehem. When they arrived, the whole town was delighted to see Naomi again.

Ruth 1.2b–5a, 6a, 11, 14b, 16–19a

Boaz's kindness

At that time the barley harvest was just beginning. Ruth said to Naomi: 'Let me go into the fields, and gather the corn that the workers leave behind.' Naomi gave her permission. While Ruth was gathering corn in a particular field, the owner of the field arrived. His name was Boaz, and he was related to Naomi by marriage. He asked the foreman of his workers: 'Who is that young woman?' The foreman replied: 'She is a foreigner, who came from Moab with Naomi. She has been working here since dawn.'

So Boaz went over to speak to Ruth: 'Let me give you some advice. Remain in this field; do not go elsewhere to gather corn. I shall order my men not to molest you. And whenever you are thirsty, you may drink from the water jars which they have filled.' Ruth bowed down, her face touching the ground, and said: 'Why are you so kind to me? I am a foreigner.' Boaz replied: 'I have heard how devoted you have been to your mother-in-law since the death of your husband. May you be richly rewarded by the Lord, the God of Israel, under whose wings you have sought refuge.' Ruth said: 'Your kind words give me comfort – even though I am lower in status than the lowest of your servants.'

At the mealtime Boaz said to Ruth: 'Come and eat with me and my workers. Have some bread, and dip it in the wine vinegar.' After the meal Boaz ordered his workers to pull some corn from the bundles, for her to pick up.

Ruth 1.22b; 2.2a, 3a, 4a, 5–6a, 7b–8a,
9b–11a, 12b, 13b–14a, 16

The marriage of Boaz and Ruth

A few days later Naomi said to Ruth: 'We must find a husband for you.' So that evening, at Naomi's instruction, Ruth washed and perfumed herself, and put on her finest clothes. Then she went to the barn where Boaz was threshing the barley. She did not let him see her. After he had finished threshing, Boaz ate a meal, lay down on a pile of barley, and fell asleep. Ruth lifted his blanket, and lay at his feet.

During the night Boaz woke suddenly, and was surprised to find a young woman lying at his feet. 'Who are you?' he asked. She answered: 'I am Ruth. Since you are a relative, you are responsible for taking care of me. So please marry me.' Boaz said: 'Every young man in the town admires your beauty; you could have gone after one of them. In the morning I shall find out whether God intends me to marry you.'

In the morning Boaz went to see the nearest relative of Naomi's husband, and said: 'Naomi wants to sell her husband's field. You have the right to buy it; and if you refuse, the right passes to me.' The man said: 'I shall buy it.' Boaz said: 'You must also take Ruth, Naomi's daughter-in-law.' So the man said: 'In that case my children could not inherit the field; so you may buy it.' According to the custom of that time, the man took off his sandal and gave it to Boaz, as a sign of their agreement. Boaz then announced to the leaders of the town that he would marry Ruth.

Ruth had a son, Obed, whose own son, Jesse, was father to King David.

Ruth 3.1a, 3, 7b–9, 10b–11a, 13b; 4.1a,
3, 4b–6a, 7a, 8a, 10a, 13b, 17b

Samuel's prophetic leadership

The Lord called a young man named Samuel to be a prophet
to the Israelites; and the Israelites, from one end of the
country to the other, acknowledged his prophetic power.
Samuel said to them: 'I urge you to dedicate yourselves to the
Lord with all your hearts. You must rid yourselves of all
foreign gods, and worship the Lord alone, serving only him.
He will rescue you from the hands of the Philistines.' So the
Israelites destroyed their idols, and worshipped only the Lord.
Then Samuel formed the men of Israel into an army.

The Philistine rulers heard of Samuel's action, and set out
to attack the Israelites. When the Israelites saw the Philistine
army, they began to tremble with fear. They said to Samuel:
'Pray to the Lord our God to save us from the Philistines.'
Samuel slaughtered a young lamb, and burnt it whole as a
sacrifice. Then he prayed to the Lord – and the Lord answered
his prayer. As the Philistines moved forward, the Lord caused
thunder to roar in the sky above them. This threw them into
a panic, and they fled. The Israelites pursued them, and killed
them all.

The Lord kept the Philistines away from the Israelites for
as long as Samuel lived. Once a year Samuel travelled around
the Israelite territory, and settled disputes. For the rest of the
year he remained at his home, where people came to seek his
advice.

1 Samuel 3.19b–20; 7.3b–4, 7–11a, 13b, 16–17a

Asking for a king

When Samuel was old, the leaders of Israel went to his home, and said: 'Appoint a king to rule over us. We want to have a king, as other nations do.' This request upset Samuel, so he prayed to the Lord. The Lord answered: 'Listen to all the people are saying to you. In asking for a king, they are rejecting not only your leadership, but also mine. From the time I brought them out of Egypt they have turned away from me, and worshipped other gods; now they are doing to you what they have always done to me. So listen to them; but solemnly warn them of how their king will treat them.'

Samuel said to the leaders: 'This is how your king will treat you. He will turn some of your sons into soldiers; they will ride in chariots pulled by horses, or march in front of the chariots. He will appoint a few of them officers in charge of a thousand men or fifty men. He will compel your other sons to plough his fields, harvest his crops, and make weapons of war. Your daughters will have to make perfumes for him, and cook food for his table. He will take your best fields, vineyards and olive-groves, and give them to his officials. He will take a tenth of your corn and your grapes, and give them to his attendants. He will take your servants, and your best cattle and donkeys, and make them work for him. And he will take a tenth of your flocks of sheep. You yourselves will become his slaves. When that day comes, you will cry out to be saved from the king you have demanded; but the Lord will not listen to you.'

1 Samuel 8.1a, 4a, 5b–18

Anointing Saul as king

The leaders of Israel paid no attention to Samuel's warning, and said: 'We are determined to be like other nations, with a king ruling over us. He will lead us out to war, and fight our battles.' Samuel related these words to the Lord, who replied: 'Do what they want – give them a king.'

A short while later the Lord said to Samuel: 'Tomorrow I shall send you a man from the tribe of Benjamin. Anoint him as king of my people Israel.' The following day Samuel caught sight of a handsome, well-built man called Saul. The Lord said to Samuel: 'This is the man I told you about; he will govern my people.'

Saul came over to Samuel, and said: 'I am looking for the prophet who is said to live in this place.' Samuel replied: 'I am the prophet.' Samuel sent Saul to the local place of worship, and later joined him. They ate together there; then Samuel took Saul to his own home, and he made a bed for him on the roof.

The following morning Samuel took a jar of olive oil, and poured it over Saul's head. He kissed Saul, and said: 'The Lord anoints you as king of his people Israel. You will govern his people, and protect them from their enemies.'

1 Samuel 8.19–22a; 9.15–16a, 17–19a, 24b–25; 10.1a

Saul's transformation

Then Samuel said to Saul: 'Go now to Gibeah, where there is a Philistine camp. At the entrance of the town you will meet a group of prophets, who will be dancing and singing. The Spirit of the Lord will suddenly take control of you, and you will join their singing and dancing; you will be transformed.' Saul did as Samuel instructed. When he began dancing and singing, he was seen by people who already knew him. They said to one another: 'What has happened to Saul? Has he become a prophet?'

Samuel called together the people of Israel. He picked out Saul, who was a head taller than anyone else, and declared: 'This is the man that the Lord has chosen as your king. There is no one to match him.' The people shouted: 'Long live the king!' Then Samuel said: 'If you and your king follow the Lord, all will go well for you. But if you and your king rebel against the Lord, flouting his laws, he will raise his hand against you.'

Saul picked three thousand men to fight the Philistines. The Philistines responded by assembling a vast army, with thirty thousand war chariots. The Philistines had allowed no blacksmiths to work in Israel, to prevent the Israelites from making swords and spears. So, as the two armies faced one another, none of the Israelites possessed a sword, except Saul himself and his son Jonathan.

1 Samuel 10.5–6, 11, 17a, 23b–24;
12.14–15; 13.2a, 5a, 19, 22

Victory against the Philistines

Jonathan said to the young man who carried his weapons: 'Let us go to an outpost of the Philistine army – just you and I. Perhaps the Lord will help us. If he does, it will indicate that he will give victory to our army – even though we are few in number.' The young man answered: 'Whatever you want to do, I am with you.' Jonathan said: 'Come, then. We shall walk towards their men, and let them see us.'

Jonathan and the young man appeared from behind some large rocks. The Philistines soldiers said to one another: 'The Hebrews are coming out of the places where they have been hiding.' Jonathan said to the young man: 'Follow me. The Lord has given Israel victory.' Jonathan attacked the Philistine outpost, knocking down about twenty soldiers; and the young man, who was running behind him, killed them.

Seeing this skirmish, the whole Philistine army panicked. As the confusion grew worse, Saul and his men took the opportunity to march into battle. Some Hebrews, who had joined the Philistine army, now changed sides, adding to the confusion. Within a short time the entire Philistine army was fleeing, with Saul and his men in hot pursuit.

Thus the Lord saved Israel on that day.

1 Samuel 14.6–8, 11, 12b–14a, 15a, 19b–22a, 23a

Saul's curse

Prior to the battle Saul had said: 'A curse on anyone who eats any food, before I take revenge on my enemies.' So the Israelite men had eaten nothing that day, and were now weak with hunger. As they pursued the Philistines, they came to a wood where there was honey everywhere. Jonathan, unaware of his father's curse, dipped a stick into a honeycomb, and ate some honey; at once he felt better. One of the men then told him of the curse. Jonathan said: 'What a terrible thing my father has done! If our men had been well fed, they would have slaughtered even more Philistines.'

At dusk Saul said to his men: 'We shall attack the Philistines again at night, plundering them until dawn.' But the priest, who kept by his side, said: 'Let us consult God first.' So Saul asked God: 'Shall I attack the Philistines? Will you give us victory?' God did not answer. Saul declared: 'Someone has sinned. I swear by the living God, who protects Israel, that the guilty man will be put to death – even if it is my son Jonathan.'

Then Jonathan said: 'Here I am. I ate a little honey. I am ready to die.' Saul exclaimed: 'May God strike me dead, if I do not put you to death.' But the men protested: 'It cannot be right to kill Jonathan – he won this great victory for Israel. We swear by the living God that he will not lose a single hair from his head.'

So the Israelite men saved Jonathan from death. Saul stopped pursuing the Philistines, and led the men back to their own territory.

1 Samuel 14.24, 27–28a, 29–30,
36–39a, 43b–45a, 46

The anointment of David

The Lord said to Samuel: 'I am sorry that I made Saul king. Take some olive oil, and go to Bethlehem, where you will meet a man called Jesse. I have chosen one of his sons to be king.' Samuel said: 'If Saul hears about this, he will kill me.' The Lord said: 'Take a calf with you, and say that you have come to offer a sacrifice to the Lord. Invite Jesse to the sacrifice.'

Samuel did as the Lord instructed. When Samuel saw Jesse's eldest son, he said to himself: 'This surely is the one that the Lord has chosen.' But the Lord said to him: 'Pay no attention to how tall and handsome he is; I have rejected him. I do not judge as humans judge; humans look at the outward appearance, but I look at the heart.' One by one Jesse brought seven of his sons to Samuel. But Samuel said: 'The Lord has not chosen any of these. Have you any more sons?' Jesse replied: 'There is still the youngest; but he is tending the sheep.' Samuel said: 'Tell him to come here. We shall not offer the sacrifice until he comes.'

So Jesse sent for his youngest son, called David. He had fine features, a ruddy complexion, and sparkling eyes. The Lord said to Samuel: 'This is the one; anoint him.' Samuel poured the olive oil over David, in front of all his brothers. At once the Spirit of the Lord took control of David, and remained with him.

1 Samuel 15.10–11a; 16.1b–3a, 4a, 6–7, 10–13a

David's harp

The Spirit of the Lord departed from Saul; and an evil spirit, sent by the Lord, tormented him. Seeing his condition, his servants said to him: 'Let us search for someone who can play the harp. Then, when the evil spirit comes upon you, the sound of the harp will soothe you.' Saul agreed to this suggestion.

Soon afterwards one of Saul's servants said: 'I have found a good musician – David, a son of Jesse from the town of Bethlehem. He is also handsome, brave and eloquent. The Lord is with him.' So Saul sent for David, and David entered his service. Saul liked David, and appointed him to carry his weapons. From then on, whenever the evil spirit came upon Saul, David would take his harp and play; the evil spirit would leave, and Saul would feel better.

1 Samuel 16.14–17a, 18–19a, 21, 23

Goliath's challenge

The Philistines gathered their forces for war against the Israelites; and Saul responded by assembling his army. The Philistines occupied one hill, and the Israelites occupied another, with a valley between them.

A man named Goliath came out from the Philistine camp to challenge the Israelites. He was extremely tall, and wore bronze armour with a bronze helmet; he carried a spear as thick as the rod on a weaver's loom, with a huge iron head. Goliath called out to the Israelites: 'Choose one of your men to fight me. If he wins and kills me, we shall become your subjects; but if I win and kill him, you will become our subjects.' When Saul and his men heard Goliath's challenge, they were terrified.

Goliath challenged the Israelites every morning and evening for forty days. Eventually David said to Saul: 'No one should be afraid of this Philistine. I shall go and fight him.' Saul replied: 'You are only a boy, whereas he has been a soldier all his life. You could not possibly defeat him.' David said: 'When a lion or bear has attacked my father's sheep, I have grabbed it by the throat and killed it. Since I can defeat lions and bears, I can defeat this Philistine – who defies the army of the living God.' Saul said: 'Go; and may the Lord be with you.'

Saul offered his armour for David to wear. But when David strapped the armour on, he could barely walk; so he took it off. He picked five smooth stones from a nearby stream, and put them in a bag. Then he walked towards Goliath.

1 Samuel 17.1a, 2a, 3–5a, 7a, 8b–9, 11,
16, 32–36, 37b–38, 39b–40

Goliath's defeat

When Goliath saw David, he was filled with contempt, and shouted: 'I shall turn your handsome young body into food for the birds and wild beasts.' David replied: 'You come with a sword and spear, but I come in the name of the Lord almighty, the God of the Israelite army, whom you have defied. This very day the Lord will hand your life to me; I shall defeat you, and cut off your head. And I shall turn the bodies of the Philistine soldiers into food for the birds and wild animals. Then the whole world will know that Israel is possessed by God. People will know that the Lord does not need swords and spears to save his people; every battle belongs to God, and he overpowers his enemies.'

Goliath walked towards David, and David ran towards him. Then David put his hand in his bag, took out a stone, and slung it at Goliath. The stone hit Goliath on the forehead, and broke his skull; he fell face downwards to the ground. David ran over to him, took Goliath's sword out of its sheath, and cut off Goliath's head.

When the Philistines saw that their hero was dead, they fled. The Israelites let out a loud shout, and pursued them.

1 Samuel 17.42, 44–49, 51–52a

Jonathan's love and Saul's jealousy

Jonathan had come to love David as much as he loved himself, and he swore a covenant with him. He took off the robe he was wearing, and gave it to David, together with his armour, sword, bow and belt.

The Israelite army returned home, and women from every town came out to greet them. They danced, and played tambourines and lyres. And they sang: 'Saul has killed thousands, but David has killed tens of thousands.' Saul hated this song, and became angry, exclaiming: 'They will be making David king next!'

Saul was now filled with jealousy of David, and was deeply suspicious of him. The next day, when Saul had returned to his house, an evil spirit from God gained control of him. He began raving like a madman. David was playing the harp, as he did every day. Saul took a spear, and said to himself: 'I shall pin him to the wall.' He threw the spear twice at David; but David dodged each time.

Saul decided that he would make David his son-in-law, on condition that he agreed to fight bravely against the Philistines. Saul hoped that the Philistines would kill David, to save him having to kill David himself. Before the day of the wedding David assembled a group of soldiers, and killed two hundred Philistines. He took their foreskins to Saul and counted them out, to show that he was worthy to be his son-in-law. David then married Saul's daughter Michal; and Saul was terrified of David.

1 Samuel 18.3–4, 6b–8a, 9–11,
17b, 26b–27, 29a

David's escape

Saul told Jonathan and his officials that he planned to kill David. Jonathan warned David, whom he loved deeply, of Saul's intentions. Then he returned to Saul, and pleaded with him: 'Do not kill your most loyal servant, who has done you no harm, and done you great good.' Jonathan continued to praise David highly. Saul was persuaded by Jonathan's words, and agreed to spare David.

But that night an evil spirit from the Lord again took control of Saul. He sent men to watch David's house, and to kill David in the morning. Michal said to David: 'If you do not escape tonight, tomorrow you will be dead.' She let David down from a window, and he fled. In the morning, when Saul heard that David had escaped, he summoned her, and asked why she had tricked him. She replied: 'He said he would kill me if I did not help him escape.'

David went to a large cave near the town of Adullam. When his brothers and the rest of his family heard that he was there, they joined him. And people who were oppressed, in debt, or discontented, also came. Soon he had about four hundred men under his command.

1 *Samuel* 19. 1–2a, 4, 6, 9a, 11–12, 17; 22. 1–2

David's conscience and Saul's remorse

Saul took three thousand of the best soldiers in Israel, and went in search of David. Saul came to the cave where David and his men were hiding, and sat down at its entrance. David's men said to him: 'This is your opportunity!' David crept towards Saul, and cut off a piece of his robe without his noticing. Then his conscience began to trouble him. He said to his men: 'May the Lord keep me from harming my master, whom the Lord chose as king.'

Saul rose up, and went on his way. David ran after him, and cried out: 'My master the king!' Saul turned round, and David prostrated himself, with his face to the ground. Then David said: 'Why do you listen to those who say that I am trying to harm you? When you entered the cave just now, the Lord put you in my power – as you have seen. Some of my men urged me to kill you, but I spared you, because God chose you as king. Dear father, look at the piece of cloth in my hand! I could have killed you, but instead I merely cut your robe. Who are you, the king of Israel, pursuing? A dead dog! A flea! The Lord will be our judge, and decide between us.'

Saul started to weep. Then he said to David: 'You are right, and I am wrong. Today you have demonstrated your goodness to me. May the Lord bless you for what you have done today. Now I am sure that you will be king of Israel.'

1 Samuel 24.2a, 3a, 4–6, 7b–11a,
14–15a, 16b–18a, 19b–20a

David and Abigail

David and his men went to the desert of Paran, where a rich landowner called Nabal lived. He was surly and mean, but his wife Abigail was intelligent and beautiful. David sent ten young men to Nabal to wish him well, and to ask for food. Nabal responded by calling David and his men runaway slaves, and refusing their request.

One of Nabal's servants told Abigail that her husband had insulted David, adding: 'This could bring disaster to our master and all his family.' Abigail quickly collected two hundred loaves of bread, two leather bags of wine, five roasted sheep, a large amount of roasted corn, a hundred bunches of raisins, and two hundred cakes of pressed figs; and she loaded the food onto donkeys. Then she rode out to David.

When she saw him, she dismounted, and threw herself at his feet. 'My lord,' she said, 'let me take the blame. Pay no attention to my wicked husband. I beg you to accept this gift of food, and share it with your men. And forgive me for any wrong I have done. I know that the Lord will make you king, because you are fighting his battles; and you will found a great and lasting dynasty.'

David replied: 'Praise the Lord, the God of Israel, for sending you to meet me today. May he bless you for keeping me from the crime of murder.' Then David accepted her gift. That night Nabal suffered a stroke; and ten days later he died. David asked Abigail to marry him, and she became his wife. In the meantime Saul had given Michal, David's first wife, to another man.

1 Samuel 25.1b, 3, 5a, 8b, 10b–11a, 14a, 17b–18, 20a, 23–25a, 27–28a, 32–33a, 35a, 37b–38, 39b, 43b–44a

Saul's death

The Philistines attacked the Israelite army at Mount Gilboa. Many Israelites were killed there; and the rest, including Saul and his sons, fled. The Philistines caught up with them, and killed Jonathan. The fighting grew fierce around Saul, and he himself was badly wounded by Philistine arrows.

He said to the young man who carried his weapons: 'Draw your sword and kill me – to deprive these godless Philistines of the pleasure of doing it.' But the young man was too afraid; so Saul took his own sword, and threw himself on it. When the young man saw that the king was dead, he threw himself on his sword, and died also. When the Philistines found Saul's body, they cut off his head, and put his weapons in their temple.

A messenger ran to tell David of the Israelite defeat, and of the deaths of Saul and Jonathan. David tore his clothes in grief, and all his men did the same. Then the leaders of all the tribes of Israel came to David, and said: 'The Lord promised that you would lead his people, and be their king.' So they anointed David, and declared him king of Israel. David was thirty years old when he became king, and he ruled for forty years.

1 Samuel 31.1–2a, 3–5, 8b–9a, 10a;
2 Samuel 1.2a, 4b, 11; 5.1a, 2b, 3b–4

David's dancing

King David decided to march on the city of Jerusalem, and seize it from the people who lived there. The people were confident that David would not succeed, so they sent him a message: 'Even the blind and the lame could keep you out.' But David captured Jerusalem, and lived in its fortress. He then rebuilt Jerusalem, which became known as the city of David.

David went to collect the covenant box, and bring it to Jerusalem. When the men carrying the covenant box had taken six steps, David ordered them to stop, while he sacrificed a bull and a fattened calf to the Lord. Then he told the men to continue towards Jerusalem. David, wearing only a linen cloth round his waist, danced with all his might in honour of the Lord. And the people accompanying him shouted with joy, and blew trumpets.

As the covenant box was being brought into the city, Michal, Saul's daughter, watched from her window. When she saw King David leaping and dancing in honour of the Lord, she despised him. The covenant box was put in the tent that David had pitched for it; and David offered more sacrifices. Then he blessed the people in the name of the Lord almighty, giving each man and woman bread, meat and raisins.

That evening Michal accused David of disgracing himself. David replied: 'I shall continue to dance in honour of the Lord – and disgrace myself even more!'

2 Samuel 5.6–7, 9a; 6.12b–20a, 21b–22a

Nathan's prophecy and David's prayer

The king built a palace for himself in Jerusalem. One day he summoned a prophet called Nathan, and said: 'I am living in a palace made from cedar, but God's covenant box is in a tent!' That night Nathan received a message from God for David: 'You are not the one to build a temple for me. From the day I rescued the Israelites from Egypt, I have moved from place to place, living in a tent. In all that time I have never asked the leaders of Israel – whom I myself appointed – to build me a temple. When you die, and are buried with your ancestors, I shall make one of your sons king, and he will rule with strength. He will build a temple for me, and I shall uphold his dynasty for ever.'

Then King David went to the tent where the covenant box was kept. He sat down, and prayed: 'Sovereign Lord, I am not worthy, nor is my family, of what you have already done. Yet now you are doing even more: you are making promises about my descendants. What can I say to you? You are acting in accordance with your will and purpose. How great you are, sovereign Lord! There is no one like you; we know that you alone are God. And there is no nation on earth like Israel; you have made the Israelites your own people, and you have become their God. Through Israel your fame will spread.'

Soon afterwards King David attacked the Philistines, and defeated them – and thus he ended their control over the land.

2 Samuel 7.1a, 2, 5–7, 12–13, 18–19a,
20a, 21a, 22–23a, 24, 26a; 8.1a

Ziba and Mephibosheth

David summoned a servant of Saul's family, called Ziba, and asked: 'Is there anyone in Saul's family to whom I can show kindness?' The servant answered: 'There is a son of Jonathan, called Mephibosheth, who is crippled in both feet.'

So King David sent for Mephibosheth, and said: 'Do not be afraid. I wish to be kind to you, for the sake of your father Jonathan. I shall give back to Saul's family all the land that belonged to Saul. And you yourself will always be welcome at my table.' Mephibosheth bowed, and said: 'I am not better than a dead dog, sir. I do not deserve your kindness.' Then King David turned to Ziba, and said: 'You and your sons will farm the land that belonged to your master Saul, to provide food for Saul's family.'

From that day onward Mephibosheth always ate at the king's table, as if he were one of the king's sons.

2 Samuel 9.3, 5, 7–9a, 10a, 11b

Uriah and Bathsheba

The following spring David dispatched the Israelite army, under the command of Joab, to besiege the city of Rabbah. David himself remained in Jerusalem.

One afternoon, as he was walking on his palace roof, David saw a woman bathing. She was very beautiful. A servant informed him that she was Bathsheba, the wife of Uriah. He ordered a messenger to fetch her; then he had intercourse with her. She became pregnant, and sent a message to David, informing him.

David summoned Uriah, who was fighting with Joab. When Uriah arrived, David asked him if Joab and the troops were well, and how the battle was going. Then he said: 'Go home, and rest a while.' Uriah left. But he did not go home; instead he slept at the palace gate with the king's guards. When David heard this, he said to him: 'You have just returned after a long absence. Why did you not go home?' Uriah answered: 'The Israelite soldiers are away at war, and are camping in the open. How could I go home, eat and drink, and sleep with my wife?'

The next morning David wrote a letter to Joab: 'Put Uriah in the front line, where the fighting is heaviest; then retreat, and let him be killed.' Then he gave the letter to Uriah, to take to Joab. So Joab sent Uriah to a place that was strongly defended; and Uriah was killed. When Bathsheba heard that her husband was dead, she mourned. Then David invited her to his palace. She became his wife, and bore him a son.

2 Samuel 11.1, 2, 4a, 5, 6b–8a,
9–11a, 14–16, 17b, 26, 27b

Nathan's rebuke

The Lord sent the prophet Nathan to David. Nathan said to David: 'There were once two men who lived in the same town; one was rich, and the other poor. The rich man had many cattle and sheep, while the poor man had only one lamb, which he had bought. The poor man kept the lamb in his home, and it grew up with his children; it shared his food, drank from his cup, and even slept in his arms. The lamb was like a daughter to him. One day a visitor arrived at the rich man's home. The rich man had to slaughter an animal, in order to feed the visitor. But he did not want to kill one of his own animals; so he took the poor man's lamb, and roasted it.'

David burned with anger at the rich man, and exclaimed to Nathan: 'I swear by the living God that the rich man should die.' Nathan replied: 'You are such a man. The Lord has rescued you from Saul, and given you his kingdom and his wives. If that had not been enough, he would have given you even more. So why did you disobey the Lord's commands? Why did you have Uriah killed in battle, and take his wife?'

David said: 'I have sinned against the Lord.' Nathan said: 'The Lord forgives you, so you will not die. But as a consequence of showing such contempt for the Lord, the son born to you will die.'

2 Samuel 12.1–5, 7–9a, 13–14

The death of Bathsheba's child

The Lord caused the son that Bathsheba had borne, to become very ill. David pleaded with God to cure the child. He fasted, and he spent every night lying on the floor of his room. His servants urged him to sleep on his bed, and to eat with them; but he remained silent.

After a week the child died. The court servants were afraid to inform David, saying to one another: 'While the child was alive, the king refused to speak to us. How can we tell him that the child is dead? He might do himself some injury.' When David noticed his servants whispering, he inferred that his child had died. So he asked them: 'Is the child dead?' 'Yes, he is,' they replied.

David rose from the floor, had a bath, combed his hair, and changed his clothes. Then he went and worshipped the Lord. When he returned to the palace, he asked for food, and ate it as soon as it was served. His servants said to him: 'We are baffled. While the child was alive, you wept for him, and would not eat; but now that he is dead, you get up and eat.' David replied: 'While the child was alive, I fasted and wept, in the hope that the Lord might be merciful, and spare the child. But now that the child is dead, why should I fast? Could I bring the child back to life? One day I shall go to him, but he will not return to me.'

Then David went to comfort Bathsheba. He had intercourse with her, and she bore a son, whom he named Solomon.

2 Samuel 12.15b–24a

Absalom's conspiracy

David's third son, Absalom, who was born before David became king of Israel, was famous for his handsome appearance; from his head to his feet he did not have a single blemish. His hair was very thick, and he cut it once a year when it grew too long and heavy.

He provided himself with a chariot and horses, and an escort of fifty men. Each morning he rose early, and stood at the gate of Jerusalem. People frequently arrived at the city with a dispute, which they wished the king to settle. Absalom would say to each one: 'I do not doubt that your claims are valid; but there is no representative of the king to hear you.' Then he would add: 'How I wish I were a judge! Then everyone with a dispute could come to me, and I should give justice.' The man would bow before Absalom; and Absalom would take hold of him, and kiss him. In this way Absalom won the loyalty of every Israelite who came to the king seeking justice.

After four years Absalom said to King David: 'Let me go to Hebron, as I wish to worship God there.' 'Go in peace,' the king replied. Then Absalom sent a secret message to all the tribes of Israel: 'When you hear the sound of trumpets, cry out that Absalom is king in Hebron.' Two hundred men from Jerusalem accompanied Absalom; and the number of his supporters quickly grew.

2 Samuel 14.25–26a; 15.1–2a, 3–7a,
8b–11a, 12b

David's departure from Jerusalem

A messenger reported to David: 'The hearts of the Israelites are with Absalom.' So David said to his officials: 'We must leave Jerusalem at once – Absalom will soon be here.' As David and his followers marched out of the city, the people wept. They were accompanied by Zadok the priest, and all the Levites, who were carrying the covenant box. The king said to Zadok: 'Take the covenant box back to the city. If the Lord favours me, he will allow me to return, and see the covenant box again in its proper place. But if he does not favour me, let him do to me what he wishes.'

Then David went to the Mount of Olives, his eyes filled with tears; he covered his head, and walked barefoot. Near the top of the hill he was met by Ziba, the servant to Mephibosheth. Ziba gave him two donkeys, laden with bread, raisins, fruit and wine. The king asked: 'Where is Mephibosheth, the grandson of your master Saul?' Ziba answered: 'He is staying in Jerusalem, because he is con-

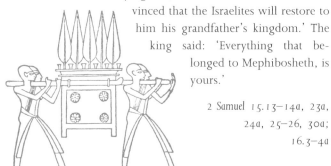

vinced that the Israelites will restore to him his grandfather's kingdom.' The king said: 'Everything that belonged to Mephibosheth, is yours.'

2 Samuel 15.13–14a, 23a, 24a, 25–26, 30a; 16.3–4a

Absalom's entry into Jerusalem

Absalom and his followers now entered Jerusalem; Ahithophel, who had been an advisor to King David, was with them. Hushai, a trusted friend of King David, came out to greet Absalom, shouting: 'Long live the king! Long live the king!' Absalom asked Hushai: 'What has happened to your loyalty to your friend David? Why did you not go with him?' Hushai replied: 'I support whoever is chosen as king by God and the people. So I shall stay with you. After all, is it not appropriate that I serve my master's son? As I served your father, so I shall serve you.'

Then Absalom turned to Ahithophel, and asked: 'Now that we are here, what should we do?' Ahithophel replied: 'Your father left ten concubines to look after the palace. Go and have intercourse with them. Then everyone in Israel will know that you are willing to humiliate your father; and this will strengthen your position.' So a tent was erected on the roof of the palace; and in public view Absalom went into the tent, and had intercourse with his father's concubines.

2 *Samuel* 16.15–22

The defeat of Absalom

Ahithophel then said to Absalom: 'Let me pursue David tonight. I shall take twelve thousand men, and attack him while he is weary and miserable. He himself will be terrified, and all his men will flee. I shall kill only the king, and bring his men to you – like a bride returning to her husband.'

Hushai said: 'Ahithophel's advice is wrong. Your father and his men are hardened fighters, and they will be as fierce as a wild bear robbed of her cubs. Besides, your father is too experienced to spend the night with his troops; even now he is probably hiding in a cave. My advice is that you gather all the Israelites together, from one end of the country to another; and that you personally lead them into battle.'

Absalom declared: 'Hushai's advice is better that Ahithophel's.'

Hushai then sent a message to David: 'Cross the Jordan at once, so that you and your men will not be caught and killed.' So by the time Absalom and his men set out after David, he was far away. David then assembled a large army, and attacked Absalom. After a terrible battle, in which twenty thousand men were killed, David's army prevailed.

During the battle Absalom rode under an oak tree, and caught his hair in its branches. A group of David's soldiers saw Absalom hanging from the tree, and told Joab, David's commander. Joab took three spears, and plunged them into Absalom's chest.

2 Samuel 17.1–3a, 7–9a, 11a, 14a, 16b, 24;
18.1a, 6b–7, 9b–10a, 14b

Joab's reprimand

Joab sent a messenger to inform King David that his army was victorious. The king asked: 'Is the young man Absalom safe?' 'My lord,' the messenger answered, 'I wish that his fate were shared by all your enemies, and by all who rebel against you.' The king was overwhelmed with grief, crying out: 'O my son Absalom! My son, my son Absalom! If only I had died in your place! O Absalom, my son, my son!'

Joab and the troops were told that the king was weeping and mourning for Absalom; so the joy of victory was turned into sadness. They marched in silence, as if they were fleeing from defeat in shame. The king covered his face, and cried loudly: 'O my son Absalom! O Absalom, my son, my son!'

That evening Joab went to the king, and said: 'Today you have humiliated your men – the men who saved your life, and the lives of your sons and daughters, your wives and your concubines. You oppose those who love you, and love those who oppose you! You have made it clear that your officers and men mean nothing to you. I can see that you would have been pleased if Absalom had survived, and all of us had died. Now go and reassure your men. I swear by the living God that, if you do not reassure them, not one will be with you by tomorrow morning. That would be the worst calamity you have ever suffered.'

The king went to his soldiers, and they gathered round him.

2 Samuel 18.21a, 31a, 32–33; 19.1–8a

Solomon's request for wisdom

When David was very old, he summoned his son Solomon, and said: 'I am close to death. Be courageous and determined, and do whatever the Lord instructs. Obey all the laws and commandments, as they are written in the Law of Moses; then you will prosper in all you do.' A short while later David died, and was buried in Jerusalem.

Soon after Solomon had become king, the Lord appeared to him in a dream, and said: 'Ask for whatever you want.' Solomon replied: 'O Lord God, you have allowed me to succeed my father as king. Yet I am little more than a boy, and do not know how to rule. So give me the wisdom I need to govern your people with justice, and to distinguish between right and wrong.'

The Lord was pleased with Solomon's answer, and said to him: 'You could have asked for a long life, or for wealth, or for the death of your enemies. Yet since you have asked for wisdom, I shall make you wiser and more discerning than anyone who has ever lived, or who ever will live. I shall also give you what you have not requested: throughout your life you will enjoy great riches and honour – more than that of any other king. And if you obey me, and keep my laws, I shall give you a long life.'

1 Kings 2.1–3, 10; 3.5, 7, 9a, 10–14

The disputed baby

One day two prostitutes came, and presented themselves to King Solomon. One of them said: 'My lord, this woman and I live in the same house. I gave birth to a boy, and two days later she also gave birth to a boy. We were by ourselves; no one else was in the house. Then one night she rolled over in her sleep, and smothered her baby. She got up, took my son from my side while I was asleep, and put her dead child in my bed. The next morning, when I awoke to feed my baby, I discovered the dead child beside me. But I looked more closely, and saw that he was not mine.'

The other woman protested: 'No! The living child is mine, and the dead child is yours.' The first woman answered: 'No! The dead child is yours, and the living child is mine.' And so they argued in front of the king.

King Solomon sent for a sword. And when it was brought, he said: 'Cut the living child in two, and give half to each woman.' The real mother, whose heart was full of love for her son, exclaimed: 'Please, my lord, do not kill the child. Give it to her.' The other woman said: 'Neither of us should have the child. Go ahead, and cut him in two.' Then Solomon said: 'Do not kill the child. Give the child to the woman who begged for his life. She is the real mother.'

When the people of Israel heard the verdict that King Solomon had given, they had the deepest respect for him; they knew that God had given him the wisdom to judge cases fairly.

1 Kings 3.16–22, 24–28

Cedars for the temple

King Hiram of Tyre had always been a friend of King David;
so when he heard that Solomon had succeeded his father as
king of Israel, he sent his envoys to him. Solomon sent back
this message to Hiram: 'The Lord my God has given me peace
on all my borders; I have no enemies, and there is no danger
of attack. Thus I intend to build a temple for the worship of
the Lord my God. I beg you to give orders that cedars of
Lebanon be cut for me. My men will work with yours; and
I shall pay your men whatever wages you decide. As you
know, my men are not so skilled in felling trees as the men
of your kingdom.'

Hiram was delighted when he received Solomon's
message, and exclaimed: 'Praise the Lord for giving David
such a wise son to rule over this great nation!' Then he sent
Solomon this message: 'I shall provide cedars and pine logs.
My men will haul them down from Lebanon to the sea; and
they will float them in rafts to wherever you specify. There
they will untie them, and your men can take them away. I
ask only that you provide food for my men.'

Thus four hundred and eighty years after the people of
Israel left Egypt, during the fourth year of his reign, Solomon
began to build the temple of the Lord.

I Kings 5. 1–2, 4, 5a, 6–9; 6. 1

The most holy place

The stones with which the temple was constructed, were dressed at the quarry; so at the site of the temple there was no noise from hammers, chisels and other iron tools. When the walls and the roof were complete, the interior was panelled with cedar, and the floor was covered with planks of pine.

A partition was erected with cedar boards at the rear of the temple, to create an inner sanctuary for the covenant box; it was called the 'most holy place'. The walls of the most holy place were overlaid with pure gold. An altar made of cedar was put there, and it too was overlaid with gold.

A pointed arch was cut into the cedar partition as the entrance to the most holy place. A double door was hung across the entrance; it was made from olive wood, and decorated with carvings of birds, trees and flowers. Two tall winged creatures were also carved out of olive wood, and covered with gold. They were carried into the most holy place, and placed on either side; their outstretched wings touched opposite walls, and touched in the middle.

The temple took seven years to build.

1 Kings 6.7, 15–16a, 20b–21a, 22b–23a,
27–28, 31–32, 38b

The covenant box in the temple

King Solomon summoned all the leaders of the tribes and clans of Israel to Jerusalem, to see the covenant box taken to the temple. When they had gathered, King Solomon led them to the covenant box, where they sacrificed so many sheep and cattle that they could not be counted. Then the priests carried the covenant box into the temple, and placed it in the most holy place, beneath the winged creatures. There was nothing inside the covenant box except the two stone tablets that Moses had put there at Mount Sinai. As the priests were leaving the most holy place, a cloud filled the temple; and within the cloud a light shone, indicating the presence of the Lord.

Then Solomon stood in front of the altar, lifted his hands towards heaven, and prayed: 'Lord God of Israel, there is no god like you in heaven above, or on the earth below. You keep your covenant of love with your people – when they obey you with all their hearts. Yet can you, O God, truly dwell on the earth? Not even all of heaven is large enough to hold you; so how can this temple, which I have built, be large enough? Lord my God, I am your servant; listen to my prayer, and grant the requests that I make today. Day and night watch over this temple, this place where you have chosen to be worshipped. Hear my prayers, and the prayers of my people, when they turn towards this place. In your home in heaven, listen to us, and forgive us.'

1 Kings 8.1, 5–6, 9a, 10–11a, 22–23, 27–30

Solomon's prayer

Solomon continued to pray: 'When one person accuses another of doing wrong, let both people be brought to this temple, and swear to tell the truth. Then, Lord, judge between them in heaven, condemning the one who is guilty, and acquitting the one who is innocent.

'When your people Israel have sinned against you, and therefore they are defeated in battle, let them come to this temple and repent. Then, Lord, listen to them in heaven. Forgive their sins, and restore to them the land which you gave to their ancestors, and which they have lost.

'When your people have sinned against you, and therefore you withhold the rain, let them come to this temple and repent. Then, Lord, listen to them in heaven. Forgive the sins of the king and the people of Israel. Teach them to do what is right. Send rain on this land, which you gave to them as a permanent inheritance.

'When foreigners from distant lands hear of the great things you have done for your people, and come to worship you in this temple, listen to their prayers in heaven, and do whatever they ask. May all the nations of the world know you and obey you, as your people Israel do.'

When Solomon had finished praying, he asked God's blessing on all the people present. Then he sent them home.

1 Kings 8.31–36, 41–43, 54a, 55, 66a

Rebellion in northern Israel

King Solomon reigned in Jerusalem over all Israel for forty years. He died, and was buried in the city; and his son Rehoboam succeeded him as king.

Rehoboam went to Shechem, where all the tribes of northern Israel had gathered. They said to him: 'Your father treated us harshly, putting a heavy yoke upon us. If you lighten the yoke, we shall be your loyal subjects.' Rehoboam replied: 'Go away, and return in three days; then I shall give you my reply.'

King Rehoboam consulted the elderly men who had advised his father. They said: 'If you give these people a favourable reply, they will always serve you well.' But he ignored their words, and consulted the younger men with whom he had grown up. They advised him to say: 'My father placed you under a heavy yoke, and I shall make the yoke heavier. My father scourged with whips; I shall scourge you with scorpions.'

Three days later the people returned to Rehoboam, and he spoke to them as his young advisors had urged. The people exclaimed to one another: 'David and his family have done nothing for us. Let us go home, and let Rehoboam look out for himself!' They rebelled against Rehoboam, and left him only with the southern territory of Judah, around Jerusalem.

1 Kings 11.42–43; 12.1, 4–6a, 7–8, 10a,
11, 12a, 14a, 16–17

Elijah and the widow

Solomon's son was forty-one years old when he became king of Judah, and he ruled for seventeen years in Jerusalem. The people of Judah sinned against the Lord, arousing his anger. On every hill they built places of worship for false gods; and both men and women served in those places as prostitutes.

In the northern territory of Israel Ahab became king. He also sinned, building a temple to Baal, and worshipping at its altar. A prophet named Elijah said to King Ahab: 'In the name of the Lord whom I serve, the living God of Israel, I tell you that there will be no dew or rain for the next few years – except at my word.'

Gradually the rivers and brook dried up for lack of rain. Then the Lord commanded Elijah to go to the town of Zarephath. As he arrived at the gate of the town, he saw a widow gathering firewood. He said to her: 'Please bring me a drink of water, and some bread as well.' She replied: 'As surely as the Lord your God lives, I have no bread. All I have is a handful of flour in a bowl, and a drop of olive oil in a jar. I am collecting firewood in order to bake my last loaf; then my son and I will starve to death.' Elijah said: 'Do not worry. Bake your last loaf, and give it to me. I assure you that the bowl will not become empty of flour, and the jar will not become empty of olive oil, until the Lord sends rain.'

When the widow found that the bowl and the jar were constantly replenished, she said to Elijah: 'You are truly a man of God.'

1 Kings 14.21*a*, 22*a*, 23*a*, 24*a*; 16.29*b*–30*a*, 32;
17.1, 7, 8–9*a*, 10–11*a*, 12–13*a*, 14, 16*a*, 24*a*

Elijah and the prophets of Baal

Elijah remained with the widow for a long time. Then in the third year of the drought, the Lord commanded Elijah to present himself to King Ahab. When Ahab saw him, he exclaimed: 'So here you are – the cause of Israel's troubles!' Elijah replied: 'I am not the cause of Israel's troubles. You are the cause – because you disobey the Lord's commands, and worship the idols of Baal. Now order all the people of Israel to meet me at Mount Carmel; and summon the four hundred and fifty prophets of Baal.'

When the Israelites and the prophets had assembled at Mount Carmel, Elijah spoke: 'How much longer will you waver between two beliefs? If the Lord is God, worship him; but if Baal is God, worship him!' The people remained silent. Then Elijah said: 'I am the only prophet of the Lord still left, whereas Baal has four hundred and fifty prophets. Let the prophets of Baal pray to their god, and I shall call on the Lord. The one who responds by sending fire – he is God.'

The prophets of Baal prayed until noon, shouting: 'Answer us, Baal!' And they danced round the altar they had erected. But no answer came. Then Elijah mocked them: 'Shout louder! Surely he is a god. Perhaps he is day-dreaming, or relieving himself; perhaps he has gone on a journey; or perhaps he is asleep, and needs to be woken.' So the prophets prayed louder, cutting themselves with knives until blood flowed. But still no answer came.

1 Kings 18.1, 17–19a, 20–22, 24a, 26b–28, 29b

Fire from God

Elijah invited the people to come closer, and they gathered round him. He took twelve stones, one for each of the twelve tribes named after the sons of Jacob – the man to whom the Lord had given the name Israel. With these stones he built an altar for the worship of the Lord. He dug a trench round it, and placed wood on top of it. He sacrificed a bull, cut it in pieces, and placed it on top of the wood. Then he ordered water to be poured over the offering. The water ran down the altar, and filled the trench.

Elijah approached the altar, and prayed: 'O Lord the God of Abraham, Isaac and Jacob, prove now that you are the God of Israel, and that I am your servant, acting on your commands. Answer me, Lord, and turn the hearts of these people back to yourself.' The Lord sent down fire, which burnt up the offering and the wood, scorched the stones and the earth, and dried up the water in the trench. When the people saw this, they threw themselves on the ground, and exclaimed: 'The Lord is God; the Lord alone is God.'

Elijah ordered: 'Seize the prophets of Baal. Do not allow any to escape.' The people seized them all. Elijah led them down to a nearby river, and killed them.

1 Kings 18.30a, 31–32a, 33, 35, 36b–40

Jezebel's threat

Elijah said to King Ahab: 'Go and eat. I hear the sound of rain approaching.' While Ahab went to eat, Elijah climbed up Mount Carmel, accompanied by a servant. At the top he bowed to the ground, with his head between his knees. Then he said to his servant: 'Go and look towards the sea.' The servant went and returned, saying: 'I saw nothing.' Seven times Elijah told him to go and look. The seventh time he returned, and said: 'I saw a cloud no bigger than a man's hand, rising from the sea.' Elijah ordered his servant: 'Go to King Ahab, and tell him to hitch up his chariot, and return home before the rain prevents him.'

Gradually the sky grew black with clouds, and the wind rose. Then heavy rain began to fall. Ahab rode off in his chariot. The power of the Lord came upon Elijah; tucking his cloak into his belt, he ran ahead of Ahab for the entire journey.

Ahab told his wife Jezebel how Elijah had humiliated the prophets of Baal, and then slaughtered them. Jezebel sent a message to Elijah: 'May the gods strike me dead, if by this time tomorrow I have not done to you, what you did to the prophets.' Elijah was afraid, and fled for his life into the desert. He prayed: 'Lord, take away my life – it is worthless.'

1 *Kings* 18.41–46; 19.1–3*a*, 4*b*

The gentle whisper of God

Elijah walked for forty days until he reached Sinai, the holy mountain. There he went into a cave to spend the night. The Lord spoke to him: 'Elijah, what are you doing here?' Elijah answered: 'Lord God almighty, I have always served you with zeal. But the people of Israel have broken their covenant with you, torn down your altars, and killed all your prophets. I am the only prophet left – and now they are trying to kill me.'

The Lord said: 'Go to the top of the mountain, and stand before me. I shall pass by.' When Elijah reached the top of the mountain, a mighty wind blew, shattering the rocks; but the Lord was not in the wind. The wind stopped, and there was an earthquake; but the Lord was not in the earthquake. After the earthquake a fire raged; but the Lord was not in the fire. After the fire came a gentle whisper.

When Elijah heard the gentle whisper, he covered his face with his cloak. The Lord said to him: 'Go to the desert near Damascus, and anoint Elisha to succeed you as prophet.' Elijah left the mountain, and eventually found Elisha ploughing with a team of oxen. Elijah took off his cloak, and put it on Elisha. Then Elisha said: 'Let me kiss my father and mother goodbye, and then I shall come with you.' Elijah replied: 'Do as you wish; I shall not stop you.'

1 Kings 19.8b–13a, 15a, 16b, 19a, 20b

Naboth's vineyard

Near King Ahab's palace was a vineyard, owned by a man named Naboth. One day Ahab offered to buy the vineyard, so that he could grow vegetables there. Naboth replied: 'I inherited this vineyard from my ancestors; the Lord forbid that I should let you have it.' Ahab became very sullen and angry; he lay on his bed, facing the wall, and he refused to eat.

When his wife Jezebel discovered the reason for his behaviour, she arranged for Naboth to be accused of blasphemy, and of cursing the king. So Naboth was stoned to death. Then she said to Ahab: 'Naboth is dead. Go and take possession of the vineyard which he refused to sell to you.' Ahab immediately went to the vineyard.

Elijah heard what had happened, and, at the Lord's command, went to the vineyard, and confronted Ahab. When he saw Elijah, Ahab exclaimed: 'So, my enemy, you have found me!' Elijah answered: 'I have found you because you do evil in the Lord's sight. The Lord will bring disaster on you.'

Three years later King Ahab went into battle against the king of Syria. During the battle an arrow pierced Ahab between sections of his armour. While the battle raged, he was propped up in his chariot, with blood running down onto the floor of the chariot. In the evening he died, and his body was taken away for burial. His chariot was washed in a pool where prostitutes bathed; and dogs licked up his blood.

1 Kings 21.1b–2a, 3–5a, 10, 15–16, 18a,
20–21a; 22.29a, 34a, 35, 37–38a

Elijah's ascension to heaven

When the time came for Elijah to be taken up to heaven, God commanded him to go to Jericho; Elisha went with him. A large group of prophets lived there. They said to Elisha: 'Do you know that the Lord will take your master away from you today?' Elisha replied: 'Yes, I know; but let us not speak about it.' Then Elijah said to Elisha: 'Stay here; the Lord has ordered me to go to the River Jordan.' Elisha replied: 'As surely as the Lord lives and you live, I shall not leave you.' So the two walked together to the Jordan, followed by fifty of the prophets.

When they reached the river, Elijah took off his cloak, rolled it up, and struck the water with it; the water divided, and he and Elisha crossed over on dry ground. Elijah asked Elisha: 'What can I do for you before I am taken away?' Elisha replied: 'Let me inherit your power' Elijah said: 'If you see me when I am taken from you, my power will be yours – otherwise not.'

Suddenly a chariot of fire, pulled by horses of fire, came between them; and Elijah was taken up to heaven in a whirlwind. Elisha saw this, and cried out: 'My father! My father! Mighty defender of Israel, you are gone!' He never saw Elijah again. In his grief he tore his clothes apart.

2 Kings 2.1a, 4b–7a, 8–9, 10b, 11b–12

The fall of Jerusalem

Zedekiah became king of Judah, and ruled in Jerusalem for eleven years. He sinned against the Lord; and the Lord became so angry with the people of Jerusalem and Judah that he banished them from his sight.

When Zedekiah had been king for nine years King Nebuchadnezzar of Babylon marched against Jerusalem with his entire army. He camped outside the city, and besieged it for two years. Finally the people had nothing left to eat. Zedekiah led his army at night through a gate close to the royal garden, and escaped. But the Babylonian army pursued Zedekiah, and caught up with him on the plains near Jericho. His soldiers deserted him, and the Babylonians captured him. On Nebuchadnezzar's orders Zedekiah's sons were executed, with Zedekiah looking on; then Zedekiah's eyes were gouged out.

The Babylonian army now entered Jerusalem. They burnt down the temple, the palace, and the houses of all the leading figures; and they tore down the city walls. Then they took away to Babylon all the skilled craftsmen, leaving only the poorest people behind. They also took away every object made of gold or silver.

2 Kings 24.18a, 19a, 20; 25.1b–2, 3b,
4b–6a, 7a, 8b–11a, 12a, 15b

Cyrus's proclamation

When Cyrus became emperor of Persia, he conquered Babylon. Then the Lord prompted him to issue this proclamation,
to be read aloud throughout his empire: 'The Lord, the God
of heaven, has given me all the kingdoms of the earth, and
ordered me to build a temple for him in Jerusalem in Judah.
God's people should return to Jerusalem, and rebuild the
temple of the Lord, the God of Israel, the God who is worshipped in Jerusalem; and may God be with his people. If any
of God's people need help in returning, their neighbours
should provide them with silver and gold, with food and livestock, and with offerings for the temple.'

So every Israelite whose heart God had moved, set out for
Jerusalem, to rebuild the house of the Lord there. And their
neighbours gave them silver utensils, gold, food and livestock, as well as many personal gifts and offerings for the
temple. Cyrus himself sent back the precious objects that
Nebuchadnezzar had removed from the temple.

When the Israelites arrived in Jerusalem, they immediately
rebuilt the altar in its original place, and offered sacrifices on
it every morning and evening.

Ezra 1.1b–4, 5b–7a; 3.3b

Starting to rebuild the temple

With Cyrus's permission, the Israelites sent food, drink and olive oil to the cities of Tyre and Sidon, in exchange for cedars from Lebanon; these were taken by sea to Joppa. So a month after arriving in Jerusalem, the Israelites began to rebuild the temple; and the Levites over twenty years of age supervised the work.

While the foundation stones were laid, the priests dressed in their sacred robes, and blew trumpets, while the Levites clashed cymbals. Then they sang God's praises, repeating the refrain: 'The Lord is good, and his love for Israel is eternal.' The people gave a great shout of praise to the Lord. The older priests, Levites and heads of clans had seen the first temple; and as they watched the foundation stones being laid for the new temple, they wept aloud with joy.

Ezra 3.7b–8a, 10a, 11–12a

Completing the temple

After the Israelites had been banished to Babylon, others had taken over their land; and these people now tried to harass and frighten the Jews, in the hope of stopping their work. They also bribed the officials of the Persian government to act against the Jews in various ways. This continued throughout the reign of Cyrus, and eventually brought the work to a standstill.

When Darius became emperor, the Persian officials in Jerusalem raised doubts as to whether permission had ever been given for the rebuilding of the temple. But God was watching over the Jewish leaders; and at their prompting, the officials wrote to Darius for guidance. Darius wrote in reply to the officials: 'Stay away from the temple, and do not interfere with its construction. Let the Jewish leaders rebuild the temple of God where it stood before. I hereby command you to help them rebuild it. Pay their expenses out of royal funds; and day by day give the priests whatever animals they need for their sacrifices. May God, who chose to be worshipped in Jerusalem, overthrow any king or nation who defies this command.'

Thus in the sixth year of the reign of Darius, the rebuilding of the temple was completed.

Ezra 4.4–5, 24; 6.3b, 5, 6b–8a, 9a, 12a, 15b

PROPHETIC VISION

Hebrew religion always made a clear distinction between priests, who performed the sacrificial rituals, and spiritual leaders, who received direct guidance from God. In the early centuries these prophets were also patriarchs and judges who wielded political power; but once the monarchy was established, their influence derived only from the force of their teachings and personalities. They often spoke with great passion against social injustice, political oppression and empty religion; and they also inspired their listeners with visions of peace and harmony on earth.

God's disgust

Here are the messages that God revealed to Isaiah.

The Lord said: 'Earth and sky, listen to my words. The children whom I raised, have rebelled against me. The ox knows its master, and the donkey knows the one who feeds it. But the people of Israel ignore their master; they reject the one who cares for them.'

You are a nation of sinners, a people loaded with guilt, a brood of evildoers, a family that has become utterly corrupt. You have abandoned the Lord; you have spurned the holy God of Israel, turning your backs on him. Why do you persist in your rebellion? Do you want further punishment? Israel, your head is already covered with wounds, and your heart and mind are ill. From the soles of your feet to the top of your head you are sick; there are bruises and sores and open wounds everywhere. None has been cleansed or bandaged or soothed with oil. Your country has been laid waste, and your cities burnt to the ground. Before your eyes foreigners have stripped your fields and ransacked your homes.

Listen to what the Lord is saying to you: 'The multitude of sacrifices which you offer to me – do you imagine that I want them? I have had more than enough burnt offerings; I am sick of the fat of your finest rams; I am weary of the blood of bulls and lambs and goats; I am disgusted with the smell of the incense you burn; I hate your religious festivals. Wash yourselves clean; stop doing wrong, and do what is right; seek justice, and uplift the oppressed; give orphans their rights, and care for widows.'

Isaiah 1.1a, 2–7, 10b–11, 13b, 16–17

Humbling the arrogant

The city that once was faithful, has become a whore. She was once full of justice; righteousness dwelt in every street. But now only murderers live there. Jerusalem, the silver of your mind has become dross, the wine of your heart has turned to water. Your rulers are rebels, companions of thieves: they love bribes and they chase gifts; they ignore the rights of orphans, and are deaf to the cries of widows.

So listen to the words of the Lord almighty, the invincible God of Israel: 'I shall take revenge on you, because you have become my enemies; I shall no longer allow you to trouble me; I shall turn my hand against you. I shall refine you as silver is refined, removing every impurity. I shall replace your rulers with wise judges, like those of long ago. Then once again Jerusalem will be called a righteous, faithful city.'

Since the Lord is just, he will save Jerusalem, and all its inhabitants who repent. But he will crush all who continue to sin, all who continue their rebellion against him. Just as straw is set on fire by a spark, so those with power will be destroyed by their own evil deeds; and no one will be able to quench the fire.

A day is coming when the arrogant will be humbled, and the proud brought low. And on that day the Lord will be exalted.

Isaiah 1.21–28a, 31; 2.11

Isaiah's calling

I saw the Lord seated on a throne, high and exalted; and the train of his robe filled the temple. Above him were angels, each with six wings; with two wings they covered their faces, with two they covered their feet, and with two they were flying. And they were calling to one another: 'Holy, holy, holy is the Lord almighty; the whole earth is full of his glory.' The sound of their voices made the foundations and the doorposts shake, and the temple was filled with smoke.

I cried: 'There is no hope for me. I am doomed, because every word I utter is unclean, and I live among people of unclean lips – and my eyes have seen the King, the Lord almighty!' One of the angels flew down to me, carrying a live coal in his hand that he had taken from the altar with tongs. He touched my lips with it, and said: 'Your guilt has been taken away, and your sins forgiven.'

Then I heard the voice of the Lord: 'Whom shall I send? Who will be my messenger?' I answered: 'Here am I. Send me!'

Isaiah 6. 1–8

Isaiah's message

The Lord ordered me to go and give the people this message:
'You will listen and listen, but not understand. You will look
and look, but not perceive. Let the hearts of these people be
callused, their ears deaf, and their eyes blind. Otherwise they
might see with their eyes, hear with their ears, and understand with their hearts – and then repent and be healed.'

I asked the Lord: 'How long will it be like this?'

The Lord answered: 'It will be like this until the cities lie
ruined and empty, the houses are abandoned and deserted,
and the fields are ruined and ravaged. It will be like this until
I have sent the people far away, and the land is utterly
desolate. Even if only one person in ten remains in the land,
the destruction will continue. But as the oak tree leaves a
stump when it is cut down, so there will be a stump in the
land from which new life will come.'

Isaiah 6.9–13

God with us

Isaiah said: 'Hear now, descendants of David! Is it not enough that you wear out the patience of human beings? Must you wear out the patience of God as well? Therefore the Lord himself will give you a sign: a young woman who is pregnant, will give birth to a son, and will name him Emmanuel – which means "God with us". When he is old enough to reject evil and choose righteousness, people will be drinking milk and eating honey.'

The Lord put his strong hand on Isaiah, and said: 'Do not follow the path which the people are treading. Do not participate in their plots and schemes, and do not fear what they fear. Remember that I, the Lord almighty, am holy; I am the one whom you should fear; I am your refuge. But for the people of Israel I am a stone on which they will stumble; I am a trap in which they will be caught.'

Isaiah 7. 13–15; 8. 11–14a

The future king

The people walking in darkness have seen a great light. They lived in a land of shadows, but now a light has dawned. Lord, you have given them great joy, and they rejoice at what you have done. You have broken the yoke that burdened them; you have shattered the rod of their oppressors. For to us a child is born, to us a son is given; and the government of our land will be on his shoulders. He will be called wonderful counsellor, mighty God, everlasting father, prince of peace. There will be no end to the increase of his rule; and his kingdom will always be at peace. He will reign on David's throne, and govern his kingdom until the end of time. His power will be founded on justice and righteousness.

The zeal of the Lord almighty will accomplish this.

Isaiah 9.2–3a, 4a, 6–7

The peaceful kingdom

The royal line of David is like a tree that has been cut down; but just as new branches sprout from a stump, so a new king will arise from among David's descendants.

The Spirit of the Lord will rest upon him – the Spirit of wisdom and understanding, the Spirit of discernment and power, the Spirit of knowledge of God's will, the Spirit of reverence for the Lord – and he will take delight in obeying the Lord.

He will not judge by what he sees with his eyes, or decide by what he hears with his ears. He will judge the needy with righteousness, and he will defend the poor from oppression. His words will be like a rod striking the earth; with the breath from his mouth he will slay the wicked. Justice will be his belt, and integrity the sash around his waist.

The wolf will live with the lamb; the leopard will lie down with the goat; calves and lion cubs will walk together, and a little child will lead them. The cow will feed with the bear, and their young will rest together; the lion will eat straw like the ox. The infant will play near the hole of the snake; the baby will put its hand in the viper's nest. On the holy mountain of God no creature will harm or destroy another creature.

As the seas are full of water, so the earth will be full of the knowledge of the Lord.

Isaiah 11.1–9

The way of holiness

The desert will be glad, and flowers will bloom in the wilderness; the desert will sing and shout for joy. It will be as beautiful as the mountains of Lebanon, and as fertile as the fields of Carmel and Sharon. Everyone will see the glory of the Lord, the splendour of our God.

Give strength to the hands that are feeble; make firm the knees that tremble. Say to those with anxious hearts: 'Be strong, and do not be afraid. God is coming to your rescue, and will vanquish your enemies.'

The eyes of the blind will be opened, and the ears of the deaf unstopped. The lame will leap like deer, and the tongues of the dumb will shout for joy. Streams will flow through the wilderness, and the burning sand will become a lake; springs will burst through the parched ground. In the haunts where jackals once lay, grass and reeds and papyrus will grow.

A highway will be there; it will be called the way of holiness. No sinners will travel on that road; and good people will not stray from it. No lions will prowl on it; no ferocious beasts will cross it. Only those whom the Lord has saved will walk on that road; those whom the Lord has rescued will walk home along it. They will enter Jerusalem with songs on their lips; everlasting joy will crown their heads. Gladness and pleasure will overtake them, and sorrow and grief will flee away.

Isaiah 35.1–10

A way for the Lord

The Lord says: 'Comfort my people; comfort the people of Jerusalem, and speak to them with tenderness. Tell them that their time of hard labour is over, that their sins have been paid for; I have punished them in full for all their evil acts.'

A voice cries out: 'Prepare in the desert a way for the Lord. Make straight in the wilderness a highway for our God. Fill every valley, and level every mountain; turn the hills into a plain, and make the rough ground smooth. The glory of the Lord will be revealed, and all humanity will see it. The mouth of the Lord has spoken.'

A voice cries out: 'Proclaim a message!' I ask: 'What message shall I proclaim?' The voice replies: 'Proclaim that all people are like grass, and their glory is like the wild flowers of the field. The grass withers and the flowers fade, when the Lord sends the wind to blow over them. Yes, people are like grass; and the grass withers and the flowers fade. But the word of our Lord lasts for ever.'

The sovereign Lord comes with power, and brings rewards for all his people. He will be a shepherd tending his flock; he will gather the lambs in his arms, and carry them close to his heart.

Isaiah 40. 1–8, 10–11a

The potter and the clay

The Lord says: 'Israel, always remember that you are my servant. I created you to be my servant, and I shall never forget you. I have swept away your offences like a cloud, your sins like the morning mist. Return to me, for I am the one who can save you.

'I am the Lord, your saviour. I created you, and I created all things; I am the Lord. I alone stretched out the sky; when I fashioned the earth, no one helped me. I make fools of fortune-tellers, and I frustrate the predictions of astrologers. I refute the words of the wise, and show that their wisdom is folly. But when my servant makes a prediction, that prediction comes true; when I send a messenger to reveal my plans, those plans are accomplished.

'Does a clay pot argue with the potter? Does the clay ask the potter what he is doing? Does the pot complain that the potter has no skill? Do children ask their parents why they made them as they are? I, the holy God of Israel, shape the future. Do you question me about what I make, or tell me what I should do? I am the one who fashioned the earth, and put human beings upon it. With my own hands I stretched out the sky; and I control the sun, the moon, and the stars.

'I do not speak in secret, or keep my purpose hidden. I do not require the people of Israel to seek me in vain. I am the Lord, and I speak the truth; I make known what is right.'

Isaiah 44.21–22, 24–26a; 45.9–12, 19

A light to the nations

Listen to me, distant nations; hear this, those who live far away. Before I was born, the Lord called me by name, and chose me as his own. He made my words as sharp as a sword; and with his own hand he protected me. He made me into a polished arrow, and concealed me in his quiver. He said to me: 'Israel, you are my servant; through you I shall display my splendour.' I said: 'I have laboured to no purpose; I have used up my strength, and accomplished nothing. Yet your hand, O Lord, is with me; you will reward my efforts.'

Then the Lord said: 'I have a great task for you: I shall restore you to greatness, in order to make you a light to the nations. Through you the whole world will be saved.'

These are the words of the Lord, the holy God of Israel, the saviour of the people. He speaks to one who was despised and abhorred by the nations, and who is the servant of rulers. Kings will see Israel released, and will rise to show their respect; princes will bow down before her.

Isaiah 49. 1–4, 6–7a

A covenant with all nations

The Lord says: 'In due time I shall come to save you; I shall hear your cries for help, and rescue you. I shall guard and protect you; and through you I shall make a covenant with all nations. I shall say to prisoners: "Go free!" I shall say to those in darkness: "Come into the light!" The people will be like sheep grazing on fertile hills; they will never be hungry or thirsty, and the heat of the desert sun will not burn them. They will be led by one who loves them, and he will lead them to springs of water. I shall make highways across the mountains; I shall prepare roads on which the people can travel. They will come from far away, from the north and the west, and from Aswan in the south.'

The people of Jerusalem reply: 'The Lord has abandoned us; he has forgotten us.' The Lord answers: 'Can a mother forget the baby at her breast; can she ignore the child she has borne? Even if a mother can forget her offspring, I shall never forget you. I have engraved your name on the palm of my hands; I never cease to watch over you.'

Isaiah 49.8–12, 14–16

The suffering of God's servant

The Lord says: 'My servant will succeed in his task; he will be raised up, and highly honoured. Many people were appalled when they saw him: he was so disfigured that he barely looked human. But many nations will marvel at him, and kings will be speechless in amazement. What they have never known, they will see; what they have never heard, they will understand.'

God's servant grew up like a tender shoot taking root in dry ground. He had no dignity or beauty to attract us; there was nothing in his appearance to draw people. We despised and rejected him, and he endured great suffering and pain. No one would even look at him; we ignored him as if he were worthless.

But he took upon himself our weaknesses, and carried our suffering. We thought that his suffering was punishment sent by God. But he was wounded for our sins; he was crushed for the evil we had done. We are healed by the punishment he suffered, made whole by the blows he received. We were like sheep that were lost, each going its own way. The Lord laid upon him the punishment that we deserved.

Isaiah 52.13—53.6

The sacrifice for sin

God's servant was treated harshly, but did not open his mouth. Like a lamb being led to the slaughter, like a sheep about to be sheared, he did not say a word. He was arrested, sentenced and led off to die; yet no one cared about his fate. He was put to death for the sins of the people. He was placed in a grave with the wicked; he was buried with the rich. Yet he had committed no crime, and had never spoken a lie.

The Lord says: 'It was my will that he should suffer; his death was a sacrifice to bring forgiveness. Yet he will live a long time, and see his children; through him my purpose will be fulfilled. After the darkness of his suffering, he will see light, and be satisfied; he will know that he did not suffer in vain. My righteous servant, in whom I am well-pleased, bears the punishment of many; and for his sake I shall forgive them. So I shall give him the place of honour, the highest place among the great and the powerful. He freely poured out his life, allowing himself to be numbered among criminals. He took the place of countless sinners, and prayed that they might be forgiven.'

Isaiah 53.7–12

The people's confession

The people of Jerusalem say: 'We look for light, but all is darkness; we look for brightness, but we walk in deep shadows. Like the blind we grope along walls; we stumble at noon, as if it were night. We live in the darkness of death. We growl like bears, and we moan like doves. We yearn for salvation, but cannot find it; we look for deliverance, but it is far away.

'Lord, our crimes against you are many; our sins accuse us. Our offences surround us, and we acknowledge them all. We have rebelled against you; we have rejected you; we have refused to follow you. We have oppressed others, and turned our backs on you. Our thoughts are false, and our words are lies. We have driven justice away, and righteousness is afraid to come near. Truth stumbles in the streets, and honesty cannot enter. Integrity is nowhere to be found, and innocent men and women are treated with contempt.'

Isaiah 59.9b–15

The eternal light

The Lord says to Jerusalem: 'You will no longer be a city forsaken and hated, a city deserted and desolate. I shall make you the pride of every generation, a source of joy for all time. Nations and their kings will cherish you, as a mother cherishes her child. You will know that I, the Lord, have saved you, that the mighty God of Israel has set you free.

'Peace will be your governor, and righteousness your ruler. The sounds of violence will never again be heard in your land; your country will never again be destroyed by warfare. Salvation will be the wall that defends you, and praise will be the gates that protect you.

'The sun will no longer be your light by day, and the moon will no longer be your light at night. I, the Lord, will be your eternal light; the light of my glory will shine upon you – a light that will continue to shine when the sun and the moon are burnt out. Cries of grief will never again be heard in your land.

'Your people will do only what is right and good; and they will possess the land forever. I planted them in your soil; they are the work of my hands. Through them my splendour will be revealed. Even your smallest and humblest family will be as great as a nation.

'When the time is right, I shall act swiftly to make all this happen. I am the Lord.'

Isaiah 60.15–16, 17b–22

Good news to the poor

The Spirit of the sovereign Lord is upon me. He has chosen me to preach good news to the poor. He has sent me to heal the broken-hearted, to proclaim freedom for captives and release for prisoners. He has sent me to declare that God will now save his people, and defeat their enemies. He has sent me to comfort all who are sad. I shall crown them with joy, in place of ashes; I shall anoint them with the oil of gladness, in place of grief; I shall dress them in a tunic of praise, in place of despair. They will be called oaks of righteousness, planted by the Lord to reveal his splendour.

My people, you will be called priests of the Lord; you will be known as servants of God. Your shame and disgrace are now ended. The Lord says: 'I love justice, and I hate oppression and crime. I shall be faithful to my people; I shall reward them by making an everlasting covenant with them. They will be famous among the nations, and their offspring will be admired throughout the world. All who see them, will know that I, the Lord, have blessed them.'

Let Jerusalem rejoice at what the Lord is doing. As a bridegroom dresses in sacred robes for his wedding, God has clothed Jerusalem with salvation. As a bride adorns herself with jewels, God has adorned Jerusalem with righteousness. As surely as soil makes seeds sprout and grow, the sovereign Lord will make justice flourish – and all nations will praise him.

Isaiah 61.1–3, 6a, 7a, 8–11

A new name

I shall not be quiet until Jerusalem's righteousness shines like
the dawn; I shall not keep silent until her salvation shines like
a blazing torch. Jerusalem, the world will see your righteousness, and every king will witness your glory. You will be
called by a new name, a name that the mouth of the Lord
will bestow. You will be like a beautiful crown for the Lord,
a royal sceptre in the hand of God. No longer will people call
you Forsaken, or your land Deserted Wife. Your new name
will be God's Delight; your land will be called Happily
Married. The Lord smiles on you with joy, and he will be like
a husband to your land. As a young man takes a virgin for
his wife, the Lord – who made you – will take you as his
own; as a groom rejoices in his bride, the Lord will rejoice
in you.

On your walls I have posted sentries; they will never be
silent day or night. They will remind the Lord of his
promises, and never let him forget them. They will give him
no rest until he restores Jerusalem, making it a city that the
whole world praises.

People of Jerusalem, go out of the city, and build a road
on which your brothers and sisters can return. Prepare a highway; clear it of stones! Raise a banner that can be seen from
afar. You will be called God's Holy People, the People of
Salvation; and Jerusalem will be called God's Beloved.

Isaiah 62.1–7, 10, 12a

Jeremiah's calling

This is an account of what the Lord said to me, Jeremiah.

The Lord says to me: 'I chose you before I formed you in the womb; before you were born, I set you apart; I appointed you as a prophet to the nations.' I reply: 'I do not know how to speak; I am too young.' But the Lord says to me: 'Do not say that you are too young. You must go to whoever I send you to; and you must say whatever I command you to say. Do not be afraid of anyone, because I am with you, and I shall protect you. I, the Lord, have spoken.'

Then the Lord reaches out his hand, touches my lips, and says: 'I am putting my words in your mouth. Today I give you authority over nations and kingdoms, to uproot and tear down, to destroy and overthrow, to build and to plant.'

Jeremiah 1.1a, 4–10

Promise of restoration

The Lord says: 'People of Israel, I shall make you well again; I shall heal your wounds. I shall restore you to your land, and cherish every family. Jerusalem and its palace will be rebuilt. You will sing my praises, and shout for joy. I shall add to your numbers, and they will never be decreased; I shall bring you honour, and you will never be disgraced. You and your descendants will live as your ancestors did in days of old; your community will be as secure and solid as it was in ancient times. Your ruler will come from among you; he will be a prince of your own blood. I shall draw him close to me, and he will devote himself to doing my will. You will be my people, and I shall be your God.

'People of Israel, I have always loved you, and I continue to love you. Once again I shall show my love. Once again you will take up your tambourines, and dance with joy. Once again you will plant vineyards on the hills, and drink the fruit of your labour.'

Jeremiah 30.17a, 18–22; 31.3b–5

The new covenant

The Lord says: 'The time is coming when I shall fill the land of Israel with people and their livestock. I took care to uproot, pull down, overthrow, destroy and demolish; now I shall take equal care to plant and build up.

'The time is coming when I shall make a new covenant with my people. It will not be like the old covenant that I made with their ancestors, when I took them by the hand and led them out of Egypt. Although I was like a husband to them, they broke that covenant. This is the covenant that I shall make with my people: I shall put my law in their minds, and write it on their hearts. I shall be their God, and they will be my people. They will not have to teach one another to know me, because all will know me, from the least to the greatest. I shall forgive their sins, and forget their wickedness. I, the Lord, have spoken.'

Jeremiah 31.27–28, 31–34

The four creatures

I, Ezekiel, a priest, was living with the Jewish exiles in Babylon. The sky opened, and I saw a vision of God. I heard the Lord speak to me, and his hand was upon me.

I looked up, and saw a storm coming from the north. Lightning was flashing from a huge cloud, and the sky around the cloud was glowing. At the centre of the storm I saw four living creatures in human form. Each creature had four faces and four wings. Their legs were straight; and they had feet in the shape of calves' hooves, which shone like polished bronze. They each had four human arms, one under each wing. Two wings of each creature were spread out; and the creatures formed a square, with their wings touching. They moved as a group, without turning their bodies. They each had a human face at the front, a lion's face at the right, a bull's face at the left, and an eagle's face at the back.

In the midst of the creatures was a light, which looked like a burning coal or a blazing torch. It sometimes became exceedingly bright, and then faded. It moved back and forth among the creatures.

As I was looking at the four creatures, I saw a wheel on the ground beside each creature. The wheels shone like precious stones; and each wheel had another wheel intersecting it, so the wheels could move in all directions. The creatures controlled the wheels; so the creatures could go wherever they wished.

Ezekiel 1.1a, 3–10, 13, 15–17, 20

The likeness of the Lord

Above the heads of the living creatures there was a dome, which sparkled like ice. The creatures stood under the dome, each with two wings stretched out, and two wings covering its body. When the creatures moved, I heard the sound of their wings; it was like the roar of the sea, or like the noise of an army marching – or like the voice of almighty God. When they stopped flying, they folded their wings.

Then I heard a voice from the dome above their heads. And I saw a throne made of sapphire. Sitting on the throne was a figure like that of a man. From the waist up he shone like molten metal, as if a fire was burning within him; and from his waist downwards there were flames. A brilliant light surrounded him, which had all the colours of the rainbow.

I knew that I was seeing the likeness and the glory of the Lord. I fell face downwards.

Ezekiel 1.22–28

Ezekiel's calling

I heard the voice of God saying: 'Mortal man, stand up. I wish to speak to you.' As the voice spoke, the Spirit of the Lord entered me, and raised me to my feet; and I could hear clearly.

'Mortal man,' the voice of God continued, 'I am sending you to the people of Israel. They have rebelled against me, turning their backs on me; and they are still rebelling, just as their ancestors did. They are stubborn and hard-hearted. So you will tell them what I, the sovereign Lord, am saying to them. Whether they listen or refuse to listen, they will know that a prophet has been among them.

'You, mortal man, must not be afraid of them, or of anything they say. They will defy and despise you. You will feel as though you are walking through briars and thorns; you will feel as though you are living among scorpions. But do not be afraid of these rebels, or of anything they say. You must speak my words to them, whether they listen or refuse to listen. Remember that they are rebels. Mortal man, listen to everything I say; do not be a rebel yourself.'

Ezekiel 2. 1—8a

Bad shepherds and the good shepherd

The Lord spoke through me to the rulers of Israel, the shepherds of his people: 'You take care of yourselves, but you never tend the sheep. You drink their milk, you wear clothes made from their wool, and you kill those who antagonize you. You show no love or compassion for them. You do not protect those who are weak; you do not heal those who are sick; you do not bandage those who are hurt; you do not search for those who have wandered from my way; and you do not guide those who are lost. Instead, you treat them cruelly. And for this reason they have been scattered from their land, and predators have attacked them. They have dispersed across the face of the earth, and no one is seeking them.

'So I myself, the sovereign Lord, will find my sheep, and tend them. As a shepherd gathers his sheep together, so I shall gather together my people from the places where they have gone. I shall guide those who are lost, bring back those who have wandered from my way, bandage those who are hurt, and heal those who are sick. But those who are fat and sleek, I shall destroy. I am a shepherd who always acts justly.'

Ezekiel 34.2–6, 11–12, 16

The valley of dry bones

The hand of the Lord was upon me, and his Spirit took me to a valley, where the ground was covered with bones. He led me all round the valley, and I saw a vast number of bones, all of which were very dry. He said to me: 'Mortal man, can these bones come back to life?' I replied: 'Sovereign Lord, you alone can answer that.' He said: 'Prophesy to these bones; command them to listen to the word of the Lord. Tell them that I, the sovereign Lord, shall put breath into them, and bring them back to life. I will attach sinews and muscles to them, and cover them with skin. I shall put breath into them, and bring them back to life. Then they will know that I am the Lord.'

So I prophesied as the Lord had ordered me. While I was speaking, I heard a rattling sound, and the bones began to join together. As I watched, I saw sinews and muscles attaching themselves to the bones, and then skin covering them. But there was no breath in the bodies.

Then God said to me: 'Mortal man, prophesy to the wind. Tell the wind that the sovereign Lord commands it to come from every direction, and enter these bodies, so they may come back to life.' So I prophesied as the Lord had ordered me. Breath entered the bodies; and they came back to life, and stood up. They were like a huge army.

Ezekiel 37. 1–10

Promise of new life

God said to me: 'Mortal man, the people of Israel are like the bones in the valley. They say that their bones are dried up – that all hope is gone, and that their hearts are in despair. So prophesy to the people of Israel. Tell them that I, the sovereign Lord, am going to open their graves, and raise them up; I shall bring them back to their land. When I open their graves, raise them up, and bring them back to their land, they will know that I am the Lord. I shall put breath in them, bring them back to life, and let them live in their own land. Then they will know that I am the Lord. I have promised that I should do this – and I shall. I, the Lord, have spoken.'

Ezekiel 37.11–14

Daniel's training

When King Nebuchadnezzar captured Jerusalem, he took some of his prisoners back to his temple in Babylon. He ordered Ashpenaz, his chief official, to select from among them some young men of royal and noble blood. They had to be handsome, intelligent, well-educated, quick to learn, and free from any physical defect; thus they would be fit to serve in the royal court. Ashpenaz was to teach them the language and literature of Babylon, and to give them food and wine from the king's table. After three years of training they were to enter the king's service. Among those chosen were Daniel, from the tribe of Judah, and three friends from the same tribe.

Daniel resolved not to defile himself with the royal food and wine, and sought the chief official's permission. The chief official refused permission. So Daniel said to the man guarding them: 'Test us for seven days, giving us nothing but vegetables to eat and water to drink. Then compare our appearance with the young men who are eating food from the royal table.' The guard agreed; and at the end of ten days Daniel and his companions looked healthier and stronger than those who had been eating the royal food. So the guard allowed them to continue eating vegetables.

God gave the four young men knowledge and skill in literature and philosophy. In addition he gave Daniel skill in interpreting visions and dreams. At the end of three years they entered the king's service.

Daniel 1.1b–2a, 3–6a, 8a, 10b, 12–18a, 19b

Nebuchadnezzar's first dream

Nebuchadnezzar had an unpleasant dream; it worried him so greatly that he could not sleep. He summoned his magicians, wizards, sorcerers and astrologers, and asked them to interpret his dream. They replied: 'May your majesty live for ever! Relate to us your dream, and we shall explain it.' The king said: 'I insist that you first relate to me my dream, and then tell me what it means. If you fail, I shall have you torn limb from limb.' They replied: 'Your majesty, if you relate your dream to us, we shall explain it.' The king exclaimed: 'You are merely trying to gain time. Tell me what the dream was, and then I shall know that you can tell me what it means.' They said: 'No one on the face of the earth could do what you are asking.' At that the king flew into a rage, and ordered the execution of all the royal advisers in Babylon – including Daniel and his companions.

Daniel heard of the king's order, and told his friends to pray to the God of heaven for help. The friends asked God to reveal the king's dream to Daniel, so they would not be killed along with the other advisors. That same night their prayer was answered. Daniel praised God in heaven: 'You are wise and powerful. You reveal that which is deep and hidden; you know what lies in darkness, and you yourself are surrounded by light. You have given me wisdom and strength, revealing to me what we asked.'

In the morning Daniel asked the guard to take him to the king.

Daniel 2.1–2a, 4–5, 7–8a, 9b, 10a, 12–13,
18–20a, 21b–22, 23b

Daniel's interpretation

When Daniel appeared before Nebuchadnezzar, he said: 'In your dream you saw before you a huge statue; it was bright and shining. You were terrified. Its head was made of the finest gold; its chest and arms were made of silver; its waist and hips were bronze; its legs were iron, and its feet were partly iron and partly clay. While you were looking at it, a great stone broke loose from a cliff, struck the iron and clay feet of the statue, and shattered them. At once the statue crumbled into dust; and the wind carried it away, leaving no trace. But the stone grew into a mountain, which covered the entire world.

'Now I shall tell your majesty what the dream means. You are the greatest of all kings; you are the head of gold. After you there will be another empire, not as great as yours, represented by the silver; then a third empire, represented by the bronze. Then there will be a fourth empire, as strong as iron, which will shatter and crush all earlier empires. The feet of iron and clay show that it will be a divided empire; part will be weak like clay, and part strong like iron. The stone which broke loose, shows what eventually happens to all empires.'

The king declared: 'Your God is the greatest of all gods, the Lord over kings; he can reveal every mystery.' Then he appointed Daniel the head of all his advisors; and at Daniel's request he put Daniel's companions in charge of the province of Babylon.

Daniel 2.31–34, 35b, 36b–37a, 38b–40a,
42, 45a, 47a, 48b–49a

The blazing furnace

King Nebuchadnezzar had a huge gold statue made, and erected on a plain in Babylon. He ordered everyone in his empire to bow down and worship the statue; and that anyone who did not do so, should be thrown into a blazing furnace.

Daniel's three friends refused to worship the statue; and their enemies, who hated all Jews, reported this to the king. The king summoned them, and asked if the report were true. They answered: 'You majesty, we shall not try to defend ourselves. The God whom we serve, has the power to save us from the blazing furnace; and he may choose to use his power. But even if he refrains from saving us, your majesty may be certain that we shall not worship your god; we shall not bow down before your statue.'

Nebuchadnezzar turned red with anger. He ordered his servants to make the furnace seven times hotter than usual. Then he commanded the strongest men in his army to tie the three men up, and throw them into it. Nebuchadnezzar stared at the furnace in astonishment. He asked his officials: 'Did we not tie three men up, and throw them in?' 'Yes, we did, your majesty,' they replied. He said: 'Why do I see four men walking about in the fire? They are not tied up, and they show no injuries – and the fourth one looks like an angel.'

So he released them, and appointed them to even higher positions.

Daniel 3. 1a, 5b–6, 8b, 12b, 13b–14a,
16–18, 19b–20, 24–26a, 30

Nebuchadnezzar's second dream

Nebuchadnezzar related a second dream: 'I saw a huge tree in the middle of the earth. It grew taller and taller, until it touched the sky, and everyone on earth could see it. Its leaves were beautiful, and its fruit was abundant – enough for every living creature in the world. Animals rested in its shade, and birds built nests in its branches; they all ate its fruit.

'While I was contemplating this tree, I saw a holy angel come down from heaven. The angel proclaimed in a loud voice: "Cut down the tree, and chop off its branches; strip off its leaves, and scatter its fruit. Drive away the animals and the birds. But leave the stump on the ground, and bind it with iron and bronze; let the grass grow round it."

'Then the angel turned to me, and said: "Let the dew drench this man, and let him live with the animals and birds. For seven years he will not have a human mind, but he will have the mind of an animal. This is the decision of all the angels, the verdict of all God's messengers. Thus all people on earth will know that the supreme God has power over human kingdoms, and that he can give them to anyone he wishes; he may even choose as king the lowliest of men."

Daniel 4.10–17

Nebuchadnezzar's repentance

When Nebuchadnezzar asked Daniel to interpret the dream, Daniel was terrified. Nebuchadnezzar said: 'Do not let the dream and its message alarm you.'

Daniel said: 'Your majesty, I wish that the dream applied to your enemies, and not to you. You will be driven away from human society, and for seven years you will live with wild animals; you will eat grass like an ox, and sleep in the open where the dew will fall on you. Then you will admit that the supreme God controls all human kingdoms, and that he can give them to anyone he wishes. The command to leave the stump on the ground means that you will become king again – when you acknowledge that God rules the world. Therefore, your majesty, I urge you to accept my advice: stop sinning, and do what is right – and make amends for your sins by being generous to the poor.'

All this happened to Nebuchadnezzar. He was driven out of human society, he ate grass like an ox, and the dew fell on his body. His hair grew as long as an eagle's feathers, and his nails as long as a bird's claws. After seven years he looked up towards heaven, and his sanity returned. He praised the supreme God, giving honour and glory to the one who lives forever. He declared: 'God will rule for all time, and his kingdom is eternal. The angels in heaven and the people on earth are under his control. No one can oppose his will, or question what he does.' Then he was restored to his kingdom, and his power was greater than ever.

Daniel 4.19, 25–28, 33b–34, 35b–36a

Daniel's loyalty to God

When Darius seized royal power, he appointed a hundred and twenty governors to rule throughout his empire; and he appointed Daniel and two others to supervise the governors. Daniel proved more capable than the other supervisors and governors, so Darius considered putting him in charge of the whole empire. In their jealousy the other supervisors and governors plotted to use Daniel's religion to undermine him. They went to Darius, and said: 'Your majesty, in order to assert your authority, we urge you to issue the following edict: for thirty days no one should pray to any god or person except you; and anyone who violates this edict should be thrown into a pit filled with lions.' Darius took their advice.

When Daniel heard about Darius's edict, he knew that he had to ignore it. He continued to go three times a day to an upstairs room, whose windows faced towards Jerusalem; and there he prayed to God. His enemies observed this, and reported it to Darius. The king was very upset, but knew that he could not withdraw his edict. So he ordered Daniel to be arrested, and thrown into the pit filled with lions.

As Daniel was taken to the pit, Darius said to him: 'May your God, whom you serve so loyally, save you.' And when Daniel was put into the pit, a stone was rolled across its entrance, so that no human being could save him. The king placed his own seal on the stone; then he returned to his palace, where he refused to eat or be entertained. That night he was unable to sleep.

Daniel 6. 1–3, 5–6a, 7b, 9–11,
13b–14a, 16–17a, 18

The pit of lions

At dawn the king rose, and hurried to the pit. When he arrived, he called out anxiously: 'Daniel, servant of the living God, has your God, whom you serve continually, saved you from the lions?' Daniel replied: 'May your majesty live for ever! God sent his angel to shut the mouths of the lions, so that they would not injure me. He knew that I was innocent, and that I have never wronged you.'

The king was overjoyed, and gave orders for Daniel to be lifted from the pit. When the soldiers brought him out, they saw that he was unharmed – for he had trusted God. Then the king ordered all Daniel's accusers to be arrested; and they were now thrown into the pit. Before they even reached the bottom, the lions pounced on them, and broke all their bones.

Darius wrote to all the nations in his empire, each in its own language: 'Greetings! I command that throughout my empire everyone must treat Daniel's God with honour and reverence. He is the living God, and he will rule forever; his kingdom will never be destroyed, and his power will never end. He rescues and saves; he performs signs and wonders in heaven and on earth. He has saved Daniel from the power of the lions.'

Daniel 6.19–27

Hosea and Gomer

The Lord spoke to the people of Israel through Hosea. He said to Hosea: 'Go, and get married. Your wife will be unfaithful, and so will your children. In the same way my people have left me, and become unfaithful.'

So Hosea married a woman called Gomer. She conceived, and gave birth to a daughter. The Lord said to Hosea: 'Name her Unloved, because I shall no longer love the people of Israel, nor shall I forgive them.' When Gomer had weaned her daughter, she became pregnant again, and gave birth to a son. The Lord said to Hosea: 'Name him Not-My-People, because the people of Israel are not my people, and I am not their God.'

Hosea 1.2–3a, 6, 8–9

Gomer as an image of Israel

Inspired by God, Hosea said to his children: 'Rebuke your mother; rebuke her, because she is no longer a wife to me, and I am no longer her husband. Beg her to remove the flirtatious look from her face; plead with her to tear all adulterous desires from her heart. If she ignores you, I shall strip off her clothes, leaving her as naked as she was on the day she was born. I shall make her into a desert; I shall turn her into a parched and barren land.

'She says: "I shall go to my lovers; they give me food and water, wool and linen, olive oil and wine." So I shall surround her with thorn bushes: I shall build a wall to block her way. She will chase her lovers, but not catch them; she will look for them, but not find them. Then she will say: "I shall go back to my husband, for I was better off with him than I am now."

'As yet she does not acknowledge all that I bestowed on her; she forgets the corn, the wine and the olive oil that I supplied to her; and she shows no gratitude for my gifts of silver and gold – which she has used in the worship of Baal. So I shall take back all these things. I shall strip her naked in front of her lovers; and no one will be able to save her from my power. I shall put an end to her religious meetings. I shall destroy her vines and fig trees, which – so she claims – her lovers gave her as a reward for pleasing them. I shall punish her for the times she forgot me, and burnt incense to Baal. The Lord has spoken.'

Hosea 2.2–3, 5b–9a, 10–11a, 12a, 13a

Israel as God's wife

Inspired by God, Hosea said: 'I shall lead her into the desert again, and win her with words of love. I shall give her back her vineyards, and take her through a gateway of hope. She will respond to me as she did when she was young – when she came out of Egypt. She will call me her husband, as she did in those early days; she will not think of me as her master, but as her lover. I shall remove the name Baal from her lips.

'At that time I shall make a covenant with all the beasts of the field, the birds of the air, and the creatures that move along the ground; they will no longer harm my people. I shall abolish all weapons of war, all bows and swords; and my people will live in peace and safety.

'Israel, I shall be your devoted husband; I shall be true and faithful, constant in compassion and mercy; I shall love you until the end of time. I shall belong to you, and you will belong to me, acknowledging me as your only Lord. I shall answer all your requests. I shall make rain fall on the earth, and the earth will bring forth abundant corn, grapes and olives. I shall plant you in your land, and you will prosper. I shall show love to those who were called Unloved. To those who were called Not-My-People, I shall say: "You are my people." And they will answer: "You are our God."'

Hosea 2.14–23

The call of the Lord

This is the Lord's message through Joel.

The Lord says: 'Even now repent; turn back to me with fasting and weeping and mourning. Tear your heart, and not your garments.'

So return to the Lord your God, for he is gracious and compassionate; he is slow to anger, and quick to forgive; he is always ready to show mercy, and not to punish. The Lord may change his mind, and bless you with abundant crops; then you can offer him corn and wine.

The Lord says: 'Blow the trumpet on the mountain tops. Declare a holy fast, and call a sacred assembly; gather the people together. Bring the old people and the children, and even the tiny babies. Let the bride and the groom leave their chamber, and come. Let the priests, who serve the Lord, standing between the porch and the altar, weep. And let them pray: "Spare your people, O Lord. Do not let other nations despise and mock us. Do not let them say that our God has abandoned us."'

Joel 1.1a; 2.12–17

The day of the Lord

The Lord says: 'I shall pour out my Spirit on all people. Your sons and daughters will proclaim my message. Your old men will have dreams, and your young men will see visions. I shall pour out my Spirit on men and women alike, and on servants as well as their masters.

'I shall give warnings of that day in the sky and on the earth. There will be bloodshed, fire, and billows of smoke. The sun will turn to darkness, and the moon will turn to blood – then the great and terrible day of the Lord will come. And all who call on the name of the Lord will be saved.'

Joel 2.28–32

The prophet's task

These are the words of Amos, who was a shepherd.

Do two people travel together, unless they have arranged to do so?

Does a lion roar in the forest, unless he has found a victim? Does a young lion roar in his den, when he has no prey?

Does a bird get caught in a trap, when no snare has been set? Does a trap spring, unless something sets it off?

When a trumpet sounds in a city, do not people tremble, fearing that an enemy approaches? Does disaster strike a city, unless the Lord has sent it?

The sovereign Lord does nothing, without first revealing his plans to his servants, the prophets.

When a lion roars, who can avoid feeling afraid? When the sovereign Lord has spoken to a prophet, can the prophet avoid prophesying?

Amos 1.1a; 3.3–8

Lament for Israel

Listen, people of Israel, to this lament that I sing: 'Virgin Israel has fallen, never to rise again. She lies abandoned in her own land, with no one to lift her up.'

The Lord says to you: 'Turn back to me, and I shall raise you up. Come to me, and you will live. I made the stars, and set them in their patterns. At the end of each day I turn light into darkness; and at the end of each night I turn darkness into light. I take water from the sea, and pour it out as rain on the earth. I can destroy the palaces of the proud; I can turn to rubble the fortresses of the powerful.'

You hate those who challenge injustice, and you despise those who speak the truth. You trample on the poor, forcing them to hand over their harvest. With the wealth which you have robbed, you have built great mansions in stone; and you have planted vineyards to provide wine. Believe me: you will never live in those mansions, nor will you drink wine from your vineyards. You oppress the righteous, and you take bribes; you prevent the weak from obtaining justice in the courts. I know the full extent of your sins; I know the number of crimes you have committed.

Seek good, and reject evil; then you will live. You claim that the Lord is already with you; if you learn to hate wickedness and love righteousness, your claim will become true. Ensure that justice prevails in the courts. Then the Lord will be merciful.

Amos 5.1–2, 4, 6a, 8–15

The day of darkness

The almighty sovereign Lord says: 'There will be wailing in every street, and cries of anguish in every public square. There will not be enough mourners to weep for all the dead; farmers will be called from distant fields to join the funeral processions. Even in vineyards there will be shouts of horror. This will happen because I, the Lord, am coming to punish you.'

Do you yearn for the day of the Lord? Do you imagine that you will enjoy the day of the Lord? That day will be terrible. For you it will be a day of darkness, not of light. It will be as though a man fled from a lion, only to meet a bear. It will be as though a man came home and rested his hand on a shelf, only to be bitten by a snake. The day of the Lord will be darker than the darkest night; not a single ray of light will shine through the gloom.

The Lord says: 'I hate your religious festivals; I despise your sacred feasts; I cannot stand your solemn assemblies. You bring me offerings of meat and grain, but I do not accept them. You sacrifice your finest animals to me, but I turn away in disgust. Stop the noise of your spiritual songs; I refuse to listen to the music of your harps. Instead, let justice flow like a river; let righteousness become a stream that never runs dry.'

Amos 5.16–24

Jonah's flight from the Lord

The word of the Lord came to Jonah: 'Go to the great city of Nineveh, and preach against it; I know that its people are very wicked.'

But Jonah set out in the opposite direction, in order to get away from the Lord. He went first to Joppa, where he found a ship bound for Spain. After paying the fare he boarded the ship, believing that in Spain the Lord would not be able to find him. But the Lord sent a mighty wind to the sea, and the storm was so violent that the ship was in danger of breaking up. The sailors were terrified, and they prayed for help, each to his own god. Then, in order to lighten the ship, they threw the cargo overboard.

Meanwhile Jonah had gone below deck, and was lying in the ship's hold, sound asleep. The captain found him there, and said: 'How can you sleep? Get up, and pray to your god for help. Perhaps he will take pity on us, and spare our lives.'

Jonah 1.1–6

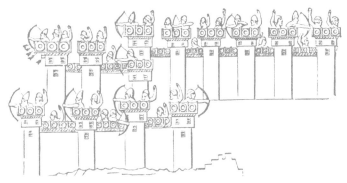

The storm at sea

The sailors said to one another: 'Let us draw lots, to find out who is responsible for this calamity.' They did so, and Jonah's name was drawn. So they said to him: 'Tell us, what are you doing here? What country do you come from? What nation do you belong to?' Jonah replied: 'I am a Hebrew; and I worship the Lord, the God of heaven, who made the sea and the land.' Jonah then explained that he was running away from the Lord.

The sailors were terrified, and exclaimed: 'What an appalling thing to do!' The storm was growing worse, and the sea was becoming rougher. So they asked him: 'What should we do?' Jonah replied: 'Pick me up, and throw me overboard; then the storm will subside. It is my fault that this storm has arisen.' At first the men could not bring themselves to throw Jonah into the sea, and they tried to row to the shore; but the sea was so wild that their efforts were futile. Then they cried to the Lord: 'O Lord, please do not punish us with death for taking this man's life. Do not hold us responsible for taking an innocent man's life. You, Lord, have caused this storm; it is your doing.'

Then they took Jonah, and threw him into the sea. At once the wind dropped, and the sea became calm. The sailors were overwhelmed with fear of the Lord; so they offered him a sacrifice, and vowed to serve him.

Jonah 1.7–16

Jonah in the whale

At the Lord's command a large fish swallowed Jonah; and he was inside the fish for three days and nights.

From deep inside the fish he prayed to the Lord: 'In my distress, O Lord, I called to you, and you answered me. From deep in the world of the dead I cried for help, and you heard me. You hurled me to the very bottom of the ocean, and the currents swirled about me; the mighty waves rolled over me. I thought I had been banished from your presence, and would never again see your holy temple. The water choked me, and seaweed wrapped itself around my head. I sank down to the roots of the mountains.

'But you, O Lord, brought me back from the depths alive. When I felt my life slipping away, I prayed to you, O Lord; and in your temple you heard me. Those who worship worthless idols, forfeit all the blessings that you can bestow. But I shall sing your praises, and offer you sacrifices. I shall do what you ask. Salvation comes from you alone.'

Then the Lord ordered the fish to spew Jonah up on the beach; and it did.

Jonah 1.17–2.10

Nineveh's repentance

The word of the Lord came to Jonah once again: 'Go to Nineveh, that great city, and proclaim to the people the message I have given to you.' So Jonah obeyed the Lord, and set out for Nineveh – a city so large that it took three days to walk through it. Jonah entered the city, and walked for a day. Then he declared: 'In forty days Nineveh will be destroyed.' The people of Nineveh believed God's message. So they decided to fast; and everyone, from the greatest to the least, put on sackcloth as a sign of repentance.

When the king of Nineveh was told God's message, he rose from his throne, and took off his robe; then he too put on sackcloth, and sat down in ashes. He issued a proclamation to the people of Nineveh: 'No one is to eat anything; all people, cattle and sheep are forbidden to eat and drink. All people, cattle and sheep must also wear sackcloth. All people must pray earnestly to God, and must give up their wicked behaviour and evil actions. Perhaps God will change his mind; perhaps his fierce anger will turn to compassion, and he will spare our lives.'

God watched them refraining from wickedness and evil; and his anger turned to compassion. He did not destroy them, as he had threatened.

Jonah 3. 1–10

Jonah's anger

Jonah was very upset that God did not carry out his threat, and became angry. He prayed: 'Lord, is this not what I foresaw before I left home? This is why I was so eager to flee to Spain. I knew that you are gracious and compassionate, patient and kind; you are always ready to relent and not to punish. Now, Lord, let me die; I should be better off dead than alive.' The Lord said: 'What right have you to be angry?'

Jonah went out to the east of the city, and sat down. He made himself a shelter, and sat in its shade, waiting to see what would happen to the city. The Lord provided a vine, and made it grow over Jonah to give greater shade; the vine eased his discomfort, and he was pleased with it. But at dawn the next day, at God's command, a worm attacked the vine, and it died. After the sun had risen, God sent a hot east wind, and the sun blazed on Jonah's head, so he felt faint. He yearned for death, and said again: 'I should be better off dead than alive.'

God said to Jonah: 'Do you have any right to be angry about the vine?' Jonah replied: 'I have every right to be angry. I am angry enough to die.' Then the Lord said to him: 'This vine sprang up in one night, and disappeared in the next. You did not tend it or make it grow; yet you feel sorry for it. How much more, then, should I have pity on Nineveh, that great city. After all, it has thousands of innocent children within it, as well as many cattle and sheep.'

Jonah 4. 1–11

JEWISH WISDOM

From the middle of the first millennium BCE a more reflective approach to religion and morality emerged, and became dominant.

The Book of Job, written by an anonymous poet around the fifth century BCE, grapples with the problem of why God allows suffering. The Book of Psalms is a collection of poems to be used in worship and private devotion; they grapple with every aspect of humanity's relationship with God. Ecclesiastes, written around 200 BCE, contemplates the vanity of human ambition.

Jesus Ben Sirach, who lived in the second century BCE, saw Wisdom as God's active presence in the universe; his book has the Latin name Ecclesiasticus. Hillel, who lived at the turn of the eras, was a rabbi in Palestine; his teachings much influenced Jesus Christ – although Jesus criticized the self-importance of Hillel's followers, the Pharisees.

After the sacking of the temple in Jerusalem in 70 CE, and the dispersal of the Jewish people, the rabbis developed a body of teaching, the Talmud, which gave detailed instruction on every aspect of daily life. The first collection of Talmudic teaching was the Mishna; and this was later supplemented by the Gemara and the Midrash.

In the following centuries rabbinical teaching became legalistic and oppressive. Hasidism was a movement amongst European Jews to revive the inner spirit of Jewish laws. Its literature, collected in various anthologies, consists of stories and aphorisms.

Satan's challenge

There was a man named Job, who was good and upright; he revered God, and shunned evil. He had seven sons and three daughters; and he owned seven thousand sheep, three thousand camels, one thousand head of cattle, and five hundred donkeys. He also had a large number of servants.

Job's sons used to take turns in holding feasts at their homes, to which the others would come; and they always invited their three sisters. On the morning after a feast, Job would rise early, and offer sacrifices for each of his children, in case they had insulted God unintentionally.

One day the angels presented themselves to the Lord. Satan was among them. The Lord asked him: 'What have you been doing?' Satan answered: 'I have been roaming the earth, wandering from one place to another.' The Lord said: 'Did you notice my servant Job? There is no one on earth as faithful and good as he is. He reveres me, and shuns evil.' Satan said: 'Would Job revere you if he derived no benefit from it? You have always protected him, his family, and his wealth. You bless everything he does. But suppose you were to take away all that he has; he would curse you to your face.'

The Lord said: 'Very well; you have power over all that he has. But you must not hurt Job himself.' Then Satan left God's presence.

Job 1.1b−3a, 4−12

Job's first test

Soon afterwards a messenger came running to Job, and said:
'We were ploughing the fields, with the donkeys grazing on
pasture nearby. Suddenly raiders came from the south, and
stole them all. They killed every one of your servants except
me; I am the only one who has escaped to tell you.'

Before the first servant had finished speaking, another servant arrived, and said: 'Lightning has struck both the sheep
and the shepherds, killing them all. I am the only one who
has escaped to tell you.' Before he had finished speaking, another servant arrived, and said: 'Three groups of raiders from
the north attacked us, took away the camels, and killed all
your servants except me. I am the only one who has escaped
to tell you.' Before he had finished speaking, another servant
arrived, and said: 'Your children were having a feast at the
home of your eldest son, when a storm swept in from the
desert. It blew the house down, and killed them all. I am the
only person who has escaped to tell you.'

Then Job rose up; he tore his clothes in grief, and shaved
his head. Then he threw himself face downwards on the
ground, and exclaimed: 'Naked I came from my mother's
womb, and naked I shall depart. The Lord gave, and the Lord
has taken away. May the name of the Lord be praised.'

Job 1.14–21

Job's second test

The angels again presented themselves to the Lord, with Satan among them. The Lord asked Satan: 'What have you been doing?' Satan answered: 'I have been roaming the earth, wandering from one place to another.' The Lord said: 'Did you notice my servant Job? There is no one on earth as faithful and good as he is. He reveres me, and shuns evil. I have allowed you to attack him without reason, yet he remains as faithful as ever.' Satan replied: 'People will give up all they possess, in order to stay alive. But suppose you were to hurt his body; he would curse you to your face.' The Lord said: 'Very well; he is in your power. But you must not kill him.' Then Satan left God's presence.

Soon afterwards Satan caused sores to break out all over Job's body, from the soles of his feet to the top of his head. Job went out, and sat by the pile of ashes; then he took a piece of broken pottery, and scraped at his sores. His wife said to him: 'You are still as faithful as ever. Curse God, and die!' Job replied: 'You are talking as a fool. We accept good things from God with gratitude. So we should not complain when he sends trouble.'

Job 2.1–10a

Job's complaint

As news of Job's sufferings spread, three of his friends came to see him, in order to offer comfort; they were Eliphaz, Bildad, and Zophar. When they saw him from a distance, they could hardly recognize him; they began to weep aloud, tearing their clothes, and throwing dust onto their heads. Then they sat on the ground with him for seven days and nights. They could not find words to say, because they could see his suffering was so great.

Finally Job broke the silence: 'May God curse the day I was born, and the night I was conceived. I wish I had died in my mother's womb, or at the moment of my birth. Why did she hold me on her knees, and let me feed at her breast? If I had died then, I should be at peace now. In the grave the wicked cease doing evil, labourers find rest, and slaves are free. Why should those who are miserable continue to live? They yearn for death, but it does not come; they desire the grave more than any earthly treasure. I mourn instead of eating, and groans pour out of me like water. My worst fears have been realized. I have no peace, no rest; my suffering never stops.'

Job 2.11–13; 3.1–3, 11–13, 17–21, 24–26

Eliphaz's first speech

Eliphaz spoke: 'Job, will you be annoyed if I speak; I cannot remain silent any longer. In the past you have given guidance to others; you have strengthened the weak, encouraged the weary, and supported those who stumbled. Now trouble has come to you, and you are driven to despair.

'You revered God, and your life was blameless; so your piety should fill you with hope. Think carefully. Can you name a single righteous person who met with disaster? I have seen people plough fields of evil, and sow seeds of wickedness; then they have reaped trouble and pain. I assure you that trouble does not grow spontaneously, and pain does not spring out of the ground without first being sown. No; people bring trouble and pain onto themselves.

'If I were you, I should appeal to God; I should lay my case before him. Happy are those whom God corrects. Do not resent the discipline of the almighty Lord.'

Job replied: 'Honest words carry conviction; but your words are nonsense. Look at me! I do not lie. You have been unjust, so take back what you have said. My integrity is at stake, so reconsider your views. Have I ever uttered any malice? Have I ever failed to distinguish right from wrong?'

Job 4.2–4a, 5–8; 5.6–7a, 8, 17;
6.25, 28–30

Bildad's first speech

Bildad spoke: 'God never perverts justice; he is always fair. Your children must have sinned against God, so he punished them as they deserved. But turn to God, and plead with him. If you are pure and upright, God will come to your aid, restoring you to your rightful position. All the wealth that you have lost, will be trivial compared to what he will give you.

'Evil people are like weeds in the sunshine, spreading through the entire garden. Their roots wrap themselves around the stones, and hold fast to every rock. Yet after they have been pulled up, no one knows they were ever there. Evil people enjoy only a brief period of pleasure; and then their place on earth is taken by others. God never gives help to those who are evil; and he never abandons those who are righteous.'

Job replied: 'How can a mortal be righteous before God? How can mere humans win their case against him? If humans argue with him, he can ask a thousand questions which cannot be answered. God is so wise and powerful, that no man or woman can stand up to him. Can I apply force to God? Can I take him to court? Even if I were innocent, my words would condemn me; even if I were blameless, my mouth would pronounce me guilty.'

Job 8.3–7, 16–20; 9.2–4, 19b–20

Zophar's first speech

Job continued: 'I loathe my life; therefore I shall freely express the bitterness of my complaint. Why do you condemn me, God? What charges do you have against me? Do you take pleasure in being cruel to me? Why do you hunt down all my sins, searching for every fault. You know that I am innocent. Can no one rescue me from you? Your hands formed and shaped me; and now those same hands destroy me. Remember that you made me from the earth; will you now crush me into dust again? Why did you allow me to be born? I should have gone straight from the womb to the grave.'

Zophar spoke: 'Job, do you think your foolish words will reduce us to silence? Do you think your mocking words will leave us speechless? How I wish that God himself would answer you! He would tell you that wisdom has many sides, and that human beings cannot know every side. But one thing is certain: God is punishing you less than you deserve. Turn your heart towards God. Reach out to him. Drive away all evil and sin. Then you will be able to face the world again, without shame or disgrace.'

Job 10.1–2a, 6–9, 18a, 19a;
11.1–3, 5–6, 13–15

Eliphaz's second speech

Job said: 'Human life is short and filled with pain. Human beings grow and wither as quickly as flowers; like fleeting shadows they do not endure. Why, God, do you fix your eyes on me? Why do you bother to judge me? Nothing pure can come from creatures as impure as humans. You decide the length of our lives before we are born; you have counted the years and months in advance, and the date of death cannot be altered. So, God, turn away from us, and leave us alone; let us derive some small pleasures from this life – if we can!'

Eliphaz spoke: 'If you had your way, Job, piety would wither, and religion fade away. Your words reveal your wickedness, even as you try to hide it with cynical wit. I do not need to condemn you, since you condemn yourself. Are you the first person ever born? Were you present when God made the mountains? Did you overhear God's plans? Does human wisdom belong to you alone? What do you know, that we do not know? What insights do you possess, that we do not possess? God offers you comfort, and yet you reject it. We have spoken gently to you on God's behalf, and yet your eyes flash in anger – and you vent your rage against God. No human being can be truly pure; no one can be counted as righteous before God.'

Job 14.1b–6; 15.4–9, 11–14

Bildad's second speech

Job said: 'Everything you utter, I have heard many times before. Your words of comfort only worsen my torment. If you were in my place and I in yours, I could say all that you are saying. I could shake my head wisely, and drown you in fine speeches. Yet neither talk nor silence relieves my pain.'

Bildad spoke: 'You are tearing yourself to pieces with your anger. Will your rage cause the earth to be abandoned? Will God move mountains to placate you? The lamps of wicked people will soon be snuffed out, and their flames will never burn again. They walk firmly today, but they are moving towards a net, which will catch their feet; a snare has been set in their path. They are now rich, but soon they will be hungry; disaster lurks on every side. They are now healthy, but soon a deadly disease will spread across their bodies, causing their arms and legs to rot. They are now respected at home and abroad, but soon they will be ignored; their descendants will pretend they never existed. This is the fate of the wicked – of those who care nothing for God.'

Job 16.1–2, 4, 6; 18.4–5, 7a, 8,
10, 12–13, 17, 19, 21

Zophar's second speech

Job spoke: 'You are my friends; so take pity on me. The hand of God has struck me down. Why must you persecute me, as God does? Will you never stop tormenting me?'

Zophar replied: 'Your rebuke upsets me, and I am impatient to reply. Surely you know that, ever since human beings were placed on the earth, no wicked person has been happy for long. Wicked people may have a brief period of greatness, when their heads reach the clouds; but they are soon blown away like dust. Those who once knew them, wonder where they have gone. They vanish, as the dreams of night vanish at dawn. And their offspring struggle to make amends to their victims, giving back the wealth they have grabbed. Evil tastes good in the mouth; but in the stomach it turns sour.'

Job said: 'Despite your words my complaint remains bitter; I cannot contain my rage against God. I wish I knew where to find him – where I could state my case to him, presenting all my arguments. I want to hear his answers. Would he oppose me with all his might? No, he would listen to me with care. I am honest, and I should defend myself honestly; and he would declare me innocent once and for all.'

Job 19.21–22; 20.1–2, 4–7, 10,
12–14*a*; 23.1–7

The Lord's answer

Then out of the storm the Lord spoke to Job: 'Who are you to question my wisdom, with your ignorant, empty words? Now I shall question you. Were you present when I laid the earth's foundation? Tell me about the creation of the world. Who decided its dimensions? Who stretched a measuring-line across it? Surely you know! Who holds up the pillars that support the earth, or laid its cornerstone? Have you seen the springs in the depths of the sea? Have you walked on the floor of the ocean? Do you know where light comes from, or the source of darkness? Have you ever visited the storerooms where I keep the snow and the hail? Have you been to the place from which the sun rises, or the place from which the east wind blows? Can you shout orders to the clouds, and cause the rain to drench the earth? Can you command the lightning to flash? Do you hunt the prey for the lioness, or supply food for the ravens? Do you know when mountain goats are born, or where the wild deer give birth? Was it you, Job, who made the horse strong, and clothed its neck with a flowing mane? Do you teach the hawk how to fly, and show the eagle how to build its nest?'

Job replied: 'I spoke foolishly, Lord. What can I say? I shall put my hand over my mouth; I have already said too much. I know that your power is invincible; no plan of yours can be thwarted. I have talked about matters which I do not understand, about marvels too great for me to know. In the past I knew only what others told me; but now I have seen you with my own eyes. I repent in dust and ashes.'

Job 38.1–6, 16, 19, 22, 34–35*a*, 39*a*, 41*a*; 39.1,
19, 26*a*, 27*a*; 40.3–5; 42.2, 3*b*, 5, 6*b*

O Lord, throughout the world

O Lord, throughout the world your name is glorified. Your praises reach to the heavens; they are on the lips even of children and babies. You have ordered your friends to praise you, in order to silence your enemies.

I look at the sky, the work of your fingers; I observe the moon and the stars, which you set in their places. And I ask: 'What are human beings, that you should think of them? What are mere men and women, that you should care for them?'

Yet you have made us inferior only to yourself; you have crowned us with glory and honour. You have appointed us rulers over all that you have made. You have put all your creation beneath us: the flocks of sheep, the herds of cattle, and the wild beasts of the forest; the birds of the air, the fish of the sea, and all the creatures that live in the sea.

O Lord, throughout the world your name is glorified.

Psalm 8. 1–9

My God, my God, why have you forsaken me?

My God, my God, why have you forsaken me? Why are you so far from helping me – despite my cries for help? My God, by day I call to you, but you do not answer; I call by night, and am never silent. Yet you are holy, enthroned on the praises of Israel. In you our ancestors put their trust; they trusted you, and you saved them. To you they cried, and were rescued; they trusted you, and were not disappointed.

But I am a worm, not a person; I am scorned and despised by everyone. All who see me, mock me; they stick out their tongues and shake their heads. They say: 'You relied on God; let God save you. If God favours you, let him come to your rescue.' You brought me from my mother's womb, and at my mother's breasts you kept me safe. From birth I was entrusted to you; since my mother bore me, you have been my God. Do not stay away from me; trouble is near, and there is no one to help me.

My strength has poured out of my body, like water spilt upon the ground. My bones are out of joint, and my heart has melted like wax within my breast. My throat is as dry as dust, and my tongue sticks to the roof of my mouth. I lie in the dust of death. A gang of evil men gather round me like a pack of dogs; they draw closer, and tear at my hands and feet. They stare at me, and gloat; they cast lots for my clothes, and divide them among themselves.

O Lord, do not remain distant; come quickly to my rescue.

Psalm 22.1–11, 14–16, 17b–19

The Lord is my shepherd

The Lord is my shepherd; I shall lack nothing. He makes me
lie down in green pastures; he leads me beside quiet waters,
and restores my soul. He guides me in the paths of righteousness, for his name's sake. If I walk through the darkest
valley, I shall fear no evil; you are with me, and your rod and
staff protect me.

   You prepare a banquet for me, in the sight of my enemies;
you anoint my head with oil, and my cup overflows. Your
goodness and love will surely follow me, all the days of my
life; and I shall dwell in your house for ever.

Psalm 23. 1–6

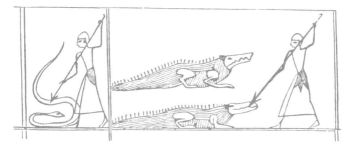

Happy are those whose sins are forgiven

Happy are those whose sins are forgiven, whose wrongs are pardoned. Happy are those whose sins are not counted against them by the Lord, and in whose spirits there is no deceit.

When I did not confess my sins, I groaned all day, causing my body to waste away. Day and night your hand was heavy upon me; my strength evaporated, like moisture in the heat of summer. Then I acknowledged my sins to you; I did not conceal my wickedness. I decided to confess my faults, and you forgave me.

So all those who are loyal to you, should pray to you in times of need. When a flood of trouble threatens to overwhelm them, it will not reach them. You are my hiding place; you will protect me from trouble, and surround me with songs of salvation.

The Lord says: 'I shall show you the path you should follow; I shall guide and advise you. Do not be foolish, like a horse or a mule who must be controlled with a bit and a bridle.'

The wicked must suffer; but steadfast love surrounds those who trust in the Lord. Rejoice in the Lord and be glad, all who are righteous. Sing, all who obey him.

Psalm 32.1–11

God is our refuge

God is our refuge and strength, a constant help in times of trouble. Therefore we shall not be afraid, even if the earth is shaken, and the mountains fall into the ocean depths; even if the seas roar and foam, and the cliffs are shaken by their surging.

There is a river whose waters make glad the city of God, the sacred house of the Most High. God is in that city, so it will never fall; at the break of day God will come to its aid. The Lord almighty is with us; the God of Jacob is our refuge.

Come and see the works of the Lord; see the wonderful things he has done on earth. He makes wars cease across the earth; he breaks the bow, shatters the spear, and sets the shield on fire. He says: 'Be still, and know that I am God. I shall be supreme among the nations, supreme over the earth.'

The Lord almighty is with us; the God of Jacob is our refuge.

Psalm 46.1–5, 7–11

Have mercy on me, O God

Have mercy on me, O God, according to your unfailing love; according to your abundant mercy, blot out my sins. Wash away my wickedness, and cleanse me of evil.

I know my wickedness; my wrongdoing is always in my mind. I have sinned against you – and you alone – and done what is evil in your sight. So you are right to speak against me, and justified in condemning me. I have been evil from the day of my birth; from the moment I was conceived I have been a sinner.

You desire truth in the depths of the soul; you teach wisdom to the heart. Cleanse me with hyssop, and I shall be clean; wash me, and I shall be whiter than snow. Fill me with joy and gladness; let the bones which you have crushed, rejoice. Close your eyes to my sins, and wipe away all my evil.

Create in me a pure heart, O God, and put a new and righteous spirit within me. Do not banish me from your presence, or take your Holy Spirit from me. Restore to me the joy of your salvation, and make my spirit willing to obey you. Then I shall teach your ways to sinners, and they will turn back to you.

O Lord, open my lips, and my mouth will declare your praise. You take no delight in sacrifices, or I should offer them. The sacrifice acceptable to God is a broken spirit; a broken and a contrite heart, O God, you will not despise.

Psalm 51.1–13, 15–17

Be gracious to us

Be gracious to us and bless us, O God, and make your face shine upon us. May your ways be known on earth; may every nation know your saving power.

Let the peoples praise you, O God; let all the peoples praise you. Let the nations be glad, and sing for joy, for you judge the peoples justly, guiding every nation on earth. Let the peoples praise you, O God; let all the peoples praise you.

Then the land will yield its harvest; God, our God, will bless us. God will bless us, and all people across the earth will honour him.

Psalm 67. 1–7

Since the days of my youth

Since the days of my youth, sovereign Lord, you have been my hope; throughout my life I have relied on you; from the day you brought me from my mother's womb, you have protected me. I shall always praise you. My life has been an example to many, because you have been my mighty defender. All day long my mouth is filled with your praises, and I proclaim your glory.

Do not cast me away now that I am old; do not abandon me now that my strength has gone. Do not withdraw from me, O God, but stay at my side and help me. I shall always have hope in you; I shall praise you more and more. I shall tell others of your goodness; all day long my lips shall declare your righteousness – though it is far greater than I can understand.

Since my youth, O God, you have taught me; and to this day I proclaim your wonderful deeds. Though I am old and grey, do not forsake me. Stay with me, and I shall proclaim your power to the next generation, your might to those who are to come.

Your righteousness, O God, reaches to the sky; you have done great things. Who, O God, is like you? Though you have sent me many bitter troubles, you have always restored my strength, and kept me from the grave. I know that you shall honour and comfort me again.

Psalm 71.6–9, 12, 14–15, 17–21

How lovely is your dwelling-place

How lovely is your dwelling-place, O Lord almighty! My soul yearns, even faints, for the courts of the Lord; my heart and my flesh cry out for the living God. Even sparrows have found a home, and swallows have made a nest; they lay their young near your altars, O Lord almighty, my king and my God. Happy are those who dwell in your house, constantly singing your praises.

One day in your courts is better than a thousand elsewhere. I should rather be a doorkeeper in the house of my God, than dwell in the tents of the wicked. For the Lord God is a sun and a shield; he bestows favour and honour. The Lord withholds no good thing from those who walk in the path of righteousness.

O Lord almighty, blessed is the man who trusts in you.

Psalm 84.1–4, 10–12

Lord, you were merciful to your land

Lord, you were merciful to your land; you forgave your people's sins, and pardoned all their wrongs. You set aside your wrath, and turned from your furious rage.

Restore us again, O God our saviour, and put away your displeasure towards us. Will you be angry with us forever? Will your anger persist through all generations? Make us strong again, that your people may rejoice in you. Show us your unfailing love, O Lord, and grant us your salvation.

I am listening to what the Lord God is saying; he promises peace, if we do not revert to our foolish ways. Surely his salvation is near to those who honour him, and his saving presence will remain in our land.

Love and faithfulness will meet; justice and peace will kiss. Human loyalty will spring up from the earth, and divine righteousness will shine from heaven. The Lord will give what is good, and our land will yield a rich harvest. Justice will go before the Lord, and prepare the way for his steps

Psalm 85.1–13

Lord, you have always been our home

Lord, you have always been our home, throughout all generations. Before the mountains were formed, or before you created the world, you were God. You are God from eternity to eternity.

You command human beings to return to dust – and you turn them back to dust. To you a thousand years is like a single day; they are like the day that has just past, or even like a single hour in the night. You sweep human beings away; they are like a passing dream. To you humans are like wild flowers, which grow and flourish in the morning, and in the evening fade and wither.

We are consumed by your burning rage, and terrified by your fury. You place our sins before you; you can see our darkest secrets. Our lives are cut short by your anger, and we finish our years with a moan. Seventy years is all we have – eighty, if we are strong – yet they bring us only trouble and sorrow; they quickly pass, and we fly away. Remind us how short are our days on earth, so that we may become wise.

How much longer will your anger last? Have compassion on your servants! Fill us each morning with your constant love, that we may sing and be glad all our lives. Make us happy for as many days as you have made us suffer; make us joyful for as many years as we have seen trouble.

Psalm 90. 1–10, 12–15

Come, let us sing for joy

Come, let us sing for joy to the Lord; let us shout aloud to the rock of our salvation. Let us come before him with thanksgiving, and extol him with music and song. For the Lord is the great God, the great king above all gods. In his hand are the depths of the earth, and the mountain peaks belong to him. The sea is his, for he made it, and his hands formed the dry land.

Come, let us bow down in worship; let us kneel before the Lord our maker. He is our God, and we are the sheep of his pasture, the flock under his care.

Today, if you hear his voice, do not harden your hearts, as you did in the desert; there your ancestors tested and tried God, though they had seen his work. For forty years God was angry with that generation, saying: 'They are a people whose hearts go astray, and they refuse to obey my commands.' So in his anger he declared on oath: 'They will never enjoy my rest.'

Psalm 95.1–11

The Lord forgives all my sins

The Lord forgives all my sins, and heals all my diseases. He keeps me from the grave, and crowns me with love and compassion. He satisfies my desires with good things, so that my youth is renewed like the eagle's.

The Lord is compassionate and gracious, slow to anger, and abounding in love. His rebukes are short, and he holds no grudges. He does not punish us as we deserve, nor repay us according to our wrongs. As high as the sky is above the earth, so great is his love for those who honour him. As far as the east is from the west, so far does he remove our sins from us. As a father is kind to his children, so the Lord is compassionate to those who worship him.

He knows of what we are made; he remembers that we are dust. We are like grass. We grow and flourish like a flower in a field; the wind blows over it, and it is gone – its place remembers it no more. But the love of the Lord lasts for ever for those who honour him; and his goodness endures for all generations to those who keep his covenant, loyally obeying his commands.

The Lord has established his throne in heaven, and he is king over all.

Psalm 103.3–5, 8–19

You are clothed with splendour

You are clothed with splendour and majesty, O Lord my God; you wrap yourself with light as if it were a garment. You stretch out the sky like a tent, and build your home on the waters above. You make the clouds your chariot, and you ride on the wings of the wind.

You set the earth on its foundations, so that it can never be moved. You covered it with the oceans like a robe; the waters covered the mountains. But at your rebuke the waters fled; at the sound of your thunder they took to flight. They flowed over the mountains, and down into the valleys, to the place you had assigned for them. You set a boundary they cannot cross; never again will they cover the earth.

You make springs flow in the valleys, and rivers run between the hills. You provide water for all the beasts of the field, for the wild donkeys to quench their thirst. The birds of the air nest in trees by the waters, and they sing among the branches. From the sky you send rain on the hills, and the earth is satisfied by your work. You create grass for the cattle, and plants for humans to cultivate. The earth brings forth food for us to eat, wine to gladden our hearts, olive oil to make our faces shine, and bread to give us strength.

Psalm 104. 1b–15

Happy are those who honour the Lord

Happy are those who honour the Lord, who find delight in obeying his commands. Their children will be mighty in the land, and their descendants will be blessed. Their families will enjoy wealth and riches, and their righteousness will endure for ever. Good people are like lights shining in the darkness; they are gracious, compassionate and just.

Happy are those who are generous, lending to the poor without interest, and treating all people fairly. They can never be shaken; their righteousness will always be remembered. They do not fear bad news, because their faith is strong and their hearts are steadfast. They are never anxious or afraid, because they know their enemies will be defeated. Their kindness to the needy never fails, and they earn respect near and far.

Wicked people look at righteous people, and are vexed. They gnash their teeth in hatred, and waste away; their ambitions come to nothing.

Psalm 112.1–10

I love the Lord

I love the Lord, for he heard my voice; he heard my cry for mercy. Since he turned his ear to me, I shall call on him as long as I live. The cords of death entangled me, and the anguish of death overwhelmed me; I was filled with sorrow and terror. Then I called on the name of the Lord: 'O Lord, save me!'

The Lord is gracious and just; our God is full of compassion. He protects the helpless; when I was in danger, he came to my aid. So be at rest, my soul, for the Lord has been good to me.

You, Lord, have delivered my soul from death; you have dried the tears from my eyes, and stopped my feet from stumbling. Now I can walk again in the land of the living. I come before you, and ask: 'How can I repay all your goodness to me?' I shall lift up the cup of salvation, and call on your name. When your people assemble, I shall offer to you all I possess.

To the Lord every person is precious, every life is holy. I am your servant, Lord; I shall serve you, just as my mother did. You have freed me from the chains of death. I shall offer you a sacrifice of thanksgiving, calling on your name.

Psalm 116.1–9, 12–17

In my anguish I cried

In my anguish I cried to the Lord, and he answered by setting me free. The Lord is with me, so I shall not be afraid. What can anyone do to me? The Lord is with me; he is my helper. It is better to trust in the Lord, than to depend on people; it is better to trust in the Lord, than to depend on human leaders.

The Lord is my strength and my song; he has become my salvation. I shall not die, but live; and I shall proclaim what the Lord has done. The Lord has chastened me severely, but he has not allowed me to die. Let the gates of righteousness be opened; I shall enter, and give thanks to the Lord – he has become my salvation.

The stone that the builders rejected, has become the capstone; the Lord has done this, and it is marvellous in our eyes. This is the day that the Lord has made; let us rejoice, and be glad in it.

O Lord, save us; O Lord, grant us success. Blessed is he who comes in the name of the Lord; from the house of the Lord we bless you. The Lord is good, and he has made his light shine upon us. With branches in your hands, join the festal procession, and march around the altar.

You are my God, and I shall give you thanks; you are my God, and I shall exalt you.

Psalm 118.5–7a, 8–9, 14, 17–19, 21a, 22–28

Teach me the meaning of your laws

Teach me the meaning of your laws, O Lord, and I shall obey
them at all times. Explain your laws to me, and I shall follow
them with all my soul. Direct me in the path of your
commandments, I shall walk on that path with joy. Turn my
heart towards your statutes, and away from selfish gain. Turn
my eyes away from worthless pleasures, and renew my life
according to your precepts. Save me from the insults I dread;
your laws are good. I yearn to obey your laws; renew my life
with your righteousness.

Show me, O Lord, the fullness of your love, and save me
according to your promise. When people mock me, I shall
answer that I trust your word. Let the truth always be in my
mouth, for I have put my hope in your laws. I shall always
obey your laws, for ever and ever. I shall live in perfect freedom, because I strive to follow your precepts. I shall speak of
your statutes before kings, and shall not be put to shame. I
take delight in obeying your commands, because I love them.
I reach out my hands to receive your laws; I love to meditate
upon your decrees.

You are righteous, Lord, and your laws are just. The rules
which you have laid down, are fair and good. Your promises
have been tested many times, and your servants can trust
them. Your instructions are always correct; let me understand
them, and I shall live.

Psalm 119, 33–37, 39–48, 137–138, 140, 144

You have examined me

You have examined me, O Lord, and you know me. You know when I sit and when I rise; you perceive my thoughts from afar. You watch me when I am going out, and when I am resting; you are familiar with all my ways. Before a word is on my tongue, you know what I shall say. You are all around me, on every side; your hand is upon me. Your understanding is too deep for me to fathom, and too high for me to reach.

Where can I escape from you? Where can I flee from your presence? If I fly up to the sky, you are there; if I lie in the deepest ocean, you are there. If I rise on the wings of the dawn, or if I settle beyond the dusk, your hand grasps me and leads me. If I ask the darkness to hide me, begging the day to become night, you see as clearly as if the sun were shining – because darkness is not dark to you.

You fashioned every part of me; you knit me together in my mother's womb. I praise you because you have made me with such skill; I honour your handiwork. I know with all my heart that all you do is wonderful. When my bones were forming in my mother's womb, you watched over me; when I was growing in secret, you cared for me. You ordained the days of my life, inscribing them in your book, before a single day had begun.

How precious to me are your thoughts, O God! How vast is their sum! If they could be counted, they would outnumber all the grains of sand.

Psalm 139.1–18a

One generation will commend your works

One generation will commend your works to the next, O Lord; each generation will proclaim your mighty acts. Older people will speak to younger people of your glory and splendour; they will tell of your awesome power. They will celebrate your abundant goodness, and joyfully sing of your righteousness. I myself will never cease to meditate on your kindness, and I shall always relate to others what you have done for me.

Lord, you are gracious and compassionate, slow to anger and rich in love. You are good to all; you are generous to what you have made. All your creatures will praise you, O Lord, and all your people will extol you. They will tell of the glory of your kingdom, and speak of your might. Your kingdom is an everlasting kingdom, and your dominion endures through all generations.

Lord, you keep your promises, and you love what you have made. You uphold those who stumble, and you raise those who are bowed down. The eyes of all creatures look to you for food, which you supply at the proper time. You open your hand, and satisfy the desires of every living thing.

Lord, you are righteous in all your ways, and loving towards all you have made. You are near to all who call on you, Lord; you want everyone to speak honestly to you. My mouth will always sing your praise; let every creature praise your holy name for ever and ever.

Psalm 145.4–11, 13–18, 21

Praise the Lord from heaven

Praise the Lord from heaven; praise him from the heights above. Praise him, all his angels; praise him, all his heavenly hosts. Praise him, sun and moon; praise him, all you shining stars. Praise the name of the Lord; he gave the command, and you were created. He set you in place for ever and ever; he issued a decree that will never pass away.

Praise the Lord from the earth; praise him, all you sea creatures in the ocean depths. Praise him, lightning and hail, snow and clouds; praise him, stormy winds that do his bidding. Praise him, mountains and hills, fruit trees and cedars; praise him, wild animals and cattle, insects and birds. Praise the Lord, all you kings and princes on earth; let every nation praise him. Praise him, young men and women; praise him, old men and women; praise him, boys and girls.

Let every creature praise the name of the Lord, for his name alone is worthy of praise. His splendour is above the earth and heaven. He makes his people strong; let praise be on the lips of all whom he loves.

Psalm 148.1–14

The vanity of life

These are the words of the Philosopher, who was king in Jerusalem.

Vanity, vanity, all is vanity! What do people gain from all their labour – from toiling under the sun? Generations come and go, but the world remains the same for ever. The sun rises and the sun sets; then it hurries back to where it rises. The wind blows to the south, and then turns to the north; round and round it goes, and back again. All rivers flow into the sea; yet the sea is never full. The water returns to where the rivers begin, and then flows again. Everything is wearisome – more wearisome than words can describe.

Our eyes can never see enough to be satisfied; our ears can never hear enough. What has happened, will happen again; what has been done, will be done again. There is nothing new under the sun. People say: 'Look! Here is something new.' But it was here already; it was here before our time. No one remembers the days of old; and no one in the future will remember today.

Ecclesiastes 1.1–11

The heavy burden on humanity

When I was king over Israel, I devoted myself to examining and exploring everything that happens under heaven. What a heavy burden God has laid on humanity! I have seen everything that is done in the world; and I assure you that it is all vanity, like chasing the wind. What is crooked, cannot be straightened; what does not exist, cannot be counted.

I said to myself: 'I have become a great king; I have become wiser than anyone who has ruled in Jerusalem before me; I have acquired much knowledge.' Then I decided to learn the difference between wisdom and folly, knowledge and madness. But this was like chasing the wind. With wisdom comes anxiety; with knowledge comes grief.

So I decided to enjoy myself, and discover the nature of happiness. But that too proved to be vanity. Laughter is foolish, and pleasure accomplishes nothing. Driven by my desire for wisdom, I decided to cheer myself with wine and embrace folly; this may be the best way for people to spend their short time on earth.

Ecclesiastes 1.12—2.3

The vanity of achievement

I undertook great projects. I built myself houses, and established vineyards. I laid out gardens and parks, planting all kinds of fruit trees in them; and I dug ponds to irrigate them. I bred sheep and cattle, so I owned more livestock than anyone in Jerusalem before me. I amassed silver and gold from the royal treasuries of the lands I ruled. I employed male and female singers to entertain me, and acquired a large harem to give me pleasure.

Yes, I was greater than anyone else who had ever lived in Jerusalem, and my wisdom never failed me. I denied myself nothing that my eyes desired; I refused my heart no pleasure. I took delight in all my work, and this was the reward for my efforts. Yet when I surveyed all that my hands had done, all that my toil had achieved, I knew that it was vanity – like chasing the wind. Nothing had been gained.

I realized that the same fate awaits us all; despite my wisdom, I must suffer the same fate as a fool. So what have I gained from being wise? Nothing. No one remembers the wise, just as no one remembers fools; in days to come we shall all be forgotten. The wise and the foolish alike must die. So I came to despise life, and work became a burden to me. I knew that every task is vanity – like chasing the wind. I must leave my achievements to the one who comes after me. He may be wise, or he may be a fool; no one knows. But he will have control over everything I have accomplished. I regretted having toiled so hard.

Ecclesiastes 2.4–11, 14b–17, 18b–20

A time for everything

There is a time for everything, and a season for every activity under heaven:

a time to be born, and a time to die;
a time to plant, and a time to uproot;
a time to kill, and a time to heal;
a time to pull down, and a time to build up;
a time to weep, and a time to laugh;
a time to mourn, and a time to dance;
a time to scatter stones, and a time to gather them;
a time to kiss, and a time to refrain from kissing;
a time to search, and a time to give up;
a time to keep, and a time to throw away;
a time to tear, and a time to mend;
a time to keep silent, and a time to speak;
a time to love, and a time to hate;
a time for war, and a time for peace.

Ecclesiastes 3. 1–8

From dust to dust

I noticed that in this world wickedness frequently takes the place of righteousness; there is evil instead of justice. I said to myself: 'God will bring to judgement both the wicked and the righteous; there is a time for every action, a time for every deed.' I concluded that God is testing us, to show us that we are no different from animals. The fate of humans is the same as that of animals; they both die. Humans and animals breathe the same air; humans have no advantage over animals. All is vanity; all creatures go to the same place; from dust they come, and to dust they will return.

Then I looked at the oppression in this world. I saw the tears of the oppressed; they have no one to comfort them. I saw that power is on the side of the oppressor; and they have no one to guide them. I declared that those who have already died, are happier than those who are still alive; but happier than them both are those who have never been born, and who therefore have not seen all the evil in the world.

I learnt why people strive so hard for success: they envy their neighbours. This too is vanity – like chasing the wind. It is said that fools fold their hands, and ruin themselves. But it is better to do little, and yet enjoy tranquillity of mind, than to be busy all day chasing the wind.

I noticed a further vanity in the world. I saw a man living alone. He had no sons or brothers; yet he was always working, and never satisfied with his wealth. Why is he working, and depriving himself of all pleasure? How miserable!

Ecclesiastes 3.16–20; 4.1–8

Awe of God

Guard your steps when you visit the temple. Go there in order to listen, rather than offer sacrifices. Only fools – those who do not know the difference between right and wrong – offer sacrifices.

Do not be quick with your mouth in making pledges to God; do not be hasty with your heart in speaking to him. God is in heaven, and you are on earth; so let your words be few. The more you worry, the more likely you are to have bad dreams; in the same way, the more you speak, the more likely you are to say something stupid.

When you make a vow to God, do not delay in fulfilling it. He takes no pleasure in fools; fulfil your vow at once. It is better not to make a vow, than to make a vow and break it. Do not let your mouth lead you into sin; do not find yourself telling the priest that you did not mean what you said. Why make God angry with you? Why let him destroy the work of your hands? Much dreaming and many words are vanity. Therefore stand in awe of God.

Ecclesiastes 5.1–7

Life and death

After long reflection I have concluded that God controls the actions of wise and righteous people; yet even they do not know whether love or hate awaits them. In fact, no one knows what lies ahead. All share a common destiny: the righteous and the wicked; the good and the bad; those who are pure, and those who are impure; those who are religious and those who ignore religion. A good person is no better off than a sinner; one who takes an oath is no better off than one who is afraid to take an oath. The same fate comes to all alike – and this is as wrong as anything that happens in this world.

While people live, their minds may be full of evil, and their hearts may be twisted with madness; then suddenly they die. Those who are alive, have hope; a live dog is better off than a dead lion. The living know they will die, but the dead know nothing. The dead have no further reward; they are completely forgotten. Their loves, their hates and their passions have died with them. They will never again play any part in the affairs of this world.

So enjoy life for the days God has given you. Eat, and be happy; drink, and be merry. Take pleasure in the company of the woman you love.

Ecclesiastes 9. 1–7, 9a

Time and chance

I have realized another thing. The race is not always won by the swift. The battle is not always won by the strong. Food does not always go to the wise. Wealth does not always accrue to the brilliant. Fortune does not always smile on the able. All are vulnerable to time and chance.

Moreover, people cannot know when their hour will come. As fish are caught in a cruel net, or birds trapped in a snare, so people can be overwhelmed by evil when they least expect it.

Ecclesiastes 9.11–12

Listening to gentle wisdom

I have seen an example of how wisdom is regarded in the world. There was once a small city, with only a few people in it. A powerful king attacked it. He surrounded it, and prepared to break through its walls. In the city there lived a man who was immensely wise and clever; he could have devised a strategy to defeat that king. But he was so poor and humble that everyone ignored him.

I have always believed that wisdom is better than strength. But the wisdom of the poor is despised, and their words go unheeded. It is better to listen to the gentle words of the wise, than to the shouts of fools – even if the fools possess power. Wisdom is superior to the weapons of war; but one sinner can destroy much good.

Ecclesiastes 9.13–18

Youth, age and death

Young people, take pleasure in your youth. Be happy while you are still young. Follow your heart's desires, for your heart will bring you joy. But remember that God will judge you for all you do. Banish anxiety from your heart, and cast troubles from your shoulders. You will not be young for long.

Remember your Creator in the days of your youth. Soon the dismal day will come, when you will say: 'I no longer enjoy life.' At that time the sun, the moon and the stars will grow dim for you, and the clouds will never pass away. Your arms, which have protected you, will tremble; and your legs, which now are strong, will weaken. Your teeth will be too few to chew your food, and your eyes too blurred to see clearly. Your ears will be deaf to the noise of the street; you will barely hear the mill as it grinds, or music as it plays – yet the song of the bird will wake you from your sleep. You will be afraid of heights, and you will fear strange places. Your hair will turn white, and your feet will drag along the ground. All desire will have gone.

When you go to your final resting-place, mourners will line the streets. Your body will return to the dust of the earth, and your spirit will return to God, who gave it.

Ecclesiastes 11.9—12.5, 7

Wise shepherds

The Philosopher was wise, and imparted his knowledge to many people. He studied many proverbs, and tested their truth. He sought words that would bring comfort to others; but his primary aim was to speak the truth. The sayings of wise people are like the sharp sticks that shepherds use to drive their sheep; and collections of their sayings are as enduring as nails that have been firmly driven. Indeed, the wisdom of the wise is bestowed by God, the shepherd of us all.

Be warned: do not try to add to the wisdom of the wise. There is no end to the writing of books; and excessive study wearies the body.

Here, then, is the conclusion to the Philosopher's teaching: honour God, and keep his commandments – that is the whole duty of humankind. God will judge all deeds, including those that are hidden, and determine whether they are good or bad.

Ecclesiastes 12.9–14

The roots of wisdom

All wisdom is from the Lord; wisdom is with him forever. Who can count the grains of sand on the bed of the sea? Who can count the drops of rain, or the days from the beginning to the end of time? Who can measure the height of the sky, the breadth of the earth, or the depths of the ocean? Wisdom was the first of all that God created; its intelligence has been present from the beginning.

Who has laid bare the roots of wisdom? Who has understood her subtlety? Only the Lord, seated upon his throne. God created her; he designed her and formed her; and he infused her into all his works. To every human being he has given her in some measure; and to those who love him, he has given wisdom in abundance.

Jesus Ben Sirach 1.1–10

A garland of joy

Devotion to the Lord brings a garland of joy; it gladdens the heart and strengthens the body. If you devote yourself to the Lord, your life will be long and happy, and your death will be peaceful.

The essence of wisdom is devotion to the Lord. When a human being is conceived in a woman's womb, wisdom is present. She lives with all people throughout their lives; she is their constant companion.

If you are devoted to the Lord, then the Lord will fill you with wisdom. You will imbibe wisdom as if you were drinking wine. The Lord has storehouses overflowing with wisdom; and from these storehouses he will give you as much wisdom as you can absorb.

Wisdom will be like a garland around your neck, with flowers of serenity and health. Your mind will have knowledge in abundance, and your hands will possess every skill. Wisdom is rooted in devotion to the Lord, and longevity grows on her branches.

Jesus Ben Sirach 1.11–20

Unjust anger can never be excused; when anger tips the scales, disaster follows. Restrain yourself until the time is ripe for anger; be patient, and keep your thoughts to yourself, until anger is right. And when your anger is just, cheerfulness will swiftly follow; and good sense will be on everyone's lips.

Wisdom possesses many shrewd proverbs, while folly is loved by sinners. If you yearn for wisdom, obey the Lord's commands; then he will give you wisdom in plenty. From devotion to the Lord comes both wisdom and self-control; serenity and gentleness are the fruits of wisdom.

Do not slacken your devotion to the Lord; and do not approach him without sincerity. Be true to yourself at all times; do not try to give a false impression of yourself to others. Guard your lips, so that no cruel words ever escape them. Do not treat others with contempt; the Lord knows your darkest secrets, and yet treats you with respect.

Jesus Ben Sirach 1.21–30

The Lord's path

My son, if you aspire to be a servant of the Lord, you should prepare yourself for testing. Set yourself on the straight course, which the Lord himself has shown you, and stay on it; do not abandon it in difficult times. Bear with fortitude every hardship that befalls you; when your reputation is attacked, be patient and calm. God is purified by fire; the Lord will purify you in the furnace of humiliation. Trust God, and he will help you; put your hope in him, and in him alone.

If you love the Lord, wait for his mercy; do not stray from his path, or you will stumble and fall. If you love the Lord, look to him for all your needs; he will never forget you. If you love the Lord, expect to be happy; joy is the reward for those who devote their lives to him.

Look at past generations. What do you observe? When people trusted in the Lord, were they ever disappointed? When people walked along his path, did he ever leave their sides? When people prayed to him, did he ever deafen his ears to their pleas? The Lord is compassionate and merciful; he forgives sins, and rescues those in danger.

Jesus Ben Sirach 2.1–11

The children of wisdom

Wisdom raises her children to greatness, and cares for those who seek her. To love wisdom is to love life; to rise early for the sake of wisdom is to be filled with joy. If you attain wisdom, the Lord will bless you; the Lord blesses the wise wherever they go. To serve wisdom is to serve God; the Lord loves those who love her. Wisdom's servants listen to her every moment of the day and night; and they teach her precepts to others. If you trust wisdom, you will possess her, and you will bequeath her to your descendants.

At first wisdom will lead you along steep and winding paths, and you will tremble with fear. You will be tempted to abandon her; you will need all your strength to remain at her side. Trust her with all your heart. Eventually she will bring you to a place of joy and gladness, and she will reveal her secrets to you. But if you leave her, she will abandon you – and your fate will be in your own hands.

Jesus Ben Sirach 4.11–19

Quick repentance

Do not rely on money, and say: 'I am independent; I do not need help.' Do not try to gratify every desire, or obey every impulse of your heart. Do not ignore the Lord, and say: 'I am my own master.'

Do not rely on the Lord's patience. Do not be so confident of his forgiveness that you sin again and again. Do not say: 'His mercy is so great that he will forgive all my sins, however many I commit.' To God belongs wrath as well as mercy, and persistent sinners suffer the full weight of his retribution. When you have sinned, repent and return to the Lord without delay. Do not put off your repentance from one day to the next, as the wrath of the Lord will soon catch up with you.

Do not rely on profits that have been gained dishonestly. Do not chase after every new idea, or follow every new teacher. Stand firmly by what you know to be true, and be consistent in what you say. Be quick to listen, but take time over your answers. If you know what to say, then speak; if not, hold your tongue. Both honour and shame can come through speech, and the tongue can bring a person down.

Avoid the little faults, as well as the great.

Jesus Ben Sirach 5.1–13, 15

The wings of wisdom

Seek wisdom while you are still young; then, when your hair is grey, you will still possess her.

Come to her like a farmer ploughing and sowing; then wait for her abundant harvest. If you cultivate her, you will work for a little while; but soon you will be eating her crops.

How harsh wisdom seems to those whose only interest is pleasure! Fools cannot abide her; she is like a burden which tests their strength to the limit – and which they quickly cast aside. Wisdom deserves her name; few are willing to cherish her.

My child, listen to my advice, and heed it. Put your feet in wisdom's fetters, and your neck into her collar. Stoop to lift her onto your shoulders, and do not chafe at her bonds. Receive her with all your heart, and follow her wherever she leads. At first she will seem like a weight upon your back; but soon she will become your wings. At first you may suffer a little; but soon your suffering will turn to joy.

Jesus Ben Sirach 6.18–28

Bride and mother

Happy are those who fix their minds upon wisdom, and think about her constantly. Happy are those who contemplate her ways and ponder her secrets.

Stalk her like a hunter stalking his prey; lie in wait beside her path. Peer through the windows of her room, and listen to her through the keyhole. Set up your tent beside her house, and drive the tent pegs into her wall. To see her, to listen to her, and to dwell beside her – these are the greatest honours that anyone can enjoy. Wisdom is like a great tree: put your children beneath her branches, and let them grow up in her shade.

If you worship the Lord, you will be wisdom's most devoted lover; she will come to you as a young bride comes to her bridegroom. If you obey the commands of the Lord, wisdom will be yours; she will care for you as a mother cares for her only son. For food she will give you the bread of knowledge, and for drink she will give you the water of insight. When you stumble, she will lift you; and when you are weary, she will hold you up.

Jesus Ben Sirach 14.20–5.4a

Fire and water

Worship cannot be sincere on the lips of sinners; true worship is prompted by the Lord. Worship is the outward expression of wisdom, and the Lord himself inspires it.

Do not say that the Lord is to blame for your sins; you have the power to avoid doing what he hates. Do not say that the Lord led you astray; he has no use for sinners. The Lord hates every kind of vice; you cannot both love sin and love the Lord.

When God created human beings, he gave them freedom to make their own decisions. If you choose, you can keep his commandments; you alone must decide whether to obey him of defy him. He offers you both fire and water; reach out and take whichever you want. God offers you both life and death; reach out and take whichever you prefer.

In his wisdom and power God sees everything. He watches over those who love him. No human action escapes his notice. He has commanded no man or woman to be wicked; he has given no one the licence to sin.

Jesus Ben Sirach 15.9–20

A drop in the ocean

There is only one being who lives forever; the creator of the universe. There is only one being who is always righteous; the Lord of all that exists.

No man or woman can know or relate the full story of his works. Who can trace his marvels to their source? No man or woman can measure the greatness of his power, nor tell the full tale of his mercies. No man or woman can increase or diminish his glory, no one can fathom the depth of his love. When human beings stretch their understanding to the limit, they barely begin to grasp his wonder; they are still perplexed.

What are human beings, and what use are they? Does it matter whether they do good or evil? The human span is at most a hundred years; compared with the whole of time, this is like a single drop in the ocean, or a grain of sand on the ocean bed. That is why the Lord is patient with humans, and lavishes his mercy upon them. He knows the harsh consequences of sin, and so strives to save them. Humans only have compassion for their neighbours; but the Lord has compassion for all people.

The Lord corrects them, trains them and teaches them; he watches over them as a shepherd watches over his flock, and brings them back when they go astray.

Jesus Ben Sirach 18. 1–13

Sweeter than honey

Hear the praise of wisdom from her own mouth, as she speaks in the presence of God, the angels and her people: 'I am the word that was spoken by God; I covered the earth like a mist. My home was in heaven, and my throne was a pillar of cloud. I travelled round the sky, and I plunged into the depths of the ocean. The ocean and the winds, the earth and all living things upon the earth, were under my sway. I looked for a home on earth, and wondered in whose territory I should settle. Then the creator of the universe commanded me to live in Israel.

'The Lord created me before the beginning of time, and I shall live forever. When the Lord established Israel, he made me its guide. I caused Jerusalem to be built, and he gave me authority over it. The Lord chose the Israelite people to be his special possession, and I took root among them.

'Come to me, all you who desire me, and eat your fill of my fruit. I am sweeter than honey dripping from the comb; and the memory of me is sweeter than syrup. If you have fed once on me, you will constantly be hungry for more; when you have drunk from me, you will constantly be thirsty for more.'

Jesus Ben Sirach 24.1–12, 19–21

The fount of happiness

There are three sights which warm my heart, and which are beautiful in the eyes of the Lord and of all people: harmony among brothers; friendship among neighbours; and unity between a husband and his wife. There are three kinds of people whose way of life disgusts me: a poor person who boasts; a rich person who lies; and anyone who commits adultery.

If you have not gained wisdom in your youth, how will you possess her when you are old? Sound judgement should be found beneath grey hairs; shrewd advice comes well from the elderly; wisdom befits those advanced in years; those close to death should give good counsel.

I can think of five types of people whom I count as happy: those who take delight in their children; those who are happily married; those who never speak what they do not mean; those who have true friends; and those who are devoted to the Lord. Indeed, devotion to the Lord is the true fount of happiness.

Jesus Ben Sirach 25.1–7a, 8a, 9a, 11

A masterpiece of wisdom

The Lord created the universe through his wisdom. As the sun in its brilliance looks down on all things, the glory of the Lord fills his creation. The Lord created the universe as a reflection of his glory.

The Lord fathoms the heart of every man, woman and child; he knows their deepest secrets. He possesses all knowledge, and observes all events. He remembers the past, and foresees the future; he penetrates the deepest mysteries. No thought escapes his notice, and no word escapes his hearing.

This world is a masterpiece of his wisdom. Nothing can be added to his wisdom, and nothing can be taken away; no advice can add to the store of his understanding. He brought his wisdom into being before time began, and it will exist after time is complete.

How beautiful is all that his wisdom has fashioned. Even the smallest spark from a fire has been designed with the utmost skill.

If you were to honour the Lord with every breath you breathe, he would still be far above your praise. If you were to summon all your strength to declare his greatness, your words would still fall short. Has anyone seen him? Can anyone describe him? Can anyone praise him as he truly is? We see only a small part of his works; there are even greater glories beyond our gaze.

Jesus Ben Sirach 42.16, 18–22a; 43.30–32

Time for action

Hillel said: 'Do you wish to know the law of God? Love peace, and cherish one another.'

Hillel also said: 'If you do not win the respect of others, you will lose their respect. If you do not increase your knowledge, it will diminish. If you refuse to learn, your mind will grow in ignorance. If you use your abilities solely for your own benefit, you will commit spiritual suicide.'

Hillel also said: 'If I am not self-reliant, on whom can I rely? But if I am selfish, what use am I? And if the time for action is not now, when is it?'

Hillel: Pirke Aboth 1.1–14

A floating skull

Hillel said: 'Do not keep aloof from the common people. Do not be confident of your own wisdom and goodness. Do not condemn another person, till you have been in the same place as that person and reacted differently. Do not say that you will delay your studies until tomorrow, because tomorrow never comes.'

Hillel also said: 'Fools do not fear sin. Self-doubters, who lack belief in their own intelligence, cannot learn. Ill-tempered people cannot teach. People preoccupied with the affairs of the world cannot acquire wisdom.'

Hillel once saw a skull floating in a lake. He said to the skull: 'Since you drowned others, you yourself were drowned. Eventually people always suffer the harm they do to others.'

Hillel also said: 'The fatter you are, the more food you will provide for the worms. The richer you are, the more worries you have. The more concubines you have, the more you are assailed by sexual desire. And the more slaves you own, the more you will be robbed. Yet the more you obey God's laws, the more fully you will love. The more you study, the wiser you will grow. The more advice you receive, the more enlightened you will become. And the more good you do, the more peace you will enjoy.'

Hillel: *Pirke Aboth* 2.5–8

A guest and a bath

Hillel was teaching his disciples. Then he rose, and started to walk away from them. 'Where are you going?' they asked. 'I am going to look after a guest,' he replied. 'Who is that guest?' they asked. He replied: 'My soul, who is a guest in my body. Today it is here, but tomorrow it may be gone.'

When Hillel was leaving his disciples on another occasion, they asked him: 'Where are you going?' He replied: 'To do a righteous deed,' he replied. 'What might that be?' they asked. 'To take a bath,' he replied. 'What is righteous about that?' they asked. Hillel answered: 'Men are paid to wash the images of kings that are set up in public places. So surely I should wash my body, which is an image of God?'

Hillel: Leviticus Rabbah 34.3

A sensible answer

A man laid a wager with a friend that he could make Hillel lose his temper. If he succeeded, he would win four hundred gold coins; and if he failed, he would lose this sum.

So he went to Hillel's house at the time when Hillel was bathing. 'Where is Hillel?' he shouted. Hillel wrapped a towel around his body, and came out. 'What do you want?' Hillel asked. The man said: 'I wish to know why Babylonians have such round heads.' Hillel replied: 'The reason is that their midwives are not as skilful as our midwives.'

The man called at Hillel's house on many more occasions at inconvenient moments: at mealtimes; while Hillel was having a nap; and when Hillel was teaching his disciples. On each occasion the man asked some foolish question; and on each occasion Hillel answered the man's inquiry with patience and courtesy.

Finally in vexation the man said: 'I have laid a wager for four hundred gold coins that I could make you lose your temper. How can you stop me from losing my money?' Hillel replied: 'That is the first sensible question you have asked. And it is the first question for which I have no answer.'

Hillel smiled, and went back into his house. The man went away, and gave four hundred gold coins to his friend.

Hillel: Shabbat 31a

A good heart

Rabbi Simeon said: 'I grew up among wise people, and have heard many wise words. But I have found nothing better than silence. It is more important to act than to speak. Saying too much encourages sin.'

Rabbi Gamaliel said: 'It is good to have a useful occupation, as well as to study religious books. The combinaton of work and study leaves you no time or inclination to sin.'

He also said: 'Beware of those with political power. They only seem friendly when it is to their own advantage; but when you are in trouble, they desert you.'

Rabbi Jochan said: 'Do not regard yourself as righteous simply because you have studied religion and morality. Righteousness consists in following the right way of life.' Then he asked his disciples: 'What is most helpful to a person in following the right way of life?' One disciple answered: 'A watchful eye.' Another answered: 'A wise friend.' Another answered: 'A kind neighbour.' Another answered: 'A listening ear.' And another answered: 'A loving heart.' Rabbi Jochan declared: 'The last answer is best, because it includes all the rest.'

Mishna

A drop of sperm

Rabbi Eliezar said: 'Let your friend's honour be as dear to you as your own. Be slow to anger, but quick to repent. Warm yourself at the fire of wise minds; but beware of those on fire with religious passion, as you will be scorched.'

Rabbi Jehoshua said: 'Keep your desires under control; otherwise you will cut yourself off from your friends.'

Rabbi Jose said: 'Let your friend's property be as dear to you as your own. Seek the truth for yourself, because you can never inherit it. And let all your actions be in the service of God.'

Rabbi Simeon said: 'Do not pray mechanically, but let your prayers come from the heart.'

Rabbi Elazar said: 'If anyone speaks falsely, have the courage to assert the truth.'

Rabbi Mahalelel said: 'Keep three things in mind, and you will avoid sin: where you came from; where you are going; and to whom you will have to give an account of yourself. Where did you come from? From a drop of sperm. Where are you going? To a graveyard, where your body will be eaten by worms. And to whom will you have to give an account of yourself? To the King of kings.'

Mishna

Two or three people

Rabbi Hanina said: 'Pray for the stability of the government. If people did not fear the government, they would swallow one another alive.'

Rabbi Hananyah said: 'When two people sit together, and discuss spiritual matters, then the spirit of God rests upon them.'

Rabbi Simeon said: 'If three people have sat at a table and eaten a meal together, but have not mentioned spiritual matters, then they have disgraced their own ancestors.'

Rabbi Hanina said: 'Those who stay up all night in order to indulge their desires, who devote the daylight hours solely to their own interests, and whose minds are filled with idle thoughts, ruin themselves.'

He also said: 'If your deeds are greater than your knowledge, then your knowledge is effective. If your knowledge is greater than your deeds, then your knowledge is futile.'

He also said: 'If your own soul is pleased with you, then you can be sure that God is pleased with you.'

Rabbi Dosa said: 'If you sleep until late in the morning, if you drink wine during the day, if you refuse to discuss serious matters, and if you keep the company of fools, then you will bring ruin on yourself.'

Mishna

Wisdom, strength, wealth and respect

Rabbi Ismail said: 'Be obedient to superiors; be generous towards those who seek your help; and be friendly towards everyone.'

Rabbi Akiba said: 'Sarcasm leads to enmity; tradition protects knowledge; hard work preserves wealth; and silence enhances wisdom.'

He also said: 'Where there is no morality, there is no generosity; and where there is no generosity, there is no morality. Where there is no wisdom, there is no friendship; and where there is no friendship, there is no wisdom. Where there is no knowledge, there is no insight; and where there is no insight, there is no knowledge. Where there is no food, there is no morality; and where there is no morality, there is no food.'

Rabbi Zoma said: 'Who are wise? Those who can learn from everyone. Who is strong? Those who can control their passions. Who are wealthy? Those who are satisfied with their lot. Who deserve respect? Those who respect all people.'

Rabbi Azai said: 'Despise no one, and treat no place with contempt. All people and all places have their moment.'

Rabbi Levitas: 'Be humble, for the destiny of all people is to be eaten by worms.'

Mishna

Busy with wisdom

Rabbi Jonathan said: 'When the poor follow God's way, they earn great spiritual wealth, and hence enjoy great happiness. When the rich abandon God's way, they make themselves spiritually poor, and hence suffer great misery.'

Rabbi Meir said: 'Be less busy with business, and more busy with wisdom. If you start to neglect wisdom, you will find more and more reasons for neglecting it.'

Rabbi Elazar said: 'Let your disciples' honour be as dear to you as a friend's. Let a friend's honour be as dear to you as your teacher's. And let your teacher's honour be as dear to you as your own.'

Rabbi Jehudah said: 'Be cautious in your teaching, because false teaching can lead others into sin.'

Rabbi Simeon said: 'There are three crowns which the world honours: the crown of scholarship; the crown of priesthood; and the crown of royalty. But greater than all these is the crown of wisdom.'

Rabbi Nehorai said: 'Go to a place where wisdom is to be found, because wisdom will not come to you.'

Rabbi Jannai said 'It is beyond our power to explain either the prosperity which many wicked people enjoy, or the poverty which many righteous people suffer.'

Mishna

The tail of a lion

Rabbi Mattihiah said: 'It is better to be the tail of a lion than the head of a fox.'

Rabbi Jacob said: 'This world is no more than the lobby of a great hall. So prepare yourself in the lobby to enter the hall – where a great banquet has been prepared.'

He also said: 'An hour of repentance is better than a lifetime of pleasure. An hour of good deeds is better than a lifetime of amusement. An hour in the next world is better than a lifetime in this world.'

Rabbi Simeon said; 'Don't try to calm a friend in a temper. Don't try to comfort a friend who has succumbed to despair. Don't question a friend whose mind is gripped by sin. If your friends know that you have witnessed their moments of disgrace, they will resent you.'

Rabbi Samuel said: 'Do not rejoice when your enemy falls; do not be glad when your enemy stumbles.'

Rabbi Elisha said: 'Listen to your teacher as if you were a child. Let your teacher write on your mind as if it were a blank sheet. If you listen as an adult, you will be like paper covered in blotches.'

Rabbi Jose said: 'Do not try and learn from those who have not yet acquired wisdom. It would be like eating unripe fruit, or drinking wine straight from the winepress.'

Mishna

A wineskin and its wine

Rabbi Judah said: 'What is the right faith for you to follow? The faith that seems right in your own sight, and causes you to speak and act in a righteous fashion.'

He also said: 'Do not look at a wineskin, but at the wine it contains. Sometimes a new pitcher is full of old wine, and sometimes an old pitcher is empty.'

Rabbi Jehudah said: 'At the age of five a person is ready to read the Bible, at ten to listen to the wisdom of rabbis, at thirteen to obey the ten commandments, at eighteen to get married, at twenty to learn a craft, at thirty to become wealthy, at forty to show discernment, at fifty to give advice to others, at sixty to feel old, at seventy to turn white, at eighty to hobble instead of walk, at ninety to become senile, and at a hundred to die.'

Rabbi Ben said: 'This is the way of life you should follow: eat bread with a little salt; drink only water; sleep on the floor; and wrestle with the Bible. If you do this, you will be happy, both in this world and the next.'

He also said: 'Do not try to be great, and do not look for honour. Do not crave to sit at the tables of kings; your table is better than theirs, and so is your crown.'

Mishna

Wise people and good disciples

Wise men and women have seven traits. They do not speak in the presence of people wiser than themselves. They do not interrupt when friends are speaking. They think carefully before speaking. They ask questions that are relevant, and give answers that are logical. They deal with first things first, and last things last. If they are ignorant about some matter under discussion, they readily admit it. And if they do or say something wrong, they are quick to apologize. Foolish people have the opposite traits.

There are four types of people. There are ordinary people, who say: 'What is mine is mine, and what is yours is yours.' There are perverse people, who say: 'What is mine is yours, and what is yours is mine.' There are saintly people, who say: 'What is mine is yours, and what is yours is yours also.' And there are wicked people, who say: 'What is mine is mine, and what is yours is mine also.'

There are four kinds of disciple. There are those who are quick to learn, but quick to forget; in them the gift is cancelled by the failing. There are those who are slow to learn, but slow to forget; in them the failing is cancelled by the gift. There are those who are quick to learn, and slow to forget; they are truly blessed. And there are those who are slow to learn, and quick to forget; they are truly cursed.

Mishna

The preservation of idols

During the time of the Roman Empire a Roman soldier asked a rabbi: 'If your God takes no pleasure in the worship of idols, why does he not destroy them?' The rabbi replied: 'If people only worshipped objects which the world does not need, then God would certainly destroy them. But some people worship the sun, the moon and the stars, which the world needs. Should God destroy the entire world which he has created, just to destroy the fools within it?'

The soldier then said: 'But people worship some objects which the world does not need. Surely your God should destroy those objects, and leave the rest.' The rabbi replied: 'That would cause great delight among those who worship the sun, the moon and the stars. In their view the divinity of the sun, the moon and the stars would have been proved – because these objects would have remained unharmed.'

Gemara

Prayers for healing

A man said to Rabbi Akiba: 'Many people claim to have been cured of sickness by praying to some idol. I am perplexed by this.'

The rabbi said: 'I shall explain this to you by means of a parable. In a certain town there was a trustworthy banker who owned a strong safe; people would let him store their valuables there without either a witness or a receipt. One day a man came with two witnesses, and deposited some gold coins. He then came each week, sometimes depositing coins, and sometimes withdrawing coins – and he always brought two witnesses. But one week he had no witnesses, and explained that both of them were away; nonetheless he deposited some gold coins. After he had gone, the banker's wife said: "Since this fellow distrusts us, teach him a lesson. When he asks for those coins back, deny that you have received them." The banker replied: "Just because another man acts wrongly towards me, should I act wrongly in return?"'

Rabbi Akiba concluded: 'So it is with sickness. When God sends a sickness, he places a time limit on it. If a sickness were to remain after its limit, it would be betraying its mission. Just because people act wrongly in praying to idols, should a sickness act wrongly in return?'

Gemara

The gold bracelet

The queen lost a gold bracelet. The chief minister issued a proclamation, which was read out in every town and village: 'If anyone returns the queen's bracelet within a month, that person will receive a reward. But if anyone is found in possession of the bracelet after a month, that person will be executed.'

The following day Rabbi Samuel happened to find the bracelet; it was lying on a road where the queen had travelled in her carriage. But the rabbi did not return it at once. Instead he waited until a month had passed. Then he went to the palace, and told the queen that he had found the bracelet a month ago. 'Did you not hear the proclamation?' the queen asked. 'Yes,' Rabbi Samuel answered. 'Then why did you not return the bracelet immediately?' the queen asked. Rabbi Samuel answered: 'If I had returned it immediately, people would have said that I feared you. I return it now because I fear God.' With those words he handed the queen her bracelet.

The queen smiled, and said: 'Your God must be the most powerful of all gods.' And with those words she handed back the bracelet to the rabbi.

Gemara

The man in the brothel

During a period of drought Rabbi Abba had a dream in which he saw a certain man, called Pentekaka, praying for rain – and the prayer was answered. When the rabbi awoke the next morning, he thought at first that the dream was meaningless. Then he found himself wondering what kind of man Pentekaka was. 'Perhaps he is the kind of man to whom God would listen,' he thought. So he decided to visit Pentekaka.

In the course of their conversation Rabbi Abba asked Pentekaka: 'What is your occupation?' 'I am a sinner,' Pentekaka replied. 'What sins do you commit?' the rabbi asked. Pentekaka replied: 'I commit five sins daily. I go to the local brothel, and have intercourse with a prostitute. I decorate the walls of the brothel with pretty paper. I wash the prostitutes' clothes. I entertain the prostitutes by singing and dancing for them. And I beat the drum at their nightly orgies.'

'Have you ever done a good deed?' the rabbi asked. The man answered: 'Once, while I was decorating the brothel, I saw a woman weeping behind one of the pillars. I asked her the reason for her tears, and she told me that her husband was in prison. In order to raise the money for his ransom, she had decided to become a prostitute – so she had come to the brothel. I immediately pawned my bed and its cover, and gave her the money; and it was just enough to redeem her husband.'

The rabbi declared: 'Your prayers will be answered. I beg you to pray for rain.' Pentekaka did so, and rain began to fall.

Gemara

Wine in plain vessels

Rabbi Joshua was extremely ugly. But he was also immensely wise, and the queen frequently invited him to the palace, to ask his advice. One day she asked him: 'Why did God see fit to put such glorious wisdom in such a hideous vessel?'

The rabbi said: 'Why do you keep wine in an earthen pitcher?' 'How else should one keep it?' she asked. The rabbi replied: 'People of your rank should keep wine in vessels of silver and gold.' So the queen ordered all the wine in the palace to be transferred from earthen pitchers to silver and gold vessels.

Within a few weeks all the wine had turned sour. So the queen summoned Rabbi Joshua, and asked him why he had given such poor advice. The rabbi replied: 'I wished to show you that wisdom, like wine, is best kept in a plain vessel.' The queen said: 'Are there not handsome sages as well?' The rabbi replied: 'Yes; but they might have been even wiser had they been ugly.'

Gemara

A tree for the future

Rabbi Honi, when he was very old, moved to a small house with a small garden in the front. He decided to plant a carob tree in the middle of the garden. He dug a hole, and put a sapling into it.

As he was pushing the earth over the sapling's roots, a man passed by, and asked: 'When do you expect that carob tree to bear fruit?' 'In seventy years,' the rabbi replied. The man laughed, and said: 'Do you expect to live a further seventy years, and see the fruit of your labour?'

The rabbi replied: 'When I was a child, I lived in a house surrounded by beautiful trees. They had been planted by people who had lived in the house before me. So I plant this tree for those who will live in this house after me.'

Gemara

The reed and the cedar

Rabbi Elazar was very proud of his scholarship; he was familiar with every commentary on the Bible that had ever been written. One day, as he was entering a certain town on his donkey, he passed a man who was horribly ugly. The man called out: 'Peace be with you, rabbi!' But, instead of returning the greeting, the rabbi said: 'Is everyone in this town as ugly as you?' The man replied: 'I don't know. You will have to ask the great craftsman who fashioned us.'

The rabbi realized he had sinned. He leapt down from his donkey, fell on his knees before the man, and begged forgiveness. But the man refused to forgive him; instead he stuck his nose in the air, and walked towards the market-place. Rabbi Elazar followed him, and continued to beg for forgiveness.

When they reached the market-place, people greeted the rabbi with respect. The man said: 'This man is not a true rabbi; he should be treated with contempt.' And he told the people what had happened. The people begged the man to forgive the rabbi. Eventually the man said to Rabbi Elazar: 'I shall forgive you, so long as you promise never to act in that manner again.' The rabbi agreed.

Rabbi Elazar frequently told this story to others. His main purpose was to warn them not to be arrogant, as he had been. But he always added: 'Be yielding like a reed, not rigid like a cedar.'

Gemara

A prayer answered

There was a man called Gizmo who was blind in both eyes, and crippled in both hands; his body was covered in leprosy, and both his feet had withered away. He was also renowned for his wisdom.

One day a man asked him: 'Since you are such a wise man, why have all these terrible afflictions befallen you?' Gizmo replied: 'The fault is entirely mine. One day I was going from my own house to my father-in-law's house. I was leading three donkeys, one laden with wine, the second laden with food, and the third laden with rare fruits. I passed by a wizened old man, who begged me for something to eat. I told him to wait until I had unloaded the donkeys.

'So I went to my father-in-law's house, and unloaded the donkeys; then I set off home. In the meantime the old man had died. When I saw his body, I threw myself on it, and prayed: "May my eyes, which had no pity on you, lose their sight. May my hands, which refused to help you, lose their strength. May my feet, which refused to stop walking, disappear. And may my whole body, which was empty of compassion, be punished."

'My prayer was immediately answered.'

Gemara

The place of honour

Rabbi Nahman was renowned for the breadth of his knowledge and the depth of his understanding. In the hope of increasing his knowledge and understanding, he frequently attended lectures at the college where young rabbis were trained; and he always sat near the back of the lecture hall.

The lecturers were embarrassed by his presence, since they knew that his knowledge was greater than theirs; and they felt bad that he sat near the back. So one day a lecturer came to him, and said: 'I beg you to sit at the front, in the place of greatest honour'

Rabbi Nahman replied: 'The place cannot honour the person; the person confers honour on the place. Mount Sinai did not confer honour on Moses; but Moses conferred honour on Mount Sinai.'

Gemara

Worthy of heaven

A rabbi was walking through a market-place. A man came up to him, and asked: 'Is there anyone in this market-place who is worthy of going to heaven?' The rabbi looked around, and said: 'No.'

At that moment two young men appeared; they were dressed in bright colours, and each wore a brightly coloured hat. The rabbi asked them: 'What is your occupation?' The young men replied: 'We make merriment. When we see people who are sad, we try to cheer them up; when we see people quarrelling, we try to make peace between them.' The rabbi said to the first man: 'My answer to your question was wrong. These two young men are worthy of going to heaven.'

Gemara

The uniqueness of each person

Rabbi Hanina said: 'Humanity is a single species fashioned by God; he stamps every person with the same die. Yet each human being is different. Therefore every human being has a right to say: "For my sake the world was created." Equally if someone destroys a single life, that person is guilty of having destroyed the entire world; and if someone rescues a single life, that person has the merit of rescuing the entire world.

'No two ears of corn are the same; each ear of corn is unique.'

Gemara

Half a loaf

Rabbi Hanina taught his disciples to regard astrology as dangerous nonsense. One day two of his disciples went into the forest to collect firewood. They met an astrologer, who predicted that they would not return alive. The two men ignored this prediction, and continued to collect wood. They each made a large bundle, and returned to the rabbi's house. The astrologer followed them, to see that his prediction was fulfilled.

On their way they met an old man, who begged them for food. They had only half a loaf of bread, and they gave it to him.

When they reached Hanina's house, they said to the astrologer: 'We have proved that your astrology is nonsense.' Then they unwrapped their bundles. In each there was a poisonous snake – which now slithered away. The astrologer put his arms in the air, and exclaimed: 'What can I do if God is placated with half a loaf of bread?'

Gemara

A comparison between two people

A rabbi from Jebnah said: 'I am a creature of God, and my neighbour is also a creature of God. My work is in the city, and his is in the countryside. I rise early for my work, and he too rises early for his work. Just as he could not excel in my work, I could not excel in his. Perhaps his work is more valuable than mine, and perhaps my work is more valuable than his. But we have both learnt that the value of your work does not matter, so long as your heart is directed to heaven.'

The same rabbi also said: 'The highest wisdom is kindness.'

The same rabbi also said: 'When someone is angry, speak softly and gently, in order to turn away anger. Try to bring peace to the hearts of sinners, so they may know happiness, both in this world and the next.'

Rabbi Hiyya said: 'Some people pray at great length, calculating that God is more likely to hear a long prayer than a short one. But long prayers merely bring pain to the heart.'

Rabbi Meir said: 'When you are addressing God, your words should always be few.'

Gemara

Lending jewels

An aristocratic lady said to Rabbi Jose: 'People often praise God for giving wisdom to the wise. Would it not be better for God to give wisdom to fools?'

Jose said to her: 'Do you possess any jewels?' 'Certainly,' she replied. Jose continued: 'If someone came to you and asked to borrow them, would you lend them?' The lady replied: 'If that person were irresponsible and careless, I should not lend my jewels. But if the person were responsible and careful, I should do so.'

Jose concluded: 'If you will not lend your jewels to an unworthy borrower, why should God confer his wisdom on fools?'

Gemara

A wicked law

During the time of the Roman Empire the Senate planned to pass a law that would have prohibited both the observance of the Sabbath and the rite of circumcision.

Rabbi Reuben disguised himself as a Roman, and came before the Senate. He spoke perfect Latin, with a Roman accent. 'Do you hate the Jews?' he asked. A leading senator replied: 'Yes, because they refuse to worship the Roman emperor as a god.' 'Do you wish, therefore, to destroy the Jewish religion?' The senator replied that they did.

Rabbi Reuben said: 'If you prohibit the observance of the Sabbath, the Jews will work seven days a week, instead of six. Thus they will become even more rich and powerful.' So the Senate set aside the first prohibition.

Then the rabbi said: 'If you prohibit circumcision, they will produce even more children – since circumcision reduces fertility.' So the Senate set aside the second prohibition.

Gemara

A painful lesson

A man purchased a field in order to grow crops. He paid a low price for the field because it was covered in stones. He decided to remove the stones, and dump them on the lane nearby. A rabbi saw what he was doing, and said: 'That which belongs to all, belongs to each.' But the man just laughed.

A few years later, while the man was ploughing the field, a wealthy merchant offered to buy it for a large bag of gold. The man eagerly agreed, and the merchant gave him the gold. The man walked along the lane, staring with glee at the gold coins inside. He stumbled on one of the stones that he had dumped on the lane. He fell to the ground, and broke a leg and an arm on other stones. As he fell, the bag flew from his hand, and the gold coins were scattered over a wide area.

A short time later a group of beggars passed by. They saw the gold coins, picked them up, and ran away. Then the rabbi passed by, and saw the man lying on the ground. He picked the man up, and carried him to a physician. As the physician was setting the broken bones, the rabbi said: 'These injuries were the only way that God could teach you.'

Gemara

Buried treasure

Rabbi Eliezer went to Antioch, to collect money for needy scholars. A devout man called Judah, who was renowned for his generosity, lived in the city. But he had lost all his wealth; and he felt ashamed that he had nothing to give.

His wife, who was even more pious, said to him: 'You still own a small field. Sell half of it, and give Rabbi Eliezer half the proceeds.' Judah did so. And, as he received the money, the rabbi said: 'May God supply all your needs.'

In the following spring Judah led his ox to the half of the field that still belonged to him, and began to plough it. His ox stumbled, and broke her hoof. As he bent down to help the animal, he saw a casket buried in the earth. He lifted the casket, and found that it was filled with precious gems.

A few months later Rabbi Eliezer came again to Antioch. Judah went to see him, and said: 'Your prayer was answered.' The rabbi answered: 'Its power came from your heart.'

Gemara

Two sons

A man once gave his father several fat chickens. The father asked: 'Can you afford this, my son?' The son replied: 'Eat what you are given, and ask no questions.'

Another man was grinding corn, while his father was sitting nearby. An official came, and demanded that one member of the family come and serve in the king's army. The son said: 'You do the grinding, father, and I shall go and serve the king. I could not allow you to endure the dangers and discomforts of army life.'

A rabbi was told of these two incidents, and said: 'The first man fed his father well, while the second man made his father work hard. But the action of the second man was finer than that of the first. So be careful when you make comparisons between people.'

Gemara

A dishonest beggar

Two rabbis in Tiberias, Johan and Simeon, went to bathe in the public baths. On their way they encountered a man dressed in rags, who begged them for money. The rabbis said they would help him on their return.

But when they returned, they found him lying dead. They felt utterly ashamed of themselves. So they said to one another: 'Since we failed to help him during his life, let us make amends by helping him in death.' So they began to prepare his body for burial.

When they took off his tunic, they found a bag of silver coins. At first they were angry with him for begging, when he had no need of money. Then they said: 'His dishonesty is no excuse for our lack of charity.' So they completed the preparation, and buried him according to the ancient rites.

Gemara

A calf and some mice

Rabbi Judah suffered from toothache for many years. He tried every kind of potion to relieve the pain, but nothing was effective. Why was he punished in this manner? He once saw a calf being taken to slaughter. The calf bleated, appealing for his help, but the rabbi said: 'You were created in order to provide food for humans. So be quiet, and walk to the slaughterhouse in peace.'

Eventually Rabbi Judah's toothache ceased. Why? He saw a litter of mice being carried to the river, in order to be drowned. He cried out: 'Let them go. God has mercy on all that he has made.'

Gemara

Boats, trees and walls

Rabbi Yannai would not board a ferry until he had examined its hull, to ensure that it was sound. He would not walk under trees on a windy day, for fear that a tree might blow over on his head. And he would not pass near a ruined wall, for fear that it might collapse.

A young boy once questioned him about his caution. The rabbi replied: 'A person should never take chances, and expect to be rescued by a miracle. By caring for myself, God can care for me more easily.'

Gemara

The former pupil and the former wife

Rabbi Johanan often said: 'A person may conform to every law and precept, and yet still act wrongly.' And he told a story to illustrate this.

A young man worked as an apprentice to a master carpenter. After he had completed his training, the young man started his own carpentry business, and became rich. He had always felt attracted to his former master's wife, and began to meet her secretly. He then decided that he wished to marry her.

So he invited his former master to his house, and said to him: 'Reliable witnesses have told me that your wife is being unfaithful to you.' 'What shall I do?' the carpenter asked. 'Divorce her,' the young man replied. The carpenter said: 'But her dowry was large; and if I were to divorce her, I should have to return it.' The young man said: 'I shall lend you the money.' So the carpenter divorced his wife.

The young man married her at once. He then sued his former master for the money he had lent. The carpenter was unable to pay it. So his former pupil and his former wife forced him to become their servant.

Rabbi Johanan concluded: 'The young man and the woman did nothing illegal. But their actions were far worse than many crimes.'

Gemara

A sliver of wood

Two rabbis, Zeira and Haggai, were walking along a lane. They passed a man who was carrying a load of wood to sell in the nearby market.

Rabbi Zeira called out to the man: 'I beg you, bring me a sliver of wood, so I can cleanse my teeth.' But Rabbi Haggai remonstrated: 'If everyone took a sliver of wood, the man would have no wood to sell – and he and his family would starve.' Rabbi Zeira said: 'I am a learned man, and so this man should regard it as an honour to serve me. If ordinary people were to ask him for slivers of wood, he would be right to refuse them.' Rabbi Haggai said: 'As a learned man, you have a duty to set an example to ordinary people. So if an ordinary person should not ask this man for a sliver of wood, nor should you.'

Throughout this argument the man with the wood had continued on his journey, and was now out of sight. So Rabbi Haggai won.

Gemara

The stolen beaker

Rabbi Mar was staying at an inn. While he was there, one of the guests stole a silver beaker that belonged to the innkeeper's wife. The innkeeper and his wife were very distressed. The rabbi said to them: 'Do not worry. I shall observe the guests very carefully. The thief will undoubtedly reveal himself.'

The rabbi watched all the guests with great care. He noticed that one of the guests left a cloak in the washroom. The rabbi remained in a corner of the washroom – behind a large tub, so he could not be seen. Then he observed people as they came into the washroom. One young man washed his hands, and then wiped them on the cloak.

The rabbi pointed out the young man to the innkeeper, and said: 'He is the thief; he has no respect for other people's property.' So the innkeeper went into the young man's room, and found the silver beaker in his bag.

Gemara

Dispute over a field

Two men, one with black hair and the other with brown hair, were involved in a legal dispute over the ownership of a field. But rather than go to court, they asked Rabbi Eliezer to judge between them.

The rabbi listened carefully to each man's arguments, but was unable to decide who was right and who was wrong. So he pointed to a carob tree, and said: 'Let this tree decide. If it moves forwards, the man with black hair should have the field; and if it moves backwards, the man with brown hair should have the field.' The carob tree moved forwards. But the man with brown hair exclaimed: 'A carob tree proves nothing.'

Rabi Eliezer pointed to a stream, and said: 'Let this water decide. If it continues flowing downwards, the man with the black hair should have the field; and if it flows upwards, the man with brown hair should have the field.' The water started flowing upwards. But the man with black hair exclaimed: 'Water in a stream proves nothing.'

At this moment a nearby wall started shaking. At once both men declared: 'That proves the field is mine.' Rabbi Eliezar turned to the wall, and said: 'Why do you care who owns the field? It's none of your business.' And with those words he walked away. So the two men were forced to go to court after all; and the cost of the case was even higher than the value of the field.

Gemara

Pearls and tinsel

Rabbi Hiyya was a great scholar, but lacked eloquence; his sermons were profound, but hard to understand. Rabbi Abba was eloquent, but had little scholarship; his sermons were amusing, but contained little substance.

The two rabbis arrived at a town on the same day. They each went to preach at a different synagogue. Most of the population went to hear Rabbi Abba, and only a few went to hear Rabbi Hiyya. In the evening someone asked Rabbi Hiyya if he was disappointed by the poor attendence at his sermon. Rabbi Hiyya said: 'Imagine two merchants arriving in a town on the one day. One merchant sells pearls, which are beautiful, but costly; while the other sells tinsel, which is merely gaudy, but cheap. To which merchant would the people throng?'

Midrash

A little puff of wind

A particular emperor was so successful at expanding the Roman Empire, that he regarded himself as divine; and he ordered his courtiers to worship him as God.

One of his courtiers was a Jew, who had trained as a rabbi. This rabbi said to the emperor: 'Please help me in my hour of need.' 'In what way do you need help?' the emperor asked. The rabbi replied: 'I own a ship that contains all that I possess. But there has been no wind for several weeks, and the ship is becalmed somewhere at sea. By now the sailors must be near to starvation; and if they die, the ship will eventually drift towards land, and break up on rocks – and I shall be ruined.'

The emperor replied: 'Very well, I shall send one of my own ships to rescue it.' The rabbi said: 'Why bother to do that? You need only send a puff of wind.' The emperor asked: 'Where am I to get wind?' The rabbi replied: 'But you told us that you are God – and God created wind.'

The emperor went red with anger, but said nothing. And he never again spoke of himself as divine.

Midrash

Frequent prayer

A man called Antonius asked Rabbi Judah: 'Should a person pray to God at least once every hour?' The rabbi replied: 'No. If people pray to God every hour, they start speaking to him falsely.'

Antonius was confused at this reply. So Rabbi Judah said: 'Suppose a man went to the emperor every hour, from dawn until dusk, of every day. What would he say to the emperor? He would probably wish the emperor health and happiness. At first his words would be honest; and the emperor might be grateful for his devotion. But soon he would merely say them without thinking. And the emperor would become irritated by his insincerity – and eventually would order him never again to enter his presence.'

Midrash

A pearl on a donkey

Rabbi Simeon was preparing flax by hand. A disciple saw him, and said: 'I shall buy you a donkey to help you; then you will not have to work so hard.'

The disciple went to the market, purchased a donkey from an Arab, and brought it to Rabbi Simeon. The rabbi stroked the donkey affectionately, and found a pearl in its mane. 'Now you will not have to work at all!' the disciple exclaimed. 'Why?' the rabbi asked. The disciple replied: 'The value of this pearl is enough to buy food for the rest of your life.'

The rabbi asked: 'Does the former owner know that there was a pearl in the donkey's mane?' 'No,' the disciple answered. 'Then you must give the pearl back to him,' the rabbi said. The disciple protested: 'Our law says that if you find something by chance, you may keep it.'

The rabbi replied: 'If you return the pearl to the Arab, he will praise God for your honesty. Surely God prefers praise than merely keeping to the letter of the law.'

Midrash

A stag in the flock

Rabbi Shetah told his disciples a story about a nobleman who owned a large flock of sheep and goats. Every morning the nobleman's shepherd took the sheep and goats to the pasture; and every evening he led them back to a large pen near the nobleman's house.

One day a stag grazed with the flock. And when the shepherd led the flock to the pen, the stag came as well. The nobleman was delighted to see the stag amidst his flock, and ordered the shepherd to treat it well. The following day the stag remained with the flock, and returned to the pen in the evening. Again the nobleman was delighted.

The shepherd now felt irritated at his master's response to the stag, and said to him: 'You give almost no attention to your sheep and goats, even though they belong to you. Yet you lavish attention on the stag, even though it belongs to no one.' The nobleman replied: 'The sheep and goats already know that I love them. But the stag is a stranger, and I must demonstrate my love.'

Rabbi Shetah concluded: 'You already know that God loves you, and so God has no need to give you special favours. But when strangers come to him, God's blessings are boundless.'

Midrash

Seed-pods and cabbages

Rabbi Akiba was on a journey with a disciple. The disciple
said to the rabbi: 'Teach me the whole of God's law in a
single sentence.' The rabbi smiled, and replied: 'Moses had to
spend forty days and nights on a mountain before he learnt
God's law – and you want me to summarize it in one sentence! Very well. Do not do to others what you would not
want done to yourself.'

The rabbi and the disciple passed a field full of seed-pods.
The disciple took several pods, and satisfied his hunger; but
the rabbi took none. Some hours later they passed a field of
cabbages. The disciple took a cabbage and satisfied his
hunger, but the rabbi took nothing. The disciple asked Rabbi
Akiba why he was taking nothing; but the rabbi remained
silent.

On the following day the disciple again took some seed-
pods from a field. But this time the rabbi seized the seed-
pods, and ate them himself. The disciple was taken aback, but
said nothing. Later the disciple took a cabbage from a field;
and the rabbi seized it from him. The disciple now reacted
angrily.

The rabbi smiled, and said: 'You think nothing of taking
seed-pods and cabbages belonging to a farmer; but you are
angry when someone takes seed-pods and cabbages which
you regard as your own. In such contradictions is the law of
God violated.'

Midrash

Wasted wisdom

Rabbi Ammi was about to die. His nephew came to see him, and found him weeping bitterly. The nephew said: 'Uncle, why are you weeping? Is there any part of God's law that you have not practised? Is there any part of God's law that you have not taught to others? I can think of none. You are acknowledged as the wisest man in the land. Surely you of all people have nothing to fear from death.'

The rabbi replied: 'You are right that I have practised and taught every part of God's law. But several times I was asked to serve as a judge; and each time I refused, because I preferred to devote my time to religious affairs. Yet a single shrewd judgement, that brings peace to those in conflict, is worth a lifetime of religion. I weep because I wasted the wisdom that God gave me.'

And with tears pouring down his cheeks the rabbi died.

Midrash

Men on a boat

Rabbi Simeon frequently spoke against greed. One day a merchant came to him, and said: 'People say that I am greedy, and they frequently quote your words against greed. But if I am sinful, this is purely my business; and if another man sins, that is his business. You have no right to condemn the sins of others.'

The rabbi told a story: 'There were a number of men crossing a river on a boat. One of them took out a drill, and began to bore a hole in the bottom of the boat. The other people protested, seized the drill, and threw it overboard. Were those people wrong to condemn that man? Should they have allowed him to continue drilling?'

The merchant went back to his home, and gave away his wealth to the poor.

Midrash

The potter and the flax dealer

Rabbi Jonathan said: 'The potter does not test cracked pots; he knows that if he were to tap them once, they would break. But he tests the good pots, because he knows that, no matter how many times he taps them, they do not break. Similarly, God does not test the wicked, but only tests the righteous.'

Rabbi Jose said: 'The flax dealer, who knows that his flax is good, pounds it, because his pounding improves it; the more he beats it, the more it glistens. But when he knows that his flax is bad, he does not dare pound it, because it would split. Similarly, God is tough with the righteous, but not with the wicked.'

Midrash

A drowning man

Rabbi Kappara was walking along the top of a cliff, when he saw a Roman proconsul struggling to swim from a shipwreck. The rabbi ran down to the sea, plunged in, and swam out to the proconsul; he then helped him to the shore. The proconsul was shivering and exhausted; so the rabbi took him home, and gave him a warm meal.

Some time later a provincial judge wrongly imprisoned a wealthy Jew. His family gave Rabbi Kappara five hundred gold coins, and begged him to pay the money as a ransom. So the rabbi went to the proconsul, and offered the coins in exchange for the wealthy Jew.

The proconsul recognized the rabbi, and said: 'Keep the gold coins as a reward for rescuing me. And the ransom for setting free the Jew is the warm meal you gave me.'

Rabbi Kappara frequently told this story, and concluded: 'Simple acts of kindness frequently bring unexpected rewards.'

Midrash

The casket of gold coins

Rabbi Jonathan was a judge, and became famous for finding amicable solutions to bitter disputes.

One day two men came to him. The first man said: 'I bought a house from this man. While I was repairing it, I found a large casket filled with gold hidden under the floor. Since the house is now mine, the casket is also mine.' The second man said: 'When I sold the house to this man, I knew nothing of the casket of gold coins. If I had known about it, I should have kept it. Therefore the casket belongs to me.'

The rabbi asked the first man: 'Do you have a son?' 'Yes,' the man replied. The rabbi asked the second man: 'Do you have a daughter?' 'Yes,' the man replied. The rabbi concluded: 'Let the son and the daughter marry, and keep the casket of gold coins as their dowry.'

Midrash

A fragile goblet

Rabbi Jose possessed a goblet, which was extremely old and fragile. He frequently showed it to people, and said: 'If I were to put hot water in this goblet, it would burst. If I were to put cold water in the goblet, then it would crack. So I must put cold water mixed with hot.

'If God were to show only mercy to people, then sin would multiply. If God were to show only justice to people, then no one would survive. So God mixes justice with mercy.'

Midrash

A sinking ship

Rabbi Tanhuma said: 'Suppose that a ship were laden with cattle and sheep, and a storm arose. If the ship were in danger of sinking, the crew would decide to lighten its load – and they would hurl the cattle and sheep into the sea. Human beings regard themselves as more important than animals, and so save their own lives in preference to the lives of animals.

'But God created both humans and animals, and he loves all his creatures equally. When he sent a flood to destroy the world, he treated humans and animals alike. When he made a covenant never again to destroy the world, the covenant included animals as well as humans. And the suffering of animals causes him as much grief as the suffering of humans.'

Midrash

Water and wine

Just as water is free to all people, the law of God is free to all people. Just as water is beyond price, so is the law of God beyond price. Just as water brings life to the world, so the law of God brings life to the world. Just as water washes away dirt, so the law of God washes away evil.

Just as wine cannot be kept in precious vessels of gold and silver, but only in cheap earthenware vessels, so the law of God can only be kept by those who are humble. Like wine, the law of God warms the heart. Just as wine improves with age, so people take greater pleasure in observing God's law as they get older.

Midrash

Valuable merchandise

A rabbi renowned for his wisdom was on board a ship with several merchants. The merchants each had valuable merchandise in the ship's hold. They asked the rabbi: 'What merchandise have you got?' The rabbi answered: 'The best merchandise in the world.' The merchants went to the ship's hold to look at his merchandise; but, when they found nothing, they laughed at him.

A storm arose, and the ship was blown onto rocks. The ship and all its cargo were destroyed; but the merchants and the rabbi swam ashore. They walked to the nearby city. The merchants had nothing, and were forced to beg for food. The rabbi preached each evening in the market-place; and his wise words attracted a large crowd.

When he had finished preaching, people offered him money as a sign of their appreciation. He only took as much as he needed. But the merchants now understood what he had meant – that he possessed the most valuable merchandise in the world.

Midrash

Money for a journey

Rabbi Judah: 'The human mind is easily burdened by un-
related facts and precepts. So if you wish to learn God's law,
do not begin with the details. Begin with the general prin-
ciples; then you can learn the details easily as you require.

'When you go on a long journey, you need money to
cover your expenses. But you do not take hundreds of copper
coins, as these would weigh you down. Instead you take a
few gold and silver coins, and change them for copper coins
as you require.'

Midrash

The courteous young man

Rabbi Yannai took a stroll each afternoon. On one occasion he encountered a young man dressed as a student; so he invited him to his house for supper.

During the meal the rabbi tried to engage the young man in scholarly conversation; but the young man proved entirely ignorant. At the end of the meal the rabbi asked the young man to offer a prayer of thanks; but the young man said that he knew no prayers.

The rabbi looked up to God, and said: 'A dog has eaten at my table!' The young man rose to his feet, seized the rabbi, and exclaimed: 'You have no right to insult me before God?' The rabbi protested: 'But what right have you to eat at my table?' The young man said: 'I am courteous to everyone; and when I see two people quarrelling, I try to make peace between them.'

The rabbi begged the young man's forgiveness – and asked him to eat again at his house whenever he wished.

Midrash

Two baskets of fruit

A king rode past a garden, and saw an old man planting a fig tree. The king stopped, and said to the old man: 'Why in your old age do you plant a fig tree? You will be dead before it bears fruit.' The old man replied: 'If it be God's will, I shall eat the fruit; if not, my children shall eat it.'

Three years later the king rode past the garden again. The old man came to him with a basket of figs, and said: 'Please accept this gift; the fruit is from the tree which I planted in your presence.' The king was delighted; and he ordered that the basket be filled with gold coins and returned to the old man, as a reward for his diligence.

The old man's wife was greedy. She filled the basket with various soft fruits, and said to her husband: 'Now take these to the king.' The old man had no idea of her intention; he innocently journeyed to the king's palace, and offered him the fruit. The king was enraged. He threw the fruit at the old man, and shouted: 'You hoped that I would again fill your basket with gold coins. How dare you try to take advantage of my kindness! Get out of my sight, and never show yourself again.'

When the old man returned, his wife asked him how he had fared. The old man replied: 'I fared well. If I had taken oranges and lemons, I should have died of the blows.'

Midrash

God's work

A wealthy woman asked Rabbi Jose: 'In how many days did God create the world?' 'In six days,' the rabbi replied. 'And what has he been doing ever since?' the woman asked. 'Making marriages,' the rabbi replied.

The woman exclaimed: 'Is that all he does? I could do that myself. I have a hundred male slaves and a hundred female slaves; in a single hour I could marry them to one another.' The rabbi replied: 'That is how you understand making marriages. But God spends as much effort on each marriage as he spent on parting the Red Sea.'

After the rabbi had left, the woman summoned all her slaves. She ordered the male slaves to stand in one line, and the female slaves to stand in another line opposite them. Then she ordered a local judge to marry the first male slave to the first female slave, the second male slave to the second female slave, and so on, until all were married. Within an hour the weddings were complete.

The following morning most of the slaves were covered with bruises and cuts, and looked utterly miserable. One by one the female slaves complained to the woman about their husbands, and the male slaves complained about their wives. Then the woman understood how hard God has to work.

Midrash

A marriage restored

A husband and wife came to Rabbi Simeon, and said: 'We have been married for ten years, and have not conceived a child. We have decided we should divorce, and each seek a new spouse.' The rabbi replied: 'Ten years ago you had a banquet to celebrate your marriage. Now you should mark your divorce with another banquet.'

At the banquet the husband became drunk; and in his drunken state, he felt great affection for his wife. He said to her: 'As a reminder of our marriage, look at my possessions, and choose what is most precious to you. Then take it back to your parents' house.' By the end of the banquet, he had fallen into a deep sleep. His wife asked two men to carry him to her parents' house.

When he awoke next morning, he asked: 'Where am I?' She replied: 'At my parents' house.' 'Why?' he asked. She replied: 'Last night you asked me to look at your possessions, and take what is most precious to me. When I reflected on the matter, I realized that you are the possession most precious to me. Indeed, there is nothing in this world more precious to me than you. That is why I have brought you here.'

They returned to Rabbi Simeon, and said that, as a result of the banquet, they had changed their minds; they now wished to remain married. He blessed them, and they lived happily together – without a child.

Midrash

Like a fool

A wealthy old man died. After the funeral, the local lawyer opened the old man's will. It stipulated that his son should inherit all his wealth – but only when the son had become a fool.

The lawyer was perplexed, and went to Rabbi Joshua for advice. When he arrived at the rabbi's house, he was astonished to see the rabbi on his hands and knees, with a reed in his mouth. 'What on earth are you doing?' the lawyer asked. 'I am playing with my young son,' the rabbi said – and then rose to his feet.

The lawyer showed Rabbi Joshua the old man's will, and asked what it meant. The rabbi laughed, and said: 'The son can only inherit his father's wealth when he has married and had a child – because as soon as a man becomes a father, he plays like a fool.'

Midrash

A neighbour in heaven

Rabbi Joshua had a dream that his neighbour in heaven would be Nanas, the butcher. The rabbi thought: 'If Nanas is to be my neighbour in heaven, this means that he and I are equal in virtue. Let me see how virtuous he is – and then I shall know whether or not I shall have a high or a low place in heaven.'

So Rabbi Joshua went to Nanas's shop, and asked him what good deeds he regularly performed. 'I try to give my customers value for money,' the butcher replied. This seemed only a small virtue in the rabbi's eyes, and he felt disappointed. Then the butcher added: 'My father and mother are both old and helpless. I give them food and drink, and I wash and dress them each day.' The rabbi smiled, and said: 'I shall be happy to have you as a neighbour in heaven.'

Midrash

Troubled marriages

Rabbi Aaron hated to see a husband and wide quarrel and separate. So he devised a method of restoring troubled marriages; and this method was invariably successful.

The rabbi would first go to the husband, and say: 'My son, why did you quarrel with your wife?' The husband would describe his wife's shameful behaviour. Rabbi Aaron would say: 'I pledge that she will never act in that way again.'

Then he would go to the wife, and say: 'My daughter, why did you quarrel with your husband?' The wife would describe her husband's shameful behaviour. Rabbi Aaron would say: 'I pledge that he will never act in that way again.'

Usually this was sufficient to bring the husband and wife back together. But if not, he would go back to the husband and wife day after day, and have the same exchange; and gradually he would wear down their resistance, until they agreed to live together again.

When a husband and wife, whose marriage had been saved by Rabbi Aaron, had a son, they invariably named him Aaron. As a result there were numerous Aarons in the rabbi's neighbourhood.

Midrash

Weary of life

An elderly Jewish man was so unhappy that he became weary of life itself, and yearned to die. At this time the Roman emperor was persecuting Jews; so the elderly man decided to hasten his death in the service of his people.

He wrote a letter to the Roman emperor, which read: 'The Jews are good citizens who oppose every kind of crime. Yet you murder and torture them because they refuse to worship you as a god. The true God, whom we worship, will punish you.'

The emperor summoned the elderly Jew, and said: 'As you must have known, your defiant letter deserves execution. But I am curious to know why you court death.' The elderly Jew replied: 'Because I am weary of life.' The emperor declared: 'Then I shall punish you by not executing you.'

The elderly Jew lived unhappily for several more years. But the emperor was sufficiently frightened by his letter, that he ordered his officials to leave the Jewish people in peace.

Midrash

Shrewd prayer

Rabbi Aha said: 'If you wish to learn how to pray, observe how women ask their neighbours for things – and imitate those that are shrewd.

'The shrewd woman always knocks at her neighbour's door, even when the door is open. And when her neighbour opens the door, she says: "Peace be with you." She asks whether her neighbour and her family are well, and is keenly interested in her neighbour's reply. The neighbour now asks her in, and offers her refreshment; she accepts with gratitude. During the course of conversation the neighbour asks her: "How can I help you?" Only then does she make her request; and the neighbour is happy to accede.

'The woman without shrewdness walks straight into her neighbour's house without knocking, and calls out her request. Her neighbour angrily refuses.'

Midrash

The wise prostitute

Rabbi Akiba's chief disciple, who was called Nahman, saw in the street a very beautiful prostitute. During the following days he could not rid his mind of the image of her, and his desire for her grew more and more ardent. Eventually he sent a servant with some money, to arrange for him to see her that night.

When Nahman arrived at the prostitute's house, she immediately recognized him as Rabbi Akiba's chief disciple. She said to him: 'If you defile yourself by having sex with me, you will ruin your career on earth, and forfeit your reward in heaven.' But this warning did nothing to cool his passion, and he began to undress. She continued: 'Please do not throw away so much, for just an hour of pleasure.'

Suddenly he came to his senses. He dressed, thanked her profusely for her wisdom, and left. Some years later, when he had become a rabbi, he sent her a message, in which he asked her to marry him. She accepted; and she proved as faithful and devoted as any husband could wish – and she frequently gave him wise advice.

Midrash

Three defects

A man called Huna had three daughters. They were all beautiful, but each had a defect: one was lazy, the second was liable to steal, and the third enjoyed slanderous gossip. Huna had imposed every kind of discipline, and inflicted every kind of punishment, but without success.

A friend called Abbahu had three sons; and he proposed to Huna that each of the daughters marry one them. Huna warned him of his daughter's defects; but Abbabu promised that these defects would be cured. So the weddings took place, and the three daughters came to live with their new husbands at Abbahu's home.

Abbahu put the first daughter in charge of the servants, so she had no need to do anything herself. But she soon grew bored with just issuing orders; and she began to work alongside the servants.

He put the second daughter in charge of the storerooms, and allowed her to take whatever she wanted for herself. So she had no incentive to steal, and soon the desire to steal faded from her heart.

As for the third one, he asked her to slander him as much as she wanted. She began to pass on all sorts of slander about him. But, since everyone in the neighbourhood knew Abbahu well, no one believed her. At first this annoyed her; but soon she lost the taste for slander.

Midrash

Weasels with meat

Rabbi Zakkei served as magistrate in a certain town. He imprisoned those who received stolen goods, and allowed the thieves themselves to go free. Many people grumbled at this policy. So he invited everyone in the town to the yard behind the courthouse; and when they had arrived, he closed the gates.

The rabbi threw pieces of meat on the ground, and released from a cage several weasels. Each weasel took a piece of meat, and ran with it to a hiding place. After a while the weasels came back in search of more meat. The rabbi ordered that the hiding places be blocked up. Then he threw some more pieces of meat on the ground. The weasels ran off with the meat; but when they found there was nowhere to hide, they brought the meat back.

Rabbi Zakkei concluded: 'If thieves have nowhere to dispose of their stolen goods, they will not steal.'

Midrash

A ship's departure and arrival

Rabbi Levi said to his disciples: 'When a baby is born, people rejoice; and when someone dies, people mourn. This is the wrong way round. When a ship leaves a port, people are sad; they are fearful of all the dangers and discomforts that the sailors will face. And when the ship returns safely, people rejoice. Similarly when a baby is born, we should be anxious about all the dangers and discomforts the baby will face in the course of life. Death by contrast should be welcomed, because at death all suffering is over, and the soul enters its true harbour.'

Midrash

A son's death

One afternoon the son of Rabbi Meir choked on a nut, and died. The rabbi was delivering a sermon in the synagogue, so his wife was alone at home with the dead body. She prayed for comfort and guidance. God prompted her to put her son's body on his bed, and cover it with a sheet.

When Rabbi Meir returned, he asked where his son was. 'He is learning the truth,' she replied. He assumed that he was reading a book, so he said nothing. She served him with bread and wine.

After he had finished, she said: 'I have a question to ask.' 'Ask it,' he said. She said: 'Many years ago someone asked me to keep something for him; and today he asked for it back. Should I give it to him?' The rabbi replied: 'Since he is the owner, you must certainly give it back.'

She then led him into their son's room, and she pulled back the sheet. The rabbi began to weep. His wife said: 'Many years ago God asked us to keep his life; now he has taken it back.' These words did not suppress the grief in their hearts; but they brought peace to their souls.

Midrash

The course of life

Rabbi Akiba said: 'At the age of one you are like a monarch; everyone loves and embraces you. At the age of two you are like a pig; you wallow in your own dirt. During your childhood you are like a kid goat; you dance and skip all day long. At the age of eighteen you are like a horse; you rejoice in your youth and strength. When you marry, you are like an ass; you carry a heavy burden. In middle age you are like a dog; you readily ask favours of others. In old age you are like a monkey; you become childish, and no one pays attention to your words.'

Midrash

A father's will

A wealthy man went with his slave to trade in a faraway country. He carried with him all his wealth, in the hope that he might double it through shrewd transactions.

But while he was in that country, he fell sick. He called a scribe; and in the presence of his slave he dictated his will. It read: 'To my slave I leave all my wealth. To my only son I leave any one possession which he may choose.' A few days later he died.

The slave was delighted; he looked forward to living in a grand house with slaves of his own. So he returned home, with all the wealth of his dead master, and showed the will to the master's son. The son took the will to Rabbi Ismael, and asked his advice.

The rabbi read it carefully, remained silent for a few moments, and then declared: 'It is an extremely shrewd will. If your father had left everything to you, the slave would have been tempted never to return. But under our law, a man can bequeath a slave to his son; the property of a slave belongs to the master.'

The son immediately understood what he must do. Under the terms of his father's will, he chose the slave – and thereby also acquired all his father's wealth.

Midrash

Coins in a cane

There was a banker named Bartholomew, who was assumed by everyone to be honest. But Bartholomew yearned to live more luxuriously, and decided that dishonesty was the only means of achieving this ambition.

A man deposited a hundred gold coins with Bartholomew; and, since he assumed that Bartholomew was honest, he did not ask for a receipt. Some time later the man asked for the coins back. 'I have already returned them to you,' Bartholomew replied. The man demanded that Bartholomew come to the local synagogue, and make the same declaration under oath before the rabbi.

Bartholomew hollowed out a cane, put the hundred gold coins inside, and pretended to use the cane as a walking stick. At the synagogue he asked the man to hold the stick while he made his declaration. Then he said to the man: 'By the Lord God on high, I swear that the coins, entrusted by you to my hands, are now in your hands.'

The man was so shocked to hear this declaration, that he dropped the cane – and all the coins fell out onto the ground. Bartholomew smiled weakly, and walked away. No one ever deposited money with him again.

Midrash

Content amidst noise

A man lived in a small house with his wife and seven children. His wife enjoyed inviting friends for cake and a chat; and his children, like all children, were boisterous. But he loved tranquillity, and was becoming utterly distraught. He was too poor to afford a larger house, where he could have a quiet room to himself. So in desperation he went to see a rabbi for advice.

'Do you have a goat in your yard?' the rabbi asked. 'Yes,' the man replied. 'Then you must bring it into the house,' the rabbi said. He did as the rabbi instructed. But the goat bleated all day and night, keeping the man awake.

So the man returned to the rabbi. 'The noise in my house is even worse,' the man said, his eyes red with exhaustion. 'Do you have any hens?' the rabbi asked. 'Yes,' the man replied. 'Then you must bring them into the house,' the rabbi said. The man brought in the hens, and the cockerel followed them. But the hens clucked all day; and at dawn, just as the man was finally dropping off to sleep, the cockerel crowed.

A week passed, and the man had no sleep at all. He staggered to the rabbi to seek further advice. The rabbi said: 'Go home, and drive the goat, the hens, and the cockerel back into the yard, where they belong.'

The man did as the rabbi instructed. His relief at no longer hearing their various noises was so great, that he hardly noticed the voices of his wife and children. And he could now sleep again. He went back to the rabbi. And exclaimed: 'A thousand blessings on you. My house is like a palace!'

Hasidism

A rich man and a poor man

Two men, one rich and one poor, happened to arrive at a rabbi's house at the same moment; both wanted the rabbi's advice on some personal matters.

The rich man was ushered in first; and the rabbi gave him a full hour of his time. Finally the poor man was ushered in, and the rabbi gave him only a few minutes.

'This is unfair,' the poor man protested. The rabbi replied: 'How foolish you are! When you entered my room, I could see at a glance that you are poor. But as for that other man – I had to listen to him for a whole hour to realize that in reality he is far poorer than you.'

Hasidism

Rich people and cows

A rabbi devoted much of his time to collecting money from the rich, in order to provide food, clothing and shelter for the poor. His method was to flatter the rich; and he was quite willing to stoop and bow before them.

One day the rabbi's son said to him: 'These rich people are far inferior to you in wisdom, scholarship and morality. Surely it is beneath your dignity to stoop and bow before them.' The rabbi replied: 'I simply follow the order of nature. Cows are inferior to human beings in wisdom, scholarship and morality. Yet human beings have to stoop and bow before cows in order to milk them.'

Hasidism

The use of money

A rabbi was asked by two merchants to arbitrate in a dispute involving a large sum of money. He performed the task to the satisfaction of both of them; and they handed him only one silver coin for his efforts.

'What is this?' the rabbi asked, looking at the coin. 'It is money,' they said. 'And what do you do with money?' he asked. They replied: 'You buy goods and sell them at a profit, and thus acquire more money.' The rabbi said: 'If that is so, I don't want it.' And he offered the coin back to them.

The merchants refused to take it, and said: 'If you do not want it, give it to your wife.' 'And what can she do with it?' he asked. 'She can buy food and furniture for the house,' they replied. The rabbi's face brightened, and he said: 'Ah, if that is the case, you should give me more.' The merchants had no choice but to give him a whole bag of coins.

Hasidism

A blow and a gift

In a time of famine a rabbi took it upon himself to raise money, in order to feed the poorest people in the community. He went from one rich person to another. Finally he reached a wealthy merchant who was notorious for his meanness and foul temper.

The rabbi asked him for money to feed the poor. But instead of giving money, the merchant slapped the rabbi's face; the blow was so hard the rabbi's cheek began to bleed. The rabbi was dazed for a moment. Then, as he wiped his cheek, he said: 'That blow was clearly meant for me. Now what will you give to the poor?' The merchant was so astonished, that he gave five gold coins.

Hasidism

Coins in a purse

A miser, who was extremely wealthy, lost his purse; and he announced that he would offer a large reward to anyone who found it. A poor man saw it lying in a ditch, and took it to the miser. The miser counted the contents, and cried out: 'There are ten coins missing. Go away, you thief!'

The poor man, who had stolen nothing, complained to the local rabbi. The rabbi went to see the miser, and asked: 'How much did your purse contain?' 'Fifty coins,' the miser said. The rabbi turned to the poor man, and asked: 'How many coins were in the purse when you found it?' 'Forty coins,' the poor man replied.

The rabbi turned back to the miser, and declared: 'It is clear, then, that this is not the purse you lost. So you must give it back to the one who found it.' And he turned to the poor man, and said: 'Keep the purse until the rightful owner appears.'

Hasidism

The window and the mirror

A miser, as he grew older, became more and more unhappy. He was perplexed by his own misery, and said to himself: 'I have every luxury that money can buy. Yet nothing gives me pleasure any more. How can this be?' So he went to the local rabbi, and asked his advice.

The rabbi led him by the hand to the window of his room. 'What do you see?' the rabbi asked. 'I see people,' the miser replied. Then the rabbi led him to a mirror, and again asked: 'What do you see?' The miser replied: 'I see myself.'

The rabbi said: 'In both the window and the mirror there is glass. But the glass in the mirror is covered with silver. And as soon as silver is added, you cease to see others, and just see yourself.'

The miser left the rabbi, and wandered through the town. For the first time he forgot about his own needs, and saw the needs of others. He decided to share his wealth with others, and kept only enough to feed and clothe himself. His misery disappeared, and he was happy.

Hasidism

The goose and the rooster

A great preacher arrived in a small town, and decided to settle there. He went to see the local rabbi, and said: 'I intend to stir people's hearts, so they will love God and obey his laws.' The rabbi replied: 'The people of this town pay me only a very small amount. If they divide this money between the two of us, we shall both starve.'

The preacher told a parable: 'There was once a goose whose owner was thoughtless. The owner frequently failed to put out any food for the goose, so the goose went hungry. One day the owner bought a rooster, and put him with the goose. The goose was alarmed, and exclaimed: "Now we shall both starve to death!" The rooster was perplexed, so the goose described how the owner often forgot to put out any food. The rooster replied: "Whenever I am hungry, I crow – and that will remind the owner to feed us both."'

Hasidism

Two scholars

Two young scholars were travelling from one city to another. They were poorly dressed, and were unknown as speakers. They arrived at a small town as the sun was setting. So they knocked at the door of a grand mansion, and asked the wealthy owner if he would provide them with food and shelter. He slammed the door in their faces. As they were walking away from the mansion, the poorest man of the town, called Reb, invited them to stay in his tiny cottage. They eagerly accepted. Reb shared his meagre supper with them; and then he gave them his bed to sleep on, while he slept on the floor.

Some years later the scholars returned to the town. By now they were famous for their learning and their eloquence; and their many admirers had showered them with gifts, so they were now rich. They dressed in fine robes, and rode in a coach pulled by six horses. The wealthy owner of the mansion came to greet them, and invited them to stay with him. They replied: 'We are the same people whom you turned away in the past. So it's not us that you welcome, but our coach and horses. Please give hospitality to our horses, while we go and stay with Reb.'

Hasidism

Words of praise

Schmelke was asked to serve as the rabbi in the town of Nikolsburg. The day before he set out for the town, he locked himself in his room. He could be heard pacing up and down, but no one knew what he was doing.

A friend decided to listen at the door. He heard Schmelke saying wonderful things about himself: how wise and scholarly he was, and how eloquent his sermons were. The friend was surprised at this apparent pride.

Finally in the evening Schmelke emerged from his room. The friend asked him what he had been doing. Schmelke replied: 'When I arrive tomorrow at Nikolsburg, I shall be greeted with words of lavish praise. I was giving that same praise to myself. No one likes to hear self-praise; so I felt utterly disgusted with myself and with the words that I was speaking. As a result, when I hear those words spoken by others, my head will not swell with pride.'

Hasidism

A neighbour and a foot

A man asked Rabbi Schmelke: 'We are told to love our neighbours as ourselves. How can I do this when my neighbour is constantly trying to harm me?'

The rabbi replied: 'Your neighbour contains God's Spirit; and this Spirit permeates every part of his body, down to the tips of his limbs. You contain God's Spirit; and this Spirit permeates every part of your body, down to the tips of your limbs. Sometimes your foot stumbles on a stone, and you fall. Do you beat your foot for causing you pain? No; you remain kind to your foot. Equally, even though he causes you pain, you should remain kind to your neighbour.'

Hasidism

The diamond ring

A beggar once called at Rabbi Schmelke's house, and the rabbi found he had no money. So he opened his wife's box of jewellery, and took out a diamond ring. The beggar was delighted at such a beautiful gift.

A little later the rabbi's wife, who had been out, returned. She unhooked some heavy earrings, and put them in her jewellery box. She noticed that the diamond ring was missing. The rabbi explained what had happened. She went red with fury, and shouted out: 'That ring was worth at least fifty gold coins!'

The rabbi ran out of the house, and went in pursuit of the beggar. When he found him, he said: 'I've just learned that the ring is worth fifty gold coins. So when you sell, let no one cheat you by giving you less.'

Hasidism

A gilded goblet

Rabbi Phineas of Koretz said: 'When someone injures or insults you, do not take revenge. Imagine that you are standing in the presence of a king, and a man strikes you on the face. You feel compelled to remain silent. The king has witnessed the blow. If he believes that you deserved the blow, then you have no right to complain; but if he believes that the blow was undeserved, he himself will punish your assailant. In truth you are always standing in the presence of the King of kings. It is for him to punish those who injure or insult you – if he judges that the injury or insult was undeserved.'

The rabbi also said: 'I devote myself constantly to study and reflection, in order to grow in wisdom. But I am constantly in fear that I will become so wise that I shall cease to be pious.'

On one occasion the rabbi's wife purchased a gilded goblet for use on the Sabbath. When Rabbi Phineas saw the goblet, he exclaimed indignantly: 'Since when have we had golden utensils in our house?' His wife, trying to justify herself, replied: 'It's not genuine gold; it's only gilded.' The rabbi said: 'You have not only brought arrogance into the house; you have brought deceit and falsehood as well.'

Hasidism

Stealing and gambling

Rabbi Wolf of Zbaraz had a wife who was pious, but who enjoyed finding fault with others; the rabbi himself always saw the goodness in others, and never the evil.

On one occasion she accused her maidservant of stealing a diamond ring. The girl denied the accusation; so the rabbi's wife decided to take her to court. As the rabbi's wife put on her coat, the rabbi put on his coat as well. She said to him: 'There is no need for you to come with me. I can conduct myself in court perfectly well.' The rabbi replied: 'That is true enough. But can that poor girl, your maidservant, defend herself? I am going to act as her counsel, so that justice is done.' His wife scowled at him, and took off her coat; she never spoke about the matter again.

On another occasion the rabbi's wife heard that certain people stayed up all night and gambled. She said to her husband: 'These people are utterly wicked. You must put a stop to their activity, and tell them to return to their families at a normal time.' The rabbi replied: 'Perhaps their intention is to learn the art of remaining awake through the night – and once they have acquired the art, they will devote the nights to study and prayer.'

Hasidism

Lower than animals

Rabbi Leib was well known for his wise aphorisms.

Whether good or bad fortune befalls you, remain calm and serene. Remember that you are a stranger on earth, who will only remain for a short time.

Why should you feel anxious about worldly matters? The world does not belong to you, but to God.

If peace is absent, nothing worthwhile is present.

Endure insults with patience. Who are you, and what is your reputation truly worth?

Think carefully before you take any action; then you will have no regrets.

You may regard yourself as a righteous servant of God. But how strong have been the temptations to do evil?

Human beings are superior to animals because they possess the power of speech. So if you abuse that power by uttering lies and slanders, you are lower than the lowest animal.

Hasidism

Donations to dowries

The rabbi of Lublin said: 'I have greater love for wicked people who know they are wicked, than for righteous people who know they are righteous. The first are truthful; and the Lord loves the truth. The latter are deceitful, for no human being is entirely free from sin; and the Lord hates deceit.'

A merchant, who had four daughters, lost his wealth; so he was unable to provide his daughters with dowries – and hence they were unable to marry. He went to the rabbi, and asked his advice. The rabbi advised him to seek donations. The man replied: 'That would corrupt my heart. If someone gave me nothing, or only a small amount, I should hate that person.' The rabbi said: 'The Lord has already decreed how much each person should give. Believe that each person's response is in accordance with the Lord's decree – then you will bear no ill will towards anyone.'

Hasidism

False moves in chess

Rabbi Simcah of Parsischa was anxious about a particular man, who was a habitual sinner; and he wanted this man to mend his ways. The man was skilled at playing chess; and the rabbi invited him to his house for a game. In the course of the game the rabbi deliberately made a move in breach of the rules. The man was about to point out the false move, and therefore declare himself the winner; but the rabbi immediately apologized, and retracted the move – and the man had little choice but to accept the apology. A few minutes later the rabbi made another false move – and immediately the man declared himself the winner. The rabbi said: 'You refuse to forgive two false moves in a game of chess; yet you expect the Lord to forgive all your numerous sins.' The man was filled with remorse – and from that day onwards obeyed God's laws.

A young man, who was vain and foolish, came to Rabbi Simcah, and said: 'My late grandfather appeared to me in a dream, and ordered me to become a rabbi.' Rabbi Simcah replied: 'When your grandfather next comes to you, tell him to appear in the dreams of other people, and order them to treat you with respect.'

When the rabbi lay dying, his wife wept bitterly. He said: 'Why do you weep? All my life has been a preparation for death.'

Hasidism

A prayer for brandy

Rabbi Yerachmiel of Parsischa fell dangerously ill. All the inhabitants of the town prayed for his recovery; but their prayers were not answered, and the illness grew worse.

A traveller arrived at the town. He went to an inn, and asked for a drink of brandy. Some local people overheard his request, and said that drinking alcohol was prohibited, in the hope that this would persuade God to answer their prayers.

The traveller went to the synagogue, and in a loud voice he prayed: 'O God, cure the rabbi quickly, so that I can have a drink of brandy.' At that moment the rabbi began to recover; and by the following day he was clearly out of danger.

Rabbi Yerachmiel heard about the traveller's prayer, and said: 'The prayer of the traveller was more acceptable to God than the prayers of the townspeople. This was because he was honest with God about his desires.'

Hasidism

The thief and the merchant

Rabbi Yerachmiel told this parable:

A thief grew old; and his limbs became so stiff that he no longer had the agility to climb into houses. As a result he had no money to buy food, and was starving to death. A wealthy merchant took pity on him, and gave him enough money to survive.

A few years later the thief and the merchant both died on the same day; and they arrived at the heavenly court at the same moment. The merchant was very gloomy, because he was convinced that the judge would send him to hell for his lifelong greed. But the judge pronounced: 'I am unable to pass judgement. So since a person is innocent unless proved guilty, I shall send you to heaven.' The merchant was delighted, and yet perplexed. 'Why can you not pass judgement?' he asked. The judge replied: 'Because the thief, with whom you arrived, has stolen the record of your deeds.'

Hasidism

Like a horse

One winter's day a young man came to Rabbi Yerachmiel, and said: 'I wish to train as a rabbi.' The rabbi asked: 'Why do you regard yourself as fit to be a rabbi?' The young man said: 'I drink only water, and I eat only bread baked from coarse grain. I put tacks on my shoes to mortify my flesh. To clean myself I roll naked in the snow. And each day I ask a friend to administer forty lashes of a whip, to suppress any sinful desires.'

At that moment a horse entered the courtyard of the rabbi's house. It drank water from a trough, and ate some coarse grain from a bag. Then it rolled naked in the snow. The rabbi said to the young man: 'That horse does everything that you do. And I am sure that its rider whips it at least forty times a day. So you are no better than a horse.'

The young man went red with anger. The rabbi added: 'I suggest that you work as a bricklayer or blacksmith for ten years – and only then consider whether to train as a rabbi.' The young man exclaimed: 'I refuse to soil my hands with bricks or metal!' The rabbi said: 'As a rabbi you would soil your mind with something much harder and tougher – the human soul.'

Hasidism

A pipe and a gun

A friend called on Rabbi Yerachmiel one Friday afternoon. He found the rabbi in his study, pacing up and down, and smoking furiously on a pipe – so the room was filled with tobacco smoke.

The friend expressed disapproval at the rabbi's excessive smoking. The rabbi replied: 'A traveller lost his way in a forest. He came across a hut, went in and saw a man lying on a bed. The piles of valuable goods inside the hut indicated that the man was a robber. The traveller saw a gun lying on a table near the door. He said to himself: "If I kill the robber, I shall be safe; and if I miss him, I shall be able to escape in the smoke."'

The rabbi concluded: 'Each Friday afternoon I try to think holy thoughts, in preparation for the Sabbath. My pipe is like that gun. It may help my thoughts to become holy. But if it fails, the tobacco fumes will dull my mind – so at least I won't think unholy thoughts.'

Hasidism

Sources of funds

Rabbi Yerachmiel lived in great luxury. A young follower asked the reason.

The rabbi replied: 'I have three sources of funds. The first is people who are especially devout and virtuous; and with their donations I purchase the necessities of life. The second is ordinary householders; I give away their donations to the needy. The third is habitual sinners. They give generously to me, in the hope of easing their consciences. I am obliged to accept these donations; and I spend them on luxuries, which I neither need nor enjoy. This shows my contempt – so the consciences of the donors are not eased.'

Hasidism

An imaginary horse

A storekeeper came to Rabbi Yerachmiel. He complained that another man was planning to open a store nearby – and this would take away his livelihood.

The rabbi asked: 'Have you ever noticed that, when a horse is led to a river for a drink, the horse stamps his foot in the water?' 'Yes,' the storekeeper answered. The rabbi continued: 'The reason is this. As the horse lowers its head to the water, it sees its shadow. It imagines that another horse is also drinking; and it fears that there will not be enough water for both of them. So it tries to kick the other horse. But the horse is doubly deluded: not only is there no other horse; but there is ample water for an entire herd of horses.'

The rabbi concluded: 'You too are kicking at an imaginary foe. God's abundance flows like a river, and there is enough for all.'

Hasidism

The signs of an enemy

Rabbi Yerachmiel told the following fable.

A mouse sent her son out in search of food. The young mouse met a rooster, and ran back in great terror. He exclaimed: 'I have seen this proud, haughty creature, with a red comb on its head.' His mother replied: 'That creature is no enemy of ours.' And she sent her son out again.

This time the son met a turkey, and was even more frightened. He exclaimed: 'Mother, I have seen this puffed-up creature with a fearsome look in its eye – as if it were ready to kill at any time.' His mother replied: 'That creature is also no enemy of ours.'

'So how can I recognize our enemies?' the son asked. She replied: 'Our enemies bow their heads in apparent humility. Their speech is polite and gentle. They give friendly smiles at every opportunity, and they perform numerous small acts of kindness. If you meet such creatures, beware!'

Hasidism

Prayers after wine

Rabbi Yerachmiel advised people to eat and drink well prior to the Day of Atonement – so they would have ample strength for worship. On one occasion a young man took this advice too far; he drank so much wine that he fell into a stupor.

When he awoke, it was too late for the evening service at the synagogue. And since he did not know the prayers by heart, he could not say them at home. So he repeated the letters of the alphabet over and over; and as he did so, he asked God to arrange them in the correct form of the prayers.

The following day he went to Rabbi Yerachmiel, and confessed that he had become so drunk that he missed the evening service. 'So what did you do?' the rabbi asked; and the young man described how he had repeated the letters of the alphabet, and asked God to arrange them properly.

Rabbi Yerachmiel beamed with pleasure, and exclaimed: 'Your prayers were more acceptable to God than mine, because you uttered them with complete devotion.'

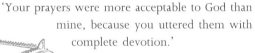

Hasidism

A fly and a coin

Rabbi Isaac said: 'There are three ways in which you can undertake a good deed. You can say: "I shall do it tomorrow." Or you can say: "I am ready to do it now." Or you can declare: "I am starting to do it now!" The first way is worst; the second way is better; the third way is best.'

He also said: 'At death you merely move from one home to another. If you are wise, you will concentrate on making your future home more beautiful than your present one.'

A man said to Rabbi Isaac that he always forgot what he had learnt. The rabbi asked him: 'When you are eating, do you ever forget to put the spoon in your mouth?' The man replied: 'No, because I cannot live without food.' The rabbi said: 'Nor can you live without learning. Remember this, and your memory will improve.'

Rabbi Isaac said: 'Many people have less fear of committing a sin than of a fly; at least when a fly alights on their shoulder, they brush it away. And many people are less willing to perform a good deed than to obtain a small coin; at least when they see a small coin on the ground, they take the trouble to pick it up.'

Rabbi Isaac and his wife lost all six of their sons in a plague. At first both were overcome with grief, and were also bitterly angry with God. Then the rabbi said: 'Let us stop grieving – then our sons will not have died in vain. Other people, when they suffer a similar tragedy, will find comfort in our example.'

Hasidism

Grains of sand

Rabbi Jacob said: 'A person is like a grain of sand. Each grain is separate and distinct; but if a pile of grains is thrown into a fire, the grains fuse together to become glass. In the same way, in normal times people each pursue their distinct interests; but in times of crisis, they unite.'

The rabbi frequently told this parable. A poor man purchased a goat at a fair, and brought it home. His wife immediately tried to milk it, but it was dry. 'This animal is useless,' she exclaimed. Her husband replied: 'She has come a long distance, and is tired, hungry and thirsty. Give her food and water, and let her rest for the night; then she will give milk.'

A man asked the rabbi whether he should study philosophy. The rabbi replied: 'On the shelves of his shop an apothecary keeps hundreds of different powders and potions. The apothecary is an expert, and can mix these powders and potions to form medicines. But if you or I were to mix them, we should probably produce poison. In the same way a philosopher has numerous ideas and theories, and he can mix them to produce valuable insights; but if someone without expertise tries to mix them, he will produce dangerous heresies. So if you wish to study philosophy, make yourself an expert.'

Hasidism

Piety and poverty

Rabbi Jacob related a dream in which he ascended to heaven. He heard an angel pleading with God to make the Jews wealthy. The angel was saying: 'Look at how pious they are, despite their poverty. If you were to give them riches, they would be even more pious.' The rabbi asked a bystander the angel's name. 'Satan,' the bystander replied. So the rabbi called out to God: 'Leave us in poverty.'

The rabbi said: 'People have the choice whether to sin or do good; so every sin is culpable. Yet a person's temperament, or the circumstances of a person's childhood, can make sin more tempting. So do not hate other people for the sins they have committed. If you had their temperament, or had endured an unhappy childhood, you might commit the same sins.'

The rabbi also said: 'There is one sin of which you should not repent: the sin of despair. If you start to repent, you sink even deeper into it.'

Hasidism

A good brain

Rabbi Leib was cheated of all his wealth. But he was quite unperturbed, and continued studying and teaching as before. His wife asked him how he could ignore his misfortune. He replied: 'Other people might spend a year worrying about such a misfortune. But the Lord gave me a good brain; so I can do the same amount of worrying in a few minutes.'

Rabbi Mordecai said: 'If you wish to acquire the habit of honesty, follow this simple method. Whenever you hear yourself telling a lie, or exaggerating the truth, apologize at once, and ask your listener to forgive you. By this means you will soon learn to control your tongue.'

Whenever Rabbi Mendel felt anger at another person's words or actions, he went at once to his library. There he looked through all the holy books, to see if anger were permissible in these circumstances. Invariably by the time he had finished his researches, his anger had subsided. So hard words never passed his lips.

Hasidism

Rabbi Henoch said: 'To sin against another person is worse than to sin against God. A person may go away, so you lose the opportunity to seek forgiveness. But God is always present, so you may seek his forgiveness at any time.'

The rabbi told this story: 'A general, in the midst of a war, received news that the enemy had massacred his finest regiment. He was greatly distressed, and his face showed his emotions. His wife overheard the news, and went into his room. She said: "I too have received news – and it is far worse than the news you have received." "What news is that?" asked the general, in a tone of irritation. She replied: "I have seen loss of courage on your face – and that is far worse than the loss of a regiment."'

Rabbi Henoch had a rule, that, when someone offended him, he never expressed his displeasure immediately. Instead he waited until the following morning, when his emotions had subsided. Then he said calmly and gently to the person: 'Yesterday you offended me.'

Hasidism

Silent sermons

In a certain town there was a wealthy merchant who loved to give money to people in need. Rabbi Meir said of him: 'That merchant is admirable, but possesses one fault. He enjoys being generous so much that he wants people always to be in need.'

For several months Rabbi Meir did not preach. At first people were too embarrassed to question him about it. But finally a young boy asked him the reason. The rabbi replied: 'There are many ways of conveying divine truth – and silence is one of them.'

When people came to Rabbi Meir in distress, his counsel was invariably wise – and they left feeling much better. Rumours began to spread that the rabbi performed miracles. So one day a person asked the rabbi's wife: 'Is it true that your husband performs miracles?' She replied: 'Many people would regard it as a miracle if God did the rabbi's will. To me it is a miracle that the rabbi always does God's will.'

Hasidism

Winter and harvest

Rabbi Cohen was renowned for his wise and witty sayings, which others recorded.

If you think you can live without others, you are mistaken. If you think others cannot live without you, you are even more mistaken.

If you believe that anything can be accomplished with money, you are likely to do anything to obtain money.

If you pursue happiness, you are flying away from contentment.

It is easier to abandon an evil habit today than tomorrow.

Ill luck usually improves people. Good luck usually makes them worse.

If you do not cultivate wisdom and knowledge, old age will be winter. But if you cultivate wisdom and learning, old age will be the season of harvest.

Fear of a misfortune is usually worse than the misfortune itself.

Hasidism

Spokes of a wheel

Be wary of those whom nobody likes. But be even more wary of those whom everybody likes.

You should be the master of your will, and the slave of your conscience.

Fear God – and also fear those who have no fear of God.

If you insist that your friends should be free of faults, you will have no friends.

Fear those who fear you.

If you have confidence in yourself, you will win the confidence of others.

If you cannot survive bad times, you will not see good times.

Let us be like the spokes of a wheel, which all unite at the centre. Let us not be like the two sides of a road, which never meet.

Hasidism

Watery juice and thick juice

Rabbi Motke was extremely tolerant of the sins and failings of others. Someone once said to him: 'You are pious and virtuous; and you make no effort to persuade others to share your way of life. Yet wicked and impious people are always eager to gain companions. Why is this?' The rabbi replied: 'A person of piety and virtue walks in the light, and so is not afraid to walk alone. But the person of wickedness and impiety walks in darkness, and so is anxious for company.'

Rabbi Motke went to visit a prison, and spoke to all the prisoners. Each prisoner asserted his innocence – except one, who admitted he had been a thief. The rabbi then said to the governor of the prison: 'Release that man who admits he was a thief. He will corrupt all the innocent prisoners.'

A person once asked Rabbi Motke about the art of reading. The rabbi said: 'If you squeeze grapes with your fingers, you extract only a watery juice, which is useless for making wine. In the same way, if you flick through the pages of a book quickly, you will gain only superficial knowledge – which is useless for making wisdom. If you squeeze grapes by treading on them, you extract a thick juice, which makes excellent wine. In the same way, if you read a book slowly and carefully, you will gain profound knowledge – which makes true wisdom.

Hasidism

JEWISH PHILOSOPHY

Through Philo (d. c. 50 CE) Judaism opened itself to the philosophy of ancient Greece. Living in the cosmopolitan city of Alexandria, he was profoundly influenced by Stoic thought, especially its theory of the divine Logos (Word) as the agent of creation. Saadya (d. 942) was head of the rabbinical academy in Baghdad, capital of the Arab empire. He too was influenced by Greek philosophy, which was now popular among Muslims; and he sought to shine the light of reason onto traditional Jewish wisdom.

Ibn Gabriol (d. c. 1090) lived in Moorish Spain, and enjoyed Sufi as well as Greek ideas. He wrote in Arabic, and was regarded as Muslim by readers in the Islamic world; his work was translated into Latin, and circulated in Europe as that of a Christian scholar.

Bahya (d. c. 1200) lived in Spain in the same period. He served as a judge in a rabbinical court. In his writings he sought to connect outward religion and morality with the inner workings of the heart.

The most famous Jewish philosopher is Maimonides (d. 1204), who grew up in Spain, and emigrated to Egypt to escape persecution. He was frequently asked to make judgements in disputes, and was called 'the second Moses.' His Guide to the Perplexed combines Greek rationalism with Jewish faith.

The Zohar, probably the work of various writers, appeared in Spain in the thirteenth century, and sought to derive mystical insights from the Hebrew Bible.

The presence of God

God fills all things. He contains, but is not contained. He alone is everywhere – and yet he is nowhere. He created space, and all the material things that fill space. God cannot be bounded by anything that he has made; any intelligent mind knows that God transcends all boundaries.

His powers extend through earth and water, air and sky. There is no part of the vast universe where he is not present.

God unites the universe. All things move in harmony, according to his will. Nothing can escape his will; his bonds can never be loosed.

Philo: The Confusion of Tongues

Sincerity in worship

God needs nothing; yet in his great love towards humanity he asks us to worship him. If we cultivate the habit of thanking him for all things, and striving to honour him in all we do, we shall purify ourselves of sin; we shall cleanse our minds of evil thoughts, our bodies of evil actions, and our mouths of evil speech.

Reflect on the purity of God. You are filthy and soiled, and so are not worthy to approach him. Yet if you sincerely repent – if in your heart you genuinely want to be pure – then he is eager to welcome you. So, before you worship God, look within yourself. Are you sincere? If so, do not hesitate to speak to God. Or do you really want to cling on to your sins? If so, remain silent.

Philo: On the Immutability of God

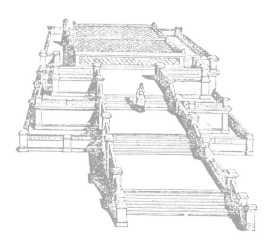

Human freedom

Human beings are distinguished from other living creatures by their capacity for reflective thought: they can consider and understand the world around them. Just as sight is the most important sense, and just as light is the most important feature of the universe, so the most important feature of a human being is the mind.

The mind is the eyes of the soul, illuminated by rays peculiar to itself; these rays disperse the darkness of ignorance. The mind was not formed out of the same elements as the body, but was made from purer and finer elements – the same elements from which the stars were fashioned.

The body can be destroyed, but the mind is indestructible. Having created the mind, God judged it worthy of freedom; he loosened the fetters of necessity, and allowed it to think and do whatever it wanted. Other living creatures, who do not possess minds, are slaves of their own instincts and urges; but through possession of a mind, human beings are their own masters.

Thus God has given human beings the capacity to choose between good and evil, between that which is noble and that which is base, between virtue and vice – in order that human beings might elevate themselves to his own status by choosing goodness, nobility and virtue.

Philo: On the Immutability of God

God as shepherd

Land and water, air and fire, plants and animals, the sun and the moon, the stars and the planets, are like a single flock, of which God is the shepherd. He leads them according to his laws; and he sets above them his Word, who rules them on his behalf.

Let all human beings also regard God as their shepherd. Let them praise him, not with words that they have learnt by rote, but with the voice of understanding and devotion. Since God is our shepherd, we can be certain that he wishes to bestow upon us joy beyond measure. He is leading us on the path of holiness, whose destination is perfect happiness.

When people strive after material wealth, they are in truth making themselves poor. But when they follow God as their shepherd, they gain wealth that can never be destroyed.

Philo: On Husbandry

God's Word

God's Word in his fullness is everywhere; so God's Word in his fullness is near us. And since he is near us, his eye observes all that we do. So let us refrain from all evil.

In all our actions our best motive is reverence for God. But if we cannot attain reverence, then let us at least be prompted by fear of his power. He is invincible; his anger is terrible; his punishment is horrible.

May the divine Word never leave us, but always live within us. When we apprehend God's Word, we feel safe and serene. God's Word is immutable.

Philo: On the Giants

God's possessions

I am made of body and soul; I possess five senses, and have a mind with which to think. Yet none of these is really mine.

Where was my body before I was born, and where will it go when I have died? At every stage through life I am different to how I was at the previous stage; the self is constantly changing. Where is the baby, the child, and the young man that I once was?

Where did the soul come from, where will it go, and how long will it remain my companion? Can I know the essence of the soul? When did I get it – before birth? Was there a time when there was no self; and will there be a time when the self has been obliterated?

In this life we are the ruled rather than the rulers, the known rather than the knowing. The soul knows me, though I do not know the soul. The soul demands that I act in certain ways, and refrain from acting in other ways; the soul is my mistress, and I am the servant. And, at a time of its own choosing, it will divorce me and depart; despite my most fervent pleas, it will escape from me – my body has no grip on the soul.

All this makes plain that we belong to another, greater being; we are God's possessions. The body and the soul are his, and we merely tend them on his behalf. He will take them back when he wants.

Philo: On the Cherubim

Strangers on earth

All of us live in this world as if we were strangers in a foreign city. Before our birth we had no knowledge of the earth, and played no part in shaping it. And we remain on earth only for a few decades before passing on.

Who, then, is a true citizen of the earth? Only God; he alone is a true citizen. If we call ourselves citizens, we are stretching the term 'citizen' beyond its breaking point; compared with God, we are merely visitors.

Foolish people do not realize this. They imagine that humanity owns the earth; and so they want to grab for themselves as big a portion of the earth as their strength and wit allow. Thus they strive for wealth and power. But in their pursuit of wealth and power they reveal their folly.

Philo: On the Cherubim

God's grace

If you are righteous, and if you explore the nature of existence, you will make a surprising discovery: that all things are gifts from God. Divine grace is not something separate from creation; it is not something added to creation. On the contrary, creation itself is divine grace. Since all things belong to God, grace too belongs to God – and all things are expressions of grace.

So if you ask what is the origin of creation, there is a simple answer: creation is the goodness and the grace of God. All things in this world, and the world itself, are free gifts from God, which come from his infinite generosity.

Philo: Allegorical Interpretation

Dedication to God

If you work with your hands, dedicate the fruits of your labour to God. If you are a scholar, dedicate to God all that you write. If you are an eloquent preacher or lecturer, dedicate to God all that you say. If you are a poet, dedicate every metre and rhyme, every metaphor and alliteration to God. If you are a sailor, dedicate every voyage to God – and trust in him to keep you safe. If you own an orchard, dedicate every tree to God. If you keep flocks of sheep and goats, dedicate every animal to God. If you are a physician, dedicate every patient to God – and trust in God to show you the right remedy for every ill. If you are a ruler, dedicate all your subjects to God – and trust in God to show you what laws to pass and what decrees to issue.

No one is too lowly or humble to come before God. No one has sunk too deeply in despair not to be raised up by God. No one is so lacking in gifts from God to have no reason for gratitude.

Philo: On the Change of Names

The practical and the contemplative life

Do you turn your back on social intercourse, and live in solitude? If so, were you once courteous and popular – or were you clumsy and awkward in company? Have you renounced the making of money? If so, were you once successful in business – or did you have a business that failed? Do you now display indifference to good food and wine? If so, did you formerly exercise moderation in eating and drinking – or were you inclined to indulge yourself? Do you despise popular esteem? If so, did you formerly enjoy a high reputation – or were you regarded by others with contempt? Do you shy away from all positions of power? If so, did you once exercise power with efficiency and compassion – or did your incompetence make you unfit for power?

In the early part of your adulthood, engage in some practical work in the world, and strive to succeed in that work. Try to make yourself pleasing to others, and make yourself worthy of their affection and respect. Only then should you consider a more solitary, contemplative way of life. The practical comes before the contemplative; it is a prelude to it. The contemplative life is harder than the practical life; and the practical challenges of the world make you fit for the tougher challenges of the spirit.

If in your youth you were to adopt the contemplative life, people would accuse you of laxity rather than piety. And perhaps they would be right.

Philo: On Flight and Finding

Disciples of God's Word

Do you wish to be a disciple of God's Word? Then you should consistently prefer moderation to indulgence, propriety to impropriety, virtue to vice. The foundations, on which you build your entire life, should be self-control, humility, and courage. Your will should be stronger than the temptations of wealth, pleasure and popularity. You should want nothing more for yourself than the necessities of life; so long as lack of food does not threaten your health, you should be content.

Indeed, true disciples of God's Word think nothing of hunger and thirst, heat and cold, and lack of rest. They happily wear cheap clothes, and would feel ashamed to put on expensive silks and brocades. They prefer to sleep on a heap of leaves, with a stone for a pillow, than on a soft couch stuffed with feathers. To them simplicity is luxury.

Philo: On Dreams

In the image of God

Nothing on earth is more like God than a human being. Of course, God does not have a human form. No, it is the human mind, the central element of the soul, which is in the image of God. The human mind is fashioned in accordance with the divine mind – which fashioned the universe.

And the human mind occupies a position in relation to the body, which reflects the position of God in relation to the universe. The mind is invisible, but through the five senses is aware of many things; God is invisible, but perceives all things. The mind is capable of exerting its will over its surroundings, but it remains free within itself; God can impose his will on all things, but remains supreme. The mind can understand things in the world, but nothing else is capable of understanding the human mind; God knows all things, but is known by nothing.

Philo: On the Creation of the World

Gratitude for the universe

When I wish to give thanks to God for the creation of the universe, I give it both for the universe as a whole, and for its parts. I think of the universe as a living creature, and its parts as its limbs.

I give thanks for the sky and the moon, the planets and the stars, the earth and the plants that grow in the earth, the sea and the rivers and the fish that live in them, the seasons of the year and the changes in weather from one season to another – yes, for all these I give thanks.

I give thanks for human beings in all their variety: for men and women, for educated people and those without education, for those living in cities and for those living in the countryside – yes, for all these I give thanks.

I give thanks for each part of the human being: for the different organs of the body, for the five senses, for the capacity for thought and speech, for the soul – yes, for all these I give thanks.

Philo: *The Special Laws*

The greatest artist

It is hard to apprehend God; but that is no reason why we should not try to search for him. Yet in searching for God two questions arise in the mind of the philosopher. The first is whether God exists – a question prompted by atheists who assert he does not.

To understand any piece of work, you must understand the workman. Who can look upon a statue or a painting without thinking about the sculptor or painter? Who can see a garment, or a ship, or a house, without thinking about the weaver, the shipwright or the builder? And when you visit a city where civil life is well managed, you find yourself admiring the city's rulers.

Consider this world. Observe its hills and valleys, teeming with animals and plants; its rivers pouring down mountains, and meandering across plains to the sea; the different temperature and atmosphere of each season; the sun ruling the day, and the moon ruling the night; the patterns of the stars in the sky – observe everything around, above and below you. Must you not think about the one who made all this – its sculptor, painter, weaver, and builder?

No work of art makes itself; it requires an artist. And since the greatest work of art is the world itself, we must assume that it was made by the greatest artist of all – whom we call God.

Philo: The Special Laws

The search for God

The second question in the mind of the philosopher concerning God is this: what is his essence? This is beyond human capacity to answer; yet the act of trying to answer it brings untold joys and pleasures.

We have the testimony of those true philosophers who devote their lives to this question – who feast day by day on it. Their souls soar above the confines of human reason, upwards to the purity of the heavenly realm; and they are dazzled by the brightness of what they perceive. Yet they do not become exhausted by their exertions; on the contrary, at each stage in their search they gain new energy and strength – and they soar higher and higher.

These mystical flights do not carry the soul to God himself; so the soul never perceives the essence of God. But they bring such profound satisfaction to the soul, that the soul takes every opportunity to make further flights.

The philosopher's search for God is like the astronomer's study of the sky. The astronomer can never with certainty determine the exact essence of the stars; and yet he eagerly persists in trying to find out – and his fulfilment is derived from the inquiry.

Philo: The Special Laws

Inactivity, folly and self-indulgence

There are eight sources of spiritual and moral ignorance.

The first is inactivity – the unwillingness to fulfil your duties, laid upon you by God's law. As soon as you begin to delay in fulfilling your duties, then you cease to regard those duties as binding. And once you cease to regard them as binding, they seem unbearably heavy. And once they seem unbearably heavy, you no longer perform them at all. You say to yourself: 'God's laws are too hard for me; I am sure he understands my weakness, and will forgive me.'

The second is folly – the foolish belief that, while God may exist, he pays no attention to the world, and thus he is irrelevant to human affairs. Suppose that you were to take this attitude towards your king – and that you conducted your life without reference to his laws and decrees. You would soon be apprehended as a rebel or a criminal, and be imprisoned or executed. How can you imagine that God is less concerned with his creation, than a king is with his kingdom?

The third is self-indulgence. Eating and drinking to excess damages the body. But obtaining the money to purchase excessive amounts of food and drink destroys the soul. If you indulge the body, you lack the energy to do an honest day's work; so you resort to various kinds of dishonesty and exploitation.

Saadya: Beliefs and Dogmas

Narrowness, pride and attachment

The fourth source of spiritual and moral ignorance is narrowness of mind. If your mind is narrow, you believe there are simple answers to every question, which can be found rapidly and without effort. You refuse to search widely, and become impatient if any question takes more than a few moments to answer. As a result your morality and spirituality is superficial – and cannot withstand difficult situations and tough challenges.

The fifth is pride. In order to acquire wisdom, you must find teachers who possess wisdom, or books by writers who possess wisdom. But if you are proud, you refuse to accept than anyone is wiser than you – so you remain ignorant.

The sixth is attachment to a particular view. At some moment in the past you may have heard a particular spiritual or moral argument that appealed to you – and to which you firmly attached yourself. While this argument may have merit, it can only contain a fraction of the truth; but in your attachment to it, you believe that it is sufficient. This closes your mind to other arguments and views, which may contain other parts of the truth.

Saadya: Beliefs and Dogmas

Consistency and perversity

The seventh source of spiritual and moral ignorance is consistency. When you hear a view or an argument that is inconsistent with your existing beliefs, you ridicule it and treat it with contempt. You only accept views and arguments that strengthen your beliefs. You say that your beliefs are held by many friends and neighbours, and that this proves their worth. But the truth is not determined by popularity. And, besides, it is surely unlikely that your existing beliefs are flawless. If you sincerely wish to know the truth, you must be open to views that are inconsistent with your own, and grapple with the contradictions.

The eighth source is pleasure in disagreement. You may have a perverse mind, which enjoys finding the faults and flaws in the arguments of others, but which pays no attention to the merits of those arguments. If you wish to make spiritual and moral progress, you should seek the merits in the arguments of others, and use those arguments to reveal the faults and flaws in your own beliefs.

Saadya: Beliefs and Dogmas

Contempt for the world

Many people say it is right to hold the world in contempt. They say the world is never stable and is constantly changing, and so it cannot be trusted. They say that all worldly goods are perishable, and hence devoid of value. They say that all worldly pleasure quickly turns to pain, that all worldly honour quickly turns to disgrace, and that all wealth quickly turns to poverty. They say that involvement in worldly affairs soon leads to dishonesty, fraud and exploitation, and so corrupts the soul. Besides, they say, life on earth is short, and may end at any moment. For all these reasons they say it is foolish to build a house, plant a vineyard, marry and have children – and it is wise to live alone in a cave in the mountains, or under a tree in a forest, and to eat wild herbs and berries.

These ideas contain some truth; but those holding them have strayed from the path of God. If it were right for human beings to live alone and have no children, God would not have implanted in them the desire for love and sex; and he would have given them the power to reproduce without intercourse. And if it were right for human beings not to build houses and plant vineyards, God would not have given them the intelligence and the skills to do these things.

The golden mean is to distinguish those worldly things that should be despised, from those worldly things that should be treasured. And God's law is our guide in making this distinction.

Saadya: Beliefs and Dogmas

Pleasures of the senses

Many people say it is right to pursue pleasures of the senses. They say that human beings have no other purpose on earth than to maximize pleasure and minimize pain. They also say that pleasure removes heaviness from the brain, and makes people bright and intelligent.

These ideas contain some truth. God has implanted within the human body the tendency to find certain things pleasurable, because they benefit the body; and he has implanted the tendency to find other things painful, because they harm the body. But it does not follow that God wants human beings to pursue pleasure for its own sake. He has given human beings the capacity for wisdom and understanding; and their ultimate purpose is to understand God himself.

The golden mean is to enjoy the degree of pleasure that is healthy for the body, but no more – and to devote the greatest effort to the acquisition of wisdom.

Saadya: Beliefs and Dogmas

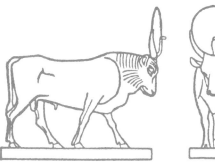

Wealth, children and longevity

Many people say it is good to gather wealth, since wealth is a measure of achievement and success – and that wealthy people have many friends. It is true that some wealth is necessary for bodily comfort. But when people have acquired great wealth, their hearts and minds are constantly anxious about losing it; they are never at ease. The golden mean is to strive for wealth in proportion to the needs of your family – and always give thanks to God for what you acquire.

Many people say it is good to have as many children as possible, since children are a delight to the eyes. It is true that children can bring great joy, and are a comfort in old age. But this joy does not increase with the quantity of children; it is their quality that matters. The golden mean is to have only as many children as you can guide and educate to the highest standard.

Many people say it is good to strive for longevity, since there are no pleasures after death. It is true that a long life gives greater time in which to acquire wisdom. Yet it is the way in which time is used, rather than its length, which matters. Some people may live to a great age, and remain fools; while others use their time well, and become wise at an early age. The golden mean is to love life on earth as an opportunity to become wise, and also to look forward to death as the gateway to a higher life.

Saadya: Beliefs and Dogmas

Power, revenge and scholarship

Many people say it is right to seek authority and power, in order to be treated with respect by others. But power is only a means of achieving some other purpose; it has no value in itself. The golden mean is to gain authority and power as the means of upholding justice, supporting the poor, and delivering the oppressed from their oppressors.

Many people say it is right to take revenge on those who have caused you injury, since revenge sets the heart at rest. But revenge only stimulates the heart to want greater vengeance. The golden mean is to seek reconciliation with your enemies, for this truly brings joy; but if this proves impossible, take revenge only to the extent that your enemy has broken God's law.

Many people say it is right to seek knowledge above all things, and that a life devoted to scholarship is most pleasing to God. The true purpose of scholarship is to reveal how life should be lived; so scholarship without action is vain. The golden mean is to balance work, study and rest – and to let scholarship inform the way in which work is undertaken and rest enjoyed.

Saadya: Beliefs and Dogmas

The best education

There are three kinds of education.

The first consists in the teacher saying to the pupil: 'Do this, and do not do that.' This is the weakest kind, because it does not indicate to the pupil the consequences of obedience and disobedience.

The second consists in the teacher saying to the pupil: 'Do this, and you will be rewarded in this way; do not do that, or you will be punished in that way.' This is stronger, because it shows how happiness and misery are connected with a person's actions.

The third consists in the teacher showing the pupil examples from history of how particular actions have particular consequences. This is the strongest, since it both convinces the pupil of the truth of the teacher's words, and it enables the pupil to remember them.

The Bible is the supreme teacher; it is filled with vivid examples, which both illustrate God's laws, and cause them to stay in the mind.

Saadya: Beliefs and Dogmas

The acquisition of wisdom

A person came to the sage, and asked: 'In what does wisdom consist?' The sage replied: 'People are only wise to the extent that they are searching for wisdom. If they imagine they have attained it, they are fools.'

A person came to the sage, and asked: 'Who is fit to rule?' The sage replied: 'A sage who has been invested with power, or a king who seeks wisdom.'

A person came to the sage, and asked: 'How is it that you are wiser than all others?' The sage replied: 'Because I spend more on oil for my lamp than they spend on wine.'

A person came to the sage, and asked: 'Who are greater, the wise or the rich?' The sage replied: 'The wise.' The person then asked: 'In which case, why do the wise come to the doors of the rich for help, whereas the rich rarely come to the doors of the wise?' The sage replied: 'Because the wise appreciate the value of wealth, whereas the rich do not appreciate the value of wisdom.'

A person came to the sage, and asked: 'How is wisdom acquired?' The sage replied: 'The first step is silence. The second step is listening. The third step is remembering. The fourth step is practice. And the fifth step is teaching others.'

Ibn Gabriol: The Choice of Pearls

Devout fools and sinful sages

A person came to the sage, and asked: 'What is the finest quality that a person can acquire?' The sage replied: 'Curiosity about the truth.'

A person came to the sage, and asked: 'At what age should a person start to seek wisdom?' The sage replied: 'The quest for wisdom in old age is like a mark on the sand. The quest for wisdom in youth is like an inscription on stone.'

A person came to the sage, and said: 'It seems to me that discussion and debate are wastes of time. What do you say?' The sage replied: 'Not to discuss wisdom is like having a hoard of gold from which nothing is ever withdrawn.'

A person came to the sage, and said: 'Human beings have a great capacity for blame. What do you say about it?' The sage replied: 'When fools do something wrong, they blame others. When seekers of wisdom do something wrong, they blame themselves. When possessors of wisdom do something wrong, they neither blame others nor blame themselves.'

A person came to the sage, and asked: 'Whose company should I avoid?' The sage replied: 'Avoid the company of fools who are devout, and sages who are sinful; both are exceedingly dangerous.'

Ibn Gabriol: The Choice of Pearls

People and power

A person came to the sage, and said: 'The company of other human beings damages the soul; so therefore I am inclined to spend my days in solitude.' The sage replied: 'That would be folly. You cannot thrive without other people, and they cannot thrive without you; you need them, and they need you. Yet when you are in human company, be like a deaf person that can hear, a blind person that can see, and a dumb man that can speak.'

A man came to the sage, and asked: 'In what does power consist?' The sage replied: 'Powerful people are those who respond to folly with humility, and who control their temper at all times. The person persisted: 'How can humility lead to power?' The sage replied: 'If you are humble, people take pleasure in assisting you.'

The person persisted: 'How can controlling your temper lead to power?' The sage replied: 'If you cannot control your own temper, how can you expect to control other people?'

Ibn Gabriol: The Choice of Pearls

Anxiety and trust

A person came to the sage, and asked: 'Why do we never perceive in you a trace of anxiety?' The sage replied: 'Because I have never possessed anything that I was afraid to lose.'

Another person came and asked the same question. On this occasion the sage replied: 'I never feel anxious because I have the fence that gives complete protection.' The person asked: 'What is this fence that gives complete protection?' The sage replied: 'Trust in God.'

A person came to the sage and asked: 'How should I cope with misfortune? And how should I respond to good fortune?' The sage replied: 'Prepare for misfortune by learning patience; and prepare for good fortune by learning gratitude.'

A person came to the sage, and said: 'I am constantly worrying about misfortunes that might occur. How can I stop worrying?' The sage replied: 'Close your eyes, and imagine that these misfortunes have already occurred.'

Ibn Gabriol: *The Choice of Pearls*

Contentment and education

A person came to the sage, and asked: 'How can I be content?' The sage replied: 'Do not strive for more than you need.'

The king came to the sage, and said: 'I am offended that you never ask any favours of me.' The sage said: 'Why should I ask favours of you? I am richer than you are.' The king asked: 'How are you richer than me?' The sage replied: 'Because I am more content with the little I possess, than you are with your great wealth.'

A person came to the sage, and said: 'I am bewildered by constant changes in fashion.' The sage said: 'Guard your tongue, and attend to your own business.'

A man came to the sage, and said: 'In every venture that I have attempted, I have failed; and my sons and daughters are ashamed of me.' The sage asked him: 'Are you happy and content?' The man replied: 'Yes, I am.' The sage declared: 'Then you are a success in all things except one: you have failed to teach your children wisdom.'

A person came to the sage, and asked: 'Is education always desirable?' The sage replied: 'Education brings happiness to the wise, but agitates the foolish – just as the sun enables humans to see, but blinds the bat.'

Ibn Gabriol: *The Choice of Pearls*

Three categories of knowledge

The noblest gift bestowed by God on humanity is knowledge. This is the life of the human soul, and the lamp of the human intellect. Through knowledge people learn how to live in harmony with God – and thus be happy both in this world and the next.

There are three categories of knowledge. The first is the science of created things. This consists in observing the material properties and behaviour, both of inanimate objects and of living things.

The second is the science of mathematics, through which order and pattern can be discerned. This category of knowledge sub-divides into arithmetic, geometry, astronomy and music.

The third is the science of religion, which is concerned with knowledge of God and his laws.

All categories of knowledge are gates that God has opened for rational beings, through which they can come to understand his creation; and through understanding his creation, they can understand something of God in himself.

Bahya: Guide to the Duties of the Heart

Outward and inward religion

The science of religion has two parts, concerned respectively with outward religion and inward religion. I have studied many books about religion, expecting to find both parts considered in equal measure. But in fact in all these books inward religion was hardly mentioned. I have reflected on this deeply; and I have concluded that inward religion is the foundation of outward religion – that unless the heart is directed towards God, religious observance counts for nothing.

As human beings we consist of both body and soul; both of them are marks of God's goodness to us. The body is visible, and the soul is invisible. It follows that we should render to God both visible and invisible service. Outward religion is visible service, and involves such things as praying, fasting, acts of charity, building temples, celebrating festivals, and so on.

Inward religion is invisible service, and involves such things as: acknowledging the unity of God in our hearts; loving God in our hearts; being humble towards him, and wishing to obey his every command; entrusting ourselves to him; abstaining from what he hates, and embracing what he loves; and meditating on his blessings.

Bahya: Guide to the Duties of the Heart

Emotions towards God

If it came into our minds that we were under no obligation to love and serve God, then our bodies would be released from all practical duties towards him. Yet it is clear that God has imposed duties upon us; so it is absurd to suppose that God does not want us to love him. Indeed unless we perform our duties with eager and willing hearts, then we are not fulfilling those duties as he wants.

When I first became convinced of the necessity of inward religion, I said to myself: 'Perhaps the necessity of inward religion is so plain, that everyone already understands it – so there is no need for a philosopher to write about it.' But when I studied human habits and attitudes through the ages, as recorded in literature, I discovered that many people are oblivious to it – that only exceptionally pious people love God with all their hearts.

I concluded that philosophers and preachers should divert their attention away from outward religion, and concentrate on people's emotions and feelings towards God.

Bahya: Guide to the Duties of the Heart

The child and the old man

There are three reasons why people are blind towards inward religion.

First, they are too absorbed in worldly affairs. They pursue happiness through worldly wealth and success; and though experience and wisdom demonstrates that this pursuit is vain, they persist in it. Whatever success they achieve, they strive for more and more; and when they look upon the success of others, they are filled with envy – so their absorption in worldly affairs in magnified.

Secondly, they take God's many blessings in this world for granted, and so are not moved to thank him for them. A small boy was once abandoned by the wayside, and a rich merchant took pity on him. The rich merchant carried him home, and raised him as his own son, providing the finest food and clothing. Then a little later this kindly merchant found an old man begging by the wayside. He took pity on him also, took him home, and treated him as his own broth-er, providing the finest food and clothing. The old man was filled with gratitude, because he compared his present privil-ege to his former deprivation. But the child showed no gratit-ude, because he had always enjoyed this privilege, and thus never stopped to consider the rich man's generosity. Most human beings are like the child: they show no gratitude for the good things of life, because they never stop to consider their source.

Bahya: Guide to the Duties of the Heart

Blind people in a home

The third reason for people's blindness towards inner religion is that they do not understand misfortune. When they suffer injury to their bodies or their property, they regard the injury as wholly negative; they do not realize that every misfortune can have beneficial consequences. They forget that God has control over every event; so every event is in accordance with his justice and wisdom.

Suppose a special home was built for blind people. It was furnished at great expense for their comfort; and the furniture was arranged to their greatest advantage. Also medicines were provided which might cure their blindness, with a skilled physician to administer them. But the blind people living in this home ignored the physician, and so did not take the medicines. And they ignored the proprietor of the home, who explained to them where the furniture was placed; so they frequently stumbled over it, and fell on their faces. As their injuries multiplied they began to complain angrily about the home, and complained that the proprietor was deliberately trying to harm them.

Most human beings are like those blind people. They do not recognize that everything in this world can work for their benefit; and they ignore those sages who can open their eyes to this. Instead they cause themselves terrible injury – and complain about the one who made the world.

Bahya: Guide to the Duties of the Heart

The prophetic gift

Most people think that God could choose anyone to be a prophet — that he could inspire anyone with the spirit of prophecy, and then confer on that person a mission. They believe that it makes no difference whether the person is wise or foolish, old or young, so long as he is morally good.

Philosophers, on the other hand, hold that only wise people, who have devoted many years to study, can be prophetic. They say that every human being possesses the faculty of prophecy, but that this faculty must be developed through the acquisition of wisdom and understanding. Thus it is impossible for a foolish or ignorant person to be a prophet; equally we should not expect young people, who have not yet had time to acquire wisdom, to make prophetic utterances.

There is a third view taught in the Bible. It coincides with the opinion of the philosophers in all points except one. A person may have developed the faculty of prophecy, but God may or may not inspire that person with prophetic insight — that is God's choice. Thus prophecy is a combination of human effort and divine will.

Maimonides: Guide to the Perplexed 2.32

The balance of good and evil

Most people think that evil in this world far outweighs goodness; they say that good things are found only rarely, while evil things are both numerous and enduring. Not only do ordinary people make this mistake, but so do people who are regarded as wise.

If you think in this way, the reason is that you judge the universe by your own narrow experience. Without ever articulating this notion to yourself, you imagine that the universe exists only for you; and so when misfortune befalls you, then you immediately conclude that the whole universe is evil. But if you could stand outside yourself, and see yourself simply as one among countless millions of men and women, then you would know the truth.

You would observe that the world is not evil, but that people bring evil upon themselves. So instead of complaining about the evils of the world, they should set about repairing the defects within themselves.

Maimonides: Guide to the Perplexed 3.12

Creation for its own sake

Many people believe that God created the universe purely for the sake of human beings, in order that they might serve him. They believe that even the sun and moon move across the sky solely for the benefit of men and women.

When you examine this notion objectively, you discover how foolish it is. Ask yourself this: could God have created human beings without creating the rest of the universe; or could he only have created human beings after creating the rest of the universe?

If you answer that he could have created human beings without creating the rest of the universe, then you must ask what is the object of those other things in creation. After all, you are asserting that they exist for the sake of humanity – and yet human beings can exist without them.

If you answer that he could only have created human beings after creating the rest of the universe, this implies that other things can exist independently of human beings – so they cannot exist purely for the sake of humanity.

Besides, is it not absurd to think that God created human beings in order that they might serve him? This implies that God needs us – which in turn implies that he is not perfect and self-sufficient.

The truth is that the universe does not exist for humanity's sake, but that God created all living beings for their own sake.

Maimonides: Guide to the Perplexed 3.13

The well-being of the body and the soul

God's laws are concerned with the well-being of both the soul and the body.

In regard to the soul, some of God's laws are imparted in plain form; these laws are to be obeyed by all people. But some are imparted in allegorical form; these laws are to be obeyed only by those who are spiritually advanced.

In regard to the body, God's laws may be summarized quite simply: you should treat other people as you would wish them to treat you. If people conducted themselves in this manner, then everyone would have ample food, clothing and shelter. To put the matter another way, people's physical needs can only be met by collective effort; if people are entirely selfish, then all will suffer.

Although the well-being of the soul is more important than the well-being of the body, the latter must take priority. If people are hungry or cold, they cannot devote attention to their souls.

Maimonides:
Guide to the Perplexed 3.27

Reduction of desire

Yet you should note a further connection between the body and the soul. In order to make progress in the spiritual sphere, you should strive to reduce your physical desires as much as possible; you should satisfy your physical desires only to the extent that the health of your body requires them to be satisfied.

If you eat and drink more than your body needs, then you damage the soul. If you engage in sexual activity more than is necessary for procreation, then you weaken the soul. When people are dominated by the desires of the body, their minds become weak and blunt. Worse still, they start to envy and resent those who posses greater wealth, and hence have greater scope for self-indulgence – and envy and resentment are like poisons to the soul.

Fools, who are ignorant of God's laws, regard physical enjoyment as an object to be pursued for its own sake. But wise people, familiar with God's laws, know that physical enjoyment should be kept to a minimum, for the sake of the soul.

Maimonides: Guide to the Perplexed 3.33

Four kinds of perfection

Human beings can acquire four kinds of perfection.

The first and lowest kind relates to property: the possession of money, garments, furniture, servants, land, and so on. Most people dedicate their lives to this kind of perfection; and a few, such as successful merchants or ruthless kings, attain it. But at any moment a merchant's business may fail, or a king may be defeated in battle by a stronger king.

The second kind relates to the body: the enjoyment of good health, and the development of great strength in the limbs. Athletes and sportsmen aspire to this; but even the greatest athlete remains weaker than a mule – and far weaker than a lion or an elephant.

The third kind relates to action: moral perfection. This is attained through developing the character. Many philosophers and sages regard this as the highest form of perfection. Yet morality exists only in connection with other people; if a person lived alone, the moral faculties would remain dormant.

The fourth kind relates to the soul: the possession of the highest spiritual faculties, which enable the soul to discern God. This is true perfection. It does not depend on the presence of others; and its attainment is the purpose for which God created humanity.

Maimonides: Guide to the Perplexed 3.53

The primal light

'And God said: "Let there be light." And there was light.'

This is the primal light. It is the light of the eye. God showed this primal light to Adam; and by means of it Adam was able to see from one end of the world to the other. God showed this light to David; and by means of it he was able to discern the perfect goodness of God. God showed this light to Moses; and by means of it he was able to see the whole of Israel, from Gilead to Dan.

After the sin of Adam and Eve, through the generation that suffered the great flood, and through the generation that built the tower of Babel, God hid the primal light. Then he gave it to Moses at the time when his mother was hiding him. When Moses was taken before the Pharaoh, God took the light away from him; and Moses did not receive it again until he stood on Mount Sinai to receive the Law. Moses then had the light for the rest of his life – and so he could not be approached by the Israelites until he had put a veil on his face.

When the world is in harmony, and people are united, God will irradiate the entire world with the primal light, from one end to the other. But until that time the light will remain hidden.

Zohar

Male and female

'He made them male and female.' This means that each person is both male and female.

A man should have a wife; and through his wife he should learn to find the female within himself. This ensures that his faith is stable, and the divine presence never leaves him.

When a man makes a journey, and is away from his wife, how does he remain both male and female? He should pray with special devotion, and embrace the divine presence with particular passion. When he has felt the warmth of the divine presence throughout his body, he should give thanks. Then, throughout every minute and hour of the day and night, he should watch over his own thoughts and actions, to ensure that the divine presence does not leave him.

During intercourse the male and the female merge, and become one. Thus sexual intercourse is a holy act; it reminds both the man and the woman of the spiritual union of male and female. Indeed, it is a sin for a man and a woman to abstain from sex.

Zohar

Three parts of the soul

'Noah had three sons.'

There are three types of people: good people, bad people, and ordinary people. Likewise there are three parts of the soul. There is the super-soul, which is the deepest power of discernment; it can discern the mysteries of God and the universe. There is the spirit, which is the faculty of imagination; it can invent images that reflect the mysteries of God and the universe. And there is vitality – that which animates the body.

Everyone is aware of vitality; and everyone, to a greater or lesser degree, possesses the faculty of imagination. But the super-soul is unknown to most people. If people try to lead holy lives, they are assisted by the super-soul; the super-soul is the source of holiness. And gradually they become aware of this source. But if people do not try to lead holy lives, the super-soul remains undiscovered within them.

Zohar

Divine blessings

'God blessed Jacob.'

Jacob had many blessings. With each problem that he faced, he used the smallest blessing that would overcome the problem. This meant that, when he was confronted by large problems, he had large blessings in store.

Jacob may be compared with a king, with thousands of soldiers at his command, who are ready to fight the strongest foe. The king is told that a small band of robbers is attacking homes in the countryside; and he orders the gatekeepers to be sent out against them. Someone says: 'Surely you could have sent a cohort of soldiers against these robbers, and not just a bunch of gatekeepers.' The king answers: 'They will be sufficient to defeat the robbers. I need to preserve my soldiers for when powerful enemies attack.'

All people, in the course of their lives, are attacked by powerful spiritual enemies; and all people have received sufficient blessings from God to defeat those enemies. But some people waste their blessings on trivial problems. The path of holiness consists in learning the lesson of Jacob: to use the smallest blessing necessary to repulse each spiritual attack.

Zohar

An old man's questions

Rabbi Hiyya and Rabbi Jose met at an inn near the tower at Tyre. Rabbi Jose said: 'Throughout my journey here I was bothered by an old man who was driving a donkey. He asked me all kinds of foolish questions. What serpent flies through the air with an ant between its teeth? What starts in union and ends in separation? What eagle has its nest in a tree that doesn't exist? Who is the beautiful virgin with no eyes? And why is she covered in ornaments that are invisible by day? But now at last I can forget this silly nonsense, and discuss the laws of God with you.'

Rabbi Hiyya asked: 'Is this old man nearby?' Rabbi Jose replied: 'Yes, he is feeding his donkey in the stable.' Rabbi Hiyya summoned the old man. And when the old man arrived, he said: 'Have two turned into three, and three into one?' Rabbi Jose exclaimed: 'I told you! This man is always spouting nonsense.'

The old man said: 'Whenever I see a rabbi, I ask questions, in the hope of learning something new about God. But today I have learnt nothing.' Rabbi Hiyya fell to his knees in front of the old man: 'The truth of God is not in the answers that rabbis might offer, but in the questions that you ask.' Rabbi Jose could not understand, and remained standing.

Zohar

BIBLIOGRAPHY

There are a number of translations of the works represented in the present volume. These are the most accessible.

Bahya, Duties of the Heart, tr. Moses Hyamson (New York, Bloch Publishing Company, 1941).

Cohen, A., (tr.), The teachings of Maimonides (London, Shapiro, Valentine & Co., 1927).

Lewy H., Altmann A., & Heinemann I., (ed.), Three Jewish Philosophers: Philo, Saadya Gaon, and Jehuda Halevi (New York, Atheneum, 1981).

Maimonides, Guide to the Perplexed, tr. Chaim Rabin (Indianapolis, Hackett Publishing Company, 1995).

Montefiore C. G. & Loewe H., (ed.), A Rabbinic Anthology (London, Macmillan and Co., 1941).

Newman, Louis J., & Spitz, Samuel, (ed.), The Hasidic Anthology (New York, Scribner, 1934).

Philo, The Works of, tr. C. D. Yonge (Peabody, Massachusetts, Hendrickson Publishers, 1993).

Zohar, The Book of Splendour, tr. G. Scholem (New York, Schocken Books, 1963).

The illustrations in this volume have been taken from Sharpe, Samuel, Texts from the Holy Bible, (London, John Russell Smith, 1869); and from Smith, William, The Old Testament History (London, John Russell Smith, 1886).

INDEX OF WRITERS

Amos	6/3–6/5
Bahya	12/16–12/20
Daniel	5/21–5/28
Ezekiel	5/15–5/20
Ezra	4/21–4/23
Former Prophets	2/28–4/20
Hasidic Teachers	10/15–11/17
Hillel	8/6–8/9
Hosea	5/29–5/31
Ibn Gabriol	12/11–12/15
Isaiah	4/24–5/11
Jeremiah	5/12–5/14
Jesus Ben Sirach	7/24–8/5
Job's poet	6/11–6/21
Joel	6/1–6/2
Jonah	6/6–6/10
Maimonides	12/21–12/26
Moses (attributed)	1/1–2/27
Philo	11/18–12/2
Philosopher (Ecclesiastes)	7/13–7/23
Psalmists	6/22–7/12
Saadya	12/3–12/10
Talmudic Rabbis	8/10–10/14
Zohar	12/27–12/31